COMPUTE!'s
AmigaDOS
Reference Guide
Third Edition

Sheldon Leemon
and
Alan R. Levitan

COMPUTE! Books
Radnor, Pennsylvania

Cover design: Anthony Jacobson
Editors: Gregg Keiser and Stephen Levy

Copyright 1986, 1987, 1989, COMPUTE! Publications, Inc. All rights reserved.

Reproduction or translation of any part of this work beyond that permitted by Sections 107 and 108 of the United States Copyright Act without the permission of the copyright owner is unlawful.

Printed in the United States of America

10 9 8 7 6 5 4 3 2 1

Library of Congress Cataloging-in-Publication Data

Leemon, Sheldon.
    AmigaDOS reference guide.

      Rev. ed. of: Compute!'s AmigaDOS reference guide / Arlan R. Levitan and Sheldon Leemon. c1986.
    Includes index.
    1. Amiga (Computer)--Programming.   2. AmigaDOS (Computer operating system)   I. Levitan, Arlan R. II. Levitan, Arlan R. Compute!'s AmigaDOS reference guide.   III. Title.
QA76.8.A177L36   1989   005.4465   89-42831
ISBN 0-87455-194-3

The authors and publisher have made every effort in the preparation of this book to ensure the accuracy of the information. However, the information in this book are sold without warranty, either express or implied. Neither the authors nor COMPUTE! Publications, Inc. will be liable for any damages caused or alleged to be caused directly, indirectly, incidentally, or consequentially by the programs or information in this book.

The opinions expressed in this book are solely those of the authors and are not necessarily those of COMPUTE! Publications, Inc.

COMPUTE! Publications Inc., Post Office Box 5406, Greensboro, NC, 27403, (919) 275-9809, is part of Chilton Company, a Capital Cities/ABC, Inc. company and is not associated with any manufacturer of personal computers. Amiga is a trademark of Commodore-Amiga, Incorporated.

Contents

Foreword v

Part 1. Using AmigaDOS 1

1. Introduction to AmigaDOS 3
Creating a CLI Disk 7

2. The CLI Environment 10
The CLI Console 11
Running a Program from a CLI 15
Starting Additional CLI Processes 17
Your Own Windows 18
Console Enhancements Under Workbench 1.3 21

3. The Filing System 26
Files and Their Characteristics 28
Directories and Subdirectories 35
File Manipulation Commands 40
Pattern Matching (Wildcards) 41

4. Devices 46
Disk Drives 46
The RAM: Disk 50
Communications Ports 51
Console and Others 53
Logical Devices 56
MOUNTable Device Drivers and Handlers 63
Redirection of Input and Output 69

5. Command Sequence Files 72
Batching Simple Commands 72
Startup-Sequence: The Autoexecuting Command File 75

6. Ed, the System Screen Editor 90
Immediate Mode 91
Extended Mode Commands 93
ED Command Summary 101

7. EDIT, the Line Editor 104
EDIT 126

Part 2. AmigaDOS Command Reference 129

Appendix 271

AmigaDOS Error Messages 273

Index 277

Foreword

Workbench, the graphics-based interface that offers icons, pull-down menus, and multiple windows, isn't the only way to operate Commodore's Amiga personal computer. A more direct method of control is also available. Called the CLI (Command Line Interface), it provides added power and flexibility.

COMPUTE!'s *AmigaDOS Reference Guide, Third Edition*, fully updated for all versions of AmigaDOS through version 1.3, shows you how to access this operating environment and how to use its commands.

How would you like to be able to set aside part of Amiga's memory as a RAM disk and electronic disk drive? You can with the CLI, and virtually eliminate disk swapping.

Learn to create batch files that automate almost any task with the CLI. You can prompt yourself to enter the date and time at each startup, or copy files automatically—all with customized command sequence files.

A full-screen editor (ED) and a traditional line editor (EDIT) are both at your disposal through the CLI.

COMPUTE!'s *AmigaDOS Reference Guide, Third Edition* shows you how, with its clear language and thorough examples. This tutorial takes you step by step through the intricacies of AmigaDOS, offering a comprehensive reference guide you'll come back to long after you're a CLI expert.

Part 1

Using AmigaDOS

Chapter 1

Introduction to AmigaDOS

The Workbench environment makes it extremely easy for first-time users to learn to use the Amiga personal computer. With its pull-down menus and pictorial representation of files and subdirectories, Workbench insulates you from the harsh realities of a command-driven DOS (Disk Operating System) environment. But this ease of use has its price. In accepting the Workbench environment, you give up some of the flexibility and power afforded by a command-driven DOS.

The question of convenience is open to debate since it's largely a matter of personal preference. While the Workbench approach has its share of advocates, many users of the old-style DOS interface insist that they can run a program faster by simply typing its name on a command line than they could by opening a disk icon and double-clicking on the program icon. Yet the greater control offered by a command-driven DOS interface is a matter of *substance*, not *style*. There are some things you just can't do from the Workbench . . . at least not yet.

The current Workbench only creates a *display* for disks, tools (program files), projects (data files), and drawers (subdirectories) for which there exists a corresponding disk file whose name ends in *.info* (for instance, *Preferences.info*). These .info files contain information about the type of object icon represents and the graphic representation of the icon itself. But there are many files on the Workbench disk that are *not* represented by icons. These files include a simple sorting utility program and a screen-oriented text editor. These programs could be well-used by many Amiga owners, but most don't even know they're there since they're not accessible from the Workbench.

Another feature of AmigaDOS that the Workbench does not directly support is the use of command sequence files (known in the MS/PC-DOS world as *batch files*). These allow you to automate a job which requires several programs to be run in sequence, such as operating a compiler and linker in order to produce an executable program. And while it's not possible to send the directory of files on a particular disk to your printer from the Workbench (unless you write a program specifically for that purpose), it's easy to do so from the CLI (Command Line Interface).

Introduction to AmigaDOS

Fortunately, you're not limited to operating in one restricted environment, not even one so friendly as the Workbench, when you have the Amiga in front of you. The Amiga was designed to provide alternative ways to use the computer, to meet the needs of as many kinds of people as possible. This philosophy is evident in the way Amiga programs allow you to substitute control key sequences for commands normally carried out by moving and clicking the mouse. Even the Workbench lets you use the keyboard instead of the mouse. It should come as no surprise, then, that the Amiga also offers the kind of command line interpreter that's so familiar to users of MS/PC-DOS and Unix. On the Amiga, this environment is known as the CLI. *COMPUTE!'s AmigaDOS Reference Guide, Third Edition* will tell you how to find this operating environment and how to use its multitude of powerful and flexible commands.

What's Here

In addition, you'll find explanations of AmigaDOS's underlying concepts. These concepts will be helpful not only when you use the CLI, but will also expand your understanding of the Workbench and how to operate within it. If you have a single-drive system, for example, you've probably noticed that when you try to get a directory of the BASIC disk from BASIC, you're prompted to put in the Workbench disk. When you swap disks, you receive a directory of the Workbench disk instead. Knowing a little bit about how DOS operates and what files it looks for can eliminate a lot of this disk swapping. The RAM disk also offers computing power impossible through the Workbench alone. With the RAM disk, you'll have instant access to commands that normally must be read from the disk, such as the one used to produce a directory listing in BASIC.

The introductory manual that comes with the Amiga personal computer assumes AmigaDOS is of interest only to software developers. That's simply not true. Thousands of people—people who don't write software for a living—are interested in knowing more about their computers and learning how to get the most out of them. If you fit that category, this book will help as you explore the power of your Amiga computer.

The Workbench Versus the CLI

The friendly Workbench environment you see when you boot up your Workbench disk is actually an application—in other words, a program—and *not* part of the operating system. In fact, the computer *starts* in CLI mode and loads the Workbench program auto-

Introduction to AmigaDOS

matically through the use of a command file (you'll hear more about command files later).

Workbench's purpose is to interpret the choices you make when you move the mouse pointer to various icons and click the button. As such, the Workbench functions often have a close correspondence to DOS concepts. The drawer icons you see on the Workbench desktop, for instance, represent the normal subdirectories created by DOS. And the Trashcan icon represents a subdirectory named *Trashcan*. When you drag an icon to the trashcan, its corresponding file and that of its icon are transferred to the *Trashcan* subdirectory. When you select Empty Trash, the files that have been moved to the *Trashcan* subdirectory are deleted.

Some similarities between the Workbench and CLI environments are more superficial. When you double-click on a tool (program file), the Workbench prepares a suitable environment and runs the program. The same thing happens when you type `RUN` *program name* from the CLI. But some Workbench programs cannot be run from a CLI, and some CLI programs cannot be run from the Workbench. In fact, none of the CLI commands found in the *c* directory of the Workbench disk can be run from the Workbench. Part of the reason for this is that the Workbench recognizes a file only if it has a corresponding file of icon information ending in .info. Since none of the CLI command files has an icon file, none of them shows up under the Workbench.

But even if these *did* have icon files, the environment that CLI prepares for a program is different enough from the environment provided by the Workbench that these early CLI command programs still could not run under the Workbench. For one thing, from the Workbench you may pass instructions to a program to load a project (a data file that the program uses) by double-clicking on the project's icon. Programs that use the CLI expect you to pass instructions by typing them on the same line with the program name. The command line

`COPY` *old file* `TO` *new file*

for instance, tells the program Copy which file to copy and what name to give the new copy.

Getting to the CLI Environment

In the System drawer of the Workbench disk, there's a program that creates a CLI window on the Workbench screen (1.3 Workbench disks have an icon for the Shell program as well, which creates an enhanced CLI window). In its original condition, however, the Workbench disk that comes with the computer may have the

Introduction to AmigaDOS

icon for this program "turned off." If this is the case, the *CLI.info* file in the *System* subdirectory has been renamed *CLI.noinfo*. This means if you open the System drawer, that icon will not appear. To use the CLI program, you must first turn the CLI icon back on. This will change the *CLI.noinfo* file to *CLI.info*.

The Preferences program contains the controls for turning the CLI icon off and on. When you start the computer, using the Kickstart and Workbench disks, an icon representing the Workbench disk appears on the screen. Open this disk by double-clicking on the icon, or by selecting it and then selecting Open from the menu. A window will appear with icons representing the programs on the disk. Start the program called Preferences—its icon looks like an Amiga with a question mark on top of it (on the Workbench 1.3 disk, this file is in its own drawer called *Prefs*). On the left side of the Preferences screen, you'll see a box marked *CLI*, just above the Reset Colors box and below the box where you choose between 60- and 80-column text. The CLI box is divided into two parts, one marked *On*, the other *Off*. The Off box is highlighted in orange to show that the CLI icon is turned off. Click the On side of the box so it turns orange. While you're at it, you can set your other preferences, such as text size and a printer driver, if you've not done so already. Save your new preferences by clicking on the Save box at the lower right of the screen. This renames *CLI.noinfo* as *CLI.info*.

Now, double-click on the System drawer to open its window. If you've already opened the System drawer before running Preferences, you must close the drawer and open it again in order to let your new preferences take effect since the Workbench checks for icon files only when it opens a drawer. The window that appears now contains an icon marked *CLI* (it looks like a box with the characters *1>* inside). Double-click on the icon. A window now displays on the screen, with the title New CLI Window in its title bar and the prompt 1> awaiting your command. (To get started, see Chapter 2.)

There's another, even easier way to get to a CLI window. During the boot-up process, and after you insert your Workbench disk, the screen turns from white to blue, and a sign-on message appears which reads *Copyright (C) 1985 Commodore-Amiga, Inc*. When you see this message, hold down the CTRL key and press the D key at the same time. This stops the execution of the command file that loads the Workbench. **BREAK - CLI shows on the screen, and under this, the familiar 1> prompt.

Creating a CLI Disk

If you're planning to use the CLI environment often, this process of opening the Workbench icon, the System drawer, and the CLI icon to get to the CLI will become time-consuming at best, frustrating at worst. You can bypass one of these steps by moving the CLI icon from the System window directly to the Workbench window. Or, you can remember to press CTRL-D at the right moment during the boot-up process so the Workbench doesn't load.

But since computers are supposed to make things easier, doesn't it seem reasonable to expect the Amiga to do all this for you? With a bit of setup work on your part, it can in fact bypass loading and running the Workbench altogether. In order to make a working CLI disk, you should make a copy of your Workbench disk, change the command file that automatically loads the Workbench when the disk starts, and delete the unnecessary Workbench files. To get you through this, the procedure is completely outlined for you below, step by step.

Make a Copy of Your Workbench Disk

You can do this either from the Workbench or from the CLI. Let's assume you'll use the CLI, since you presumably already know how to copy a disk with the Workbench. First, bring up the CLI by double-clicking its icon on the Workbench disk, or by booting the Workbench disk and then interrupting the loading process with a CTRL-D key combination when the blue screen appears. From this point, the procedure is slightly different for single- and dual-drive systems.

Single-drive systems. When the CLI prompt (1>) appears, you may use the DISKCOPY command to copy the Workbench disk. Get out a blank, new disk for the copy. Remember, any information on this disk will be lost when you copy to it. Type:

SYS:SYSTEM/DISKCOPY df0: TO df0:

and press RETURN. The copy program will prompt you when to put in the disk to copy FROM (your original Workbench disk) and when to put in the disk to copy TO (your blank disk). You'll have to swap the FROM and TO disks a number of times with a single-drive system. The copy program will tell you when the copy process is complete.

Dual-drive systems. When the CLI prompt (1>) appears, leave the Workbench disk in the internal drive, and place a new, blank disk in the external drive. Type:

SYS:SYSTEM/DISKCOPY df0: TO df1:

Introduction to AmigaDOS

and press RETURN. You'll be prompted to put the FROM disk in drive df0: and the TO disk in drive df1:, but since both disks are where they should be, merely press RETURN. The copy program will tell you when the process is completed. Place the disk that contains the copy of the Workbench into the internal drive.

Getting Going with CLI

Restart the computer with your new disk. Press the CTRL key and both Commodore/Amiga keys (the closed Amiga or Commodore key—on the left side of the space bar—and the open Amiga or Commodore key—on the right side of the space bar) at the same time to restart. Your new disk is now the system disk, which will save you some disk swapping later.

Bring up the CLI. Use the CTRL-D combination to stop the Workbench from loading during the boot process, or open the System drawer and click on the CLI icon. If you use the Workbench CLI, you may find it convenient to size this window to full-screen by moving it with the drag bar to the top left of the screen and pulling the sizing gadget down to the bottom right.

Edit the command file. This is used to load the Workbench automatically when you start the computer. You'll use the system screen editor program—called *ED*—to change the *startup-sequence* file in the *s* directory. To start the editor, enter

`ed s/startup-sequence`

at the 1> prompt (whenever you see text in this font, press the RETURN key at the end of the line). A new screen appears, showing the contents of this text file. A text cursor shows at the top left corner. If you haven't changed the default system colors, it will be orange. Use the down-arrow cursor key to move this cursor down until it covers the first letter of the line that reads *LoadWB*. Press the ESC key (found in the upper left of the keyboard). An asterisk appears at the bottom of the screen, and the cursor is now next to it. Type 2 d ; x. The two lines used to load the Workbench will be deleted and the new file saved to disk. If you wish to both load the Workbench and leave the initial CLI window intact, move the cursor to the last line of the file, press the ESC key, and type d ; x, instead.

Delete all of the unnecessary Workbench files. Since you've edited the startup command file, the new disk will not load the Workbench automatically. But there are still a number of files on the disk that will run only under the Workbench. The only files you'll want to save are the contents of these directories:

Directory
c
l
s
t
devs
libs
(and possibly) fonts

To delete the rest of the files, type in each of the following lines, just as you see them, pressing the RETURN key at the end of each.

```
delete trashcan demos#? empty utilities all
delete c/loadwb #?
```

Relabel the disk. Though not strictly necessary, for purposes of clarity it's probably better to have the title of the disk read *CLI* rather than *Copy of Workbench*. To change the disk's volume label, make sure it's in the internal drive, then enter

```
RELABEL df0: CLI
```

There you have it. A Workbench disk without the Workbench. Insert this disk in the internal disk drive any time you see the WORKBENCH prompt screen.

Make a backup copy of the disk right now, and put the original away so you can make clean copies of the disk in the future (unless you want to go through these six steps every time). If you have only one drive, you'll find it particularly convenient to have all of the CLI commands on the same disk as your application programs. To make a new disk that contains both the CLI commands and the application program, simply copy those application programs onto duplicates of this master CLI disk. If you're really pressed for space, you may have to delete some of the less useful commands, printer-driver files for printers you don't have, character font files, and so on. To determine which files you can afford to delete, see Appendix A, which lists all the files on the Workbench disk.

Chapter 2

The CLI Environment

When you insert the Workbench disk into the disk drive, the Amiga's operating system sets up a *task* (one of the programs that can run simultaneously under a multitasking system such as AmigaDOS) called a *CLI process*. The job of the CLI is to accept commands to run a program. When the CLI finds the program, it loads the program, prepares its environment, and then passes control to the program. After the program finishes, control is passed back to the CLI, which waits for the next command. Although the system starts up only one CLI, you may start others yourself to run multiple tasks simultaneously.

First, the initial CLI process checks whether there's a command file in the s directory called *Startup-Sequence*. If there is, the commands listed in that file are executed automatically (see Chapter 5 for more detailed information about command sequence files). On the standard Workbench disk, this file contains commands to load and run the Workbench and end the CLI process. But if there's no command present to load the Workbench, once the command file is executed, the CLI process prints its prompt message (1>) and waits for further orders.

The AmigaDOS CLI process performs the simplest of functions. It starts in interactive mode, which means it prints its 1> prompt and waits for you to type something. It simply sits, letting you type until it sees that you've entered a special editing character or pressed RETURN. The editing characters invoke some minor screen-editing functions described below. But when you press RETURN, the CLI looks at the whole line you've entered.

It interprets the first word (a series of characters that end with a space) as a filename. The CLI then tries to load a program file with that name. An error message and another 1> appear if it can't find the file. Assuming it finds the file, the CLI tries to load it as a program. Since program files have a structure the CLI recognizes, it can tell whether the file is an executable program. Again, an error message and the 1> prompt are displayed if the file isn't an executable program. If the file exists *and* is an executable program, the

The CLI Environment

CLI loads the program into memory, prepares a stack area for the program to use as workspace, tells the program where to find the rest of the text on the command line in case it wants that text as instructions, and passes control to the program. Once this happens, the CLI cannot accept user input until the program passes control back to it.

Let's break this simple task into its component parts and examine them in detail. We'll start with the process of accepting text characters that you type in.

The CLI Console

The console device that the CLI uses to accept keyboard input and display the results operates much like an old-fashioned Teletype terminal—it can deal with only a single line of text at a time. This *command line* may be up to 255 characters long. It's possible, therefore, that a single command line can occupy more than one line on the screen. As far as the console device is concerned, you're still entering text on the same line until you hit the RETURN key. When you've typed in 255 characters (more than three or four screen lines, depending on the column width of the screen), the console refuses to accept any additional keyboard input.

One of the less pleasant aspects of a line-oriented editor (like the console device) is that you cannot use the cursor keys to move to another command line on the screen, edit it, and use the revised line. Each time you issue a new command you have to enter the entire command line from scratch. In fact, you can't even use the cursor keys to edit the line you're on. If you make a mistake at the beginning of a line, you have to erase the whole line and start over. To remedy this situation, Workbench 1.3 added a new console device called *Newcon:*, which performs line-editing functions. We'll discuss this device a little later on.

CLI Editing

Because of its limited line-editing capabilities, the console device recognizes only a very few special characters as editing commands. Some of these are useful for working with the CLI, while others merely enable you to control the color and appearance of the text the console device prints to the screen (see Chapter 4 for more about this device). In summary, here are the editing commands:

The CLI Environment

Useful Editing Features

Key(s)	Function
BACK SPACE or CTRL-H	Erases the character to the left of the cursor
CTRL-X	Erases the entire current line (cancels the line)
CTRL-L	Clears the screen (form-feed)
RETURN or CTRL-M	Ends the line and executes the command
CTRL-J	Moves the cursor to the next line, but doesn't execute the command
;	Marks the start of a comment
CTRL-\	End-of-file indicator

Text Output Features

Key(s)	Function
TAB or CTRL-I	Moves the cursor one space to the right (inserts a tab character)
CTRL-K	Moves the cursor up one line (vertical tab)
CTRL-O	Switches to the ALTernate character set (shifts out)
CTRL-N	Switches back to the normal character set (shifts in)
ESC-[1m	Switches to bold characters
ESC-[2m	Switches character color (to black)
ESC-[3m	Italics on
ESC-[4m	Underline on
ESC-[7m	Reverse video on
ESC-[8m	Switches character color (to blue—invisible)
ESC-[0m	Switches to normal characters
ESC-C	Clears the screen and switches to normal characters

Note: When using the ESC key combinations, just press the ESC key and then enter the one to three additional characters.

As you can see, the only way to correct your typing mistakes is to delete them with the BACK SPACE key (or hold the CTRL key and press X if you want to erase the whole line) and retype. If you press the CAPS LOCK key, the red light on the key appears, and all alphabetic keys will be capitalized. This is of little practical significance since the CLI does not discriminate between lowercase and uppercase, or even mixed case.

The CLI Environment

The RETURN key is the CLI's signal to process your command line. The linefeed character (CTRL-J) moves the cursor to the beginning of the next line, just like RETURN, but it doesn't cause the CLI to process the line until RETURN is pressed. This means you can type a list of commands separated by CTRL-J and have the CLI perform them one by one. For example, if you type

DELETE *old file* <CTRL-J> DIR

the CLI first deletes the file named in *old file*, then feeds the next instruction to the following CLI prompt, which displays the new directory listing.

Though not really an editing character, the semicolon (;) is significant to the CLI. The CLI interprets anything following a semicolon as a *comment* and ignores the entire rest of the line. Comments may not be too useful for immediate mode commands which you enter at the keyboard, but they can be extremely helpful in documenting command sequence files (see Chapter 5).

The last character in the summary table of useful commands, CTRL- \, will probably make more sense after you've read Chapter 4, which covers devices. Briefly, it sends an end-of-file character to the console device. This is helpful because the Amiga is flexible about letting you use one device in place of another. For instance, you can use the COPY command (program) not only to copy one file to another, but also from one file to another device, such as the printer. Likewise, you can COPY from the console device (which in this case means the keyboard) to a disk file. Unlike a disk file, the console device does not have a natural limit to its input—you can keep typing and typing until you're too tired to type. The CTRL- \ character, therefore, lets the console device know when you've come to the end of the "file" so you can stop using the console as an output device and start using it for your CLI input again. PC/MS-DOS users will recognize that this is the equivalent of the CTRL-Z (or F6) character used by that operating system.

Most of the other special command key combinations represent output formatting commands that you may find amusing or learn to avoid. Their functions are really a byproduct of the fact that the console device supports certain standard codes that are usually applied to printer devices. The TAB key, for example, moves the cursor over one space as the space bar does. But it leaves a tab character in its wake, which the command line interpreter doesn't like at all. If you use a tab instead of a space you'll most likely receive an error message.

CTRL-O acts like an ALT-lock which permanently switches you to the ALTernate characters (you can think of these as the

The CLI Environment

Other, or *Oddball*, characters to remember the CTRL key combination). The alternate characters normally appear only when you hold the ALT key down as you type. These characters, which include accented vowels and other international symbols, are interesting to look at if you want to see what characters the standard Amiga set contains, but they're of little practical use here since the CLI doesn't recognize them. If you get into this mode by mistake, press CTRL-N (for *Normal* characters) to get out of it. You can also return to the normal character set by pressing ESC and the C key, which both clears the screen and changes the character set. When the screen clears, however, you don't get your prompt back automatically—you must hit RETURN to get a new command line. If you just want to clear the screen, CTRL-L (Linefeed) does the job.

The console device also recognizes a series of ESCape codes which change the typeface of the font printed on the screen. For example, if you press the ESC key, then the [key, 1 key, and m key, subsequent screen text is printed in boldface. Likewise, the ESC-[2m combination changes the color of the printing, ESC-[3m turns on italics, and ESC-[4m turns on underlining. These special features are cumulative. In other words, if you change to bold, then turn italics on, the result is text in bold italics. To disable all these special features and return to normal text, use the ESC-[0m combination. Pressing ESC-C clears the screen and also resets the text to normal characters. Note that although these features affect the display, CLI pays no attention to special typefaces. This sampling of escape codes was listed primarily to acquaint you with the fact that the console device responds in many ways like a standard ANSI terminal. The codes are by no means the only ones to which the console device responds. For instance, it also accepts a wide range of cursor positioning commands. These commands, however, are of little use to the average CLI user and are of greater interest to programmers who wish to use the console device in their programs.

Pausing and Restarting

Another aspect of the console device that you should be familiar with is pausing and restarting screen output. The CLI (and the command programs that use its console device) constantly watches the console for input from the keyboard. If you type a character while one of the command programs is running, the program will stop its own output to the screen so as not to mix it with your input. Even if the command program prints no messages of its own, you'll not get the CLI prompt (1>) back until you restart output. The way to do that is either to erase the line you're typing (by using the BACK SPACE or CTRL-X keys) or finish the line by entering a RETURN.

The CLI Environment

The pause is really a function of the CLI's type-ahead feature. The CLI can keep track of up to 255 characters of command instructions while it's busy running a command program and will execute these instructions after it's finished. In practical terms, however, it means you can pause a display of, say, a directory listing, by pressing the space bar and restart it later by pressing the BACK SPACE key. This roughly corresponds to the function performed by the CTRL-S, CTRL-Q combination on MS/PC-DOS machines.

If you use the RETURN key to complete the line rather than erasing it, you should be aware that the command line you've just entered will be saved by the CLI and will be executed after it finishes with the current command.

If you prefer to terminate output entirely instead of just pausing it, you can use the BREAK function. Hold down the CTRL key and press the C key, and you'll see the message **BREAK* as the CLI prompt appears once again. You may also interrupt an EXECUTE command sequence with the CTRL-D combination (see Chapter 5 for details on command sequence files). AmigaDOS reserves the CTRL-C, CTRL-D, CTRL-E, and CTRL-F combinations for interrupt functions, but the CLI uses only the first two. Other programs may use the latter two as they see fit.

As you'll soon see, it's possible to have more than one CLI window open at a time. Using the CTRL-C or other break key combinations only works for the CLI window that's *currently* active. To interrupt others, you must either make them the active CLI and use the break keys or use the BREAK command. This command interrupts the other process just as if you'd made it active and then used the break keys.

Running a Program from a CLI

The next phase of the CLI's task is running a program. Running a program from a CLI is simple—all you do is type the name of the program at the prompt, followed by pressing the RETURN key. If the program needs further input to run, you type that input on the same line as the filename. For example, to create a duplicate of one file under another name (on the same disk and in the same directory as the original), type:

COPY *old file* TO *new file*

In this command line, the word COPY is the name of the copy program file, and the rest of the line tells that program what to do.

The CLI Environment

The Complete Location
Actually, running a program isn't quite as simple as typing its name. That works only if the program is located in the current directory of the current disk, or if it's located in the current command directory. These concepts will be discussed in detail in Chapter 3, which deals with the directory structure, and Chapter 4, which explains the use of virtual devices. Generally speaking, however, when you start up the system, the current directory is the root (topmost) directory of the CLI disk that's in the internal disk drive (DF0:), and the command directory is the *c* subdirectory found on that disk. If your program is anywhere else, you have to specify its complete location by typing in the name of the disk and/or the subdirectory on that disk. For instance, to run a program called *WordWizard,* located in the *Wordprocessing* subdirectory of the external floppy drive (DF1:), you would enter

DF1:Wordprocessing/Wordwizard

There are other reasons simply typing the name of the program may not run it. There may be typing errors in either the program name or the instruction line that the program is to use. The file may not be in the executable load format AmigaDOS requires, or the disk itself may be damaged or write-protected. In most cases, AmigaDOS gives you complete error messages and may even give you a chance to remedy the error without having to redo the command. In some cases, however, these messages may not be satisfactory. You can get more information about a failure by using the WHY command—just type **WHY** after receiving an error message. Only rarely will you receive a more cryptic message, such as *Error code 218.* To find this error code's meaning, use the FAULT command. Typing **FAULT** *n,* where *n* is the error code number, will usually yield a clearer explanation. If all this fails, or if you're simply curious, consult Appendix B, which explains the various errors you might receive.

Room to Work
One rare problem you might encounter concerns the environment that the CLI provides to the program it's running. As mentioned earlier, after the CLI successfully loads the program, it prepares a stack area for the program to use as working storage. The initial allocation for this stack area is 4000 bytes. Usually, this will be enough, but in some cases there won't be enough stack space for the program to run. If you try to run the ABasiC program supplied with the first Amigas from a CLI, for example, you'll receive a message that there's not sufficient stack space. If you first increase the

The CLI Environment

stack space to 8000 bytes, however, with the STACK command (STACK 8000), the program runs. Other programs, like the SORT command—which needs a lot of working space if it's to sort a large file—may run out of stack space and cause the computer to hang up. In this case, when in doubt, increase the stack space before sorting a large file. Though most programs written for the CLI will not need their stack increased, some programs written for the Workbench environment may need a stack increase when run from the CLI. To see the stack size required, click once on the program's icon; then select the Info item from the Workbench menu. There will be a number in a box marked "Stack" which will tell you the required stack size.

A final note about the simple nature of the CLI process. Some disk operating systems (like MS/PC-DOS) have a set of intrinsic commands, commands which the DOS recognizes and executes as soon as the user types them in on the command line. As you've seen, CLI commands are all disk-based programs, and you must have the CLI disk containing the program files in the disk drive before you can use any of them. This is not as inconvenient as you might expect. For one thing, you can transfer the commands you use most often to the RAM device and add that directory to the current search path. Or, you can make the commands resident by using the Shell and the RESIDENT command (more on these later). This gives you the equivalent of a custom-tailored set of intrinsic commands that occupy no more user RAM than is really necessary. Another nice thing about having all the commands as program files is that you can rename any command to suit your preference (though for the sake of compatibility, you'll probably want to make a copy of the program with a new name, while retaining the file with the old name as well). For example, if you're used to MS/PC-DOS, you might want to use the word *ERASE* instead of *DELETE*. If you type COPY c/delete TO c/erase, you'll be able to use either form of the command. The "alias" feature of the Shell (discussed below) provides similar capabilities, without requiring multiple copies of the file.

Starting Additional CLI Processes

Though AmigaDOS is a multitasking operating system, each CLI can run only one program at a time. To run several programs simultaneously, you must create additional CLI processes. The command program NEWCLI takes care of this nicely. When you type NEWCLI, a new interactive CLI window opens up in front of the current window (the one labeled *AmigaDOS*). This window is

The CLI Environment

titled New CLI and displays the message *New CLI task 2*, followed by its prompt, 2>.

This should solve the mystery of why the prompt in the first CLI window is 1>. The number in the prompt is the task number of the CLI. By the way, you're free to change the prompt to anything you want, in any CLI window, by using the PROMPT command. For instance,

PROMPT "What is your wish, O Master?"

will change the prompt to this verbose phrase. Even ALT characters, such as foreign language accented characters, can be used in a prompt string. In fact, you can use the text output commands (within quotation marks) to change the color of your prompt, or to make it appear in reverse video, as with the command shown below.

PROMPT "<ESC>[7mReverse prompt>> <ESC>[0m "

When you create a new CLI window, it becomes the active window. You can tell which window is active by looking at the title bars. The title bar of the window that's currently active is a solid color, while the title bars of the other windows are dotty (or *ghosted*, as it's called). To change a window from inactive to active, just move the mouse pointer inside the window and click the mouse button. Whenever you type anything at the keyboard, the printing always appears in the active window. The other rules for system windows apply to CLI windows as well. You can use the normal system gadgets to change the size of the new CLI window, drag it around the screen, and move it in front of or behind other windows. You can keep opening as many as 20 CLI windows, provided there's enough available memory.

Your Own Windows

If you just type NEWCLI, the operating system decides at what position on the screen to create the window and how large the window will be. These sizes are measured in *pixels* (picture elements), which are the individual dots used to create the display. The standard DOS screen is 640 pixels across and 200 pixels high. Versions 1.3 of AmigaDOS creates new CLI windows that start at the top left corner of the screen, and are 640 pixels wide by 100 pixels high. All new CLI windows are created in the same place, in the same size, unless you specify otherwise. This means the third CLI window appears atop the second, and you'll have to drag one of them out of the way to use both.

You can create a new CLI window in a particular location and

The CLI Environment

size by describing the console device output window. The description for this device follows the format

CON:*hpos* / *vpos*/ *width*/ *height*/ *windowtitle*

where *hpos* is the horizontal position of the top left corner of the window (expressed as the number of pixels in from the left edge of the screen), *vpos* is the vertical position of the top left corner of the window (expressed as the number of pixels down from the top edge of the screen), and *width* and *height* give the size of the window in pixels. The maximum size for a CLI window is the screen size, which for the default Workbench screen is 640 × 200 pixels. The minimum is 90 × 25 pixels. The last entry, *windowtitle*, is optional. It allows you to enter the text of a title to appear in the title bar. If you don't enter any text, the title is left blank. To create a new CLI window that occupies the full screen, you would type

NEWCLI CON:0/0/640/200/

Note that the last slash mark is *required*, even though you didn't specify the title.

A title can contain special characters, such as the space character (which AmigaDOS usually interprets as separating one command word from another), but if you use them, you must put the *entire device name* in quotation marks:

NEWCLI "CON:40/40/200/100/A Standard Window"

There's one more feature of NEWCLI you should know about. When the first CLI window opens, it automatically executes a command sequence file called *s:startup-sequence*. We'll talk all about command sequence files in Chapter 5, but for now, let's just say it's a file that executes a series of CLI commands. If you want your new CLI window to automatically execute a series of commands when it starts up, you can specify a command sequence file in the NEWCLI command:

NEWCLI FROM *StartupFile*

where "StartupFile" is the name of the command sequence file you want executed. Under Workbench 1.3, if no FROM file is specified, the sequence file *S:CLI-Startup* is automatically executed when a NEWCLI command is issued.

Going Away

Anytime you want to eliminate one of your CLI windows, make that window active by clicking the mouse button inside its borders, and type ENDCLI. The message *CLI task n ending* (where *n* is the number of the CLI task) is briefly printed, and the window closes.

The CLI Environment

(In fact, the message prints so quickly that you probably won't see it.)

Always leave yourself at least *one* open CLI window—if you close the final window, you won't be able to issue any commands. You'll have no choice but to warm-start the computer by pressing CTRL and both Amiga keys at the same time. In fact, its not a bad idea to keep an extra CLI around, just in case. There are programs like the public domain *PopCLI* which allow you to open a new CLI window just by pressing a hot-key combination.

If you're using one program and want to start another, you can switch back to the Workbench screen (the one on which the CLIs reside), either by using the depth-arrangement gadgets at the top right of the screen, or by using the Amiga-N key combination to bring the Workbench screen forward and Amiga-M to send it back. (The Amiga key combinations move entire screens, not just individual windows.) This gives you access to your open CLI so you can run another program or use one of the DOS command programs.

If you have a number of CLI tasks running at the same time, some whose windows do not appear on the Workbench screen, you may lose track of them all. The STATUS command prints a list of all of the current CLI tasks and the command programs they're running.

Running Programs in a Noninteractive Process

When you want to run a program as a separate task, but don't need the interactive features (and the memory overhead) of another CLI window, you can use the RUN command program. When you type RUN followed by a command you would normally type in a CLI window, a new CLI process is created which executes the command. That new process then disappears.

Let's say you want to run a word processor program without losing your current CLI window. If you normally type wordprocessor to start the program, type RUN wordprocessor instead. The RUN command prints a message like *[CLI n]* (where *n* is the next unused CLI number) and then runs the word processor. This saves you the trouble of typing NEWCLI before entering the command and of getting rid of the CLI with ENDCLI after you're finished. It also saves you the memory that would ordinarily be taken up by the CLI window. When you finish with the word processor and exit the program, it leaves nothing behind.

Even though RUN does not provide you with a command window, it does offer a way to send additional commands to the process. At the end of the first command, type a plus sign (+) and press RETURN. You may then enter a second command on the next line. If you want to add a third, type the plus sign and RETURN at the end of the second line and add the new command on the third line. At the end of your last command line, just type RETURN. The RUN command executes each of the command lines in sequence, just as if you had typed them in a CLI window, one after the other. For example, if you want to send a sorted list of BASIC program files to the printer, enter

```
RUN LIST S .bas TO ram:temp+
   SORT ram:temp TO prt:
```

This runs the LIST program, which sends a list of all files with the characters *.bas* in their filenames to a file on the RAM disk. After LIST has finished, the CLI runs the SORT program, which sorts the lines and sends them to the printer. This CLI process doesn't disappear until the last task is finished.

Console Enhancements Under Workbench 1.3

As noted above, the default console device used by the CLI window is fairly primitive—it doesn't even offer the line-editing capabilities of the Commodore 64. This situation was remedied by a new console handler, called *NEWCON:*, introduced with Workbench 1.3. As of version 1.3, this console is not an integral part of AmigaDOS like the old one was. It resides in a file in the *L:* directory called *Newcon-Handler*, and must be added to the system with the **MOUNT** command (though this situation may change under 1.4). However, the default startup-sequence file on Workbench 1.3 mounts this console handler for you automatically. Likewise, to start a CLI window with the NEWCON: handler, you must specify it as your console in the NEWCLI command:

```
NEWCLI NEWCON:0/0/600/100/
```

Note, however, that if you use the NEWSHELL command (discussed below), NEWCON: is used as the default console handler.

NEWCON: adds two important enhancements to the standard console handler. First, it adds line editing features. With the old console, the only way to move back through a command line is with the backspace key, which erases everything as you go. The NEWCON lets you use the left- and right-arrow keys to move left and right through the line, without erasing any text. Morevoer, any additional characters you type will push ahead any existing characters to the right of them, without erasing anything. The Backspace key can be used to erase the character to the left of the cursor, while the Delete key erases the character under the cursor. The ex-

The CLI Environment

tended editing features of the NEWCON: handler are summarized below:

Key	Function
DELETE	Erases the character to the left of the cursor
CTRL-A (or Shift-LeftArrow)	Moves the cursor to the beginning of the line
CTRL-K	Erases everything from the cursor forward to the end of the line
CTRL-U	Erases everything from the cursor forward to the end of the line
CTRL-W	Moves the cursor forward to the next tab stop
CTRL-Z (or Shift-RightArrow)	Moves the cursor to the end of the line

The NEWCON: handler introduces one more subtle editing change. Control characters are now printed in reverse video, and are not acted on immediately (though they will be passed through if the screen output is directed to a file or device). This means that typing the sequence ESC-c will no longer immediately clear the screen, although if you press Return after typing it, the screen will clear when the CLI prints the error message **Can't open <ESC-c>**.

In addition to enhanced editing functions, the NEWCON: handler provides a command history buffer. This buffer saves each command line as you entered it, up to a maximum of 2,048 characters (when the buffer fills, the oldest command line is deleted each time a new one is entered). To retrieve a previous command line, merely press the UpArrow key. Each time you press this key, the next oldest command line appears. If you go past a command line, you can move forward through the buffer with the DownArrow key. To move all the way forward to the most recent (bottom) entry in the buffer, press CTRL-B (or Shift-DownArrow). This leaves you on a blank line. The command history also has a search feature that allows you to find a past command by typing part of it and then pressing Shift-UpArrow. For example, if you wanted to repeat the command:

Copy Work:Wordprocessing/Documents/MyDoc to df1:Backup

and you know you'd typed the command recently, you could just type:

Co *<Shift-UpArrow>*

and NEWCON: would display the last line that you typed that started with those two letters. If the command line you'd like to repeat showed up, you could just hit Return to reissue the command. Note, however, that the search function is case sensitive; if you type Co *<Shift-UpArrow>*, NEWCON: won't find a command

The CLI Environment

line that starts with "copy."

The command history of NEWCON: can come in very handy when you're performing repetitive tasks. For example, if you wanted to format a series of disks, you'd only have to type the Format command once. For each succeeding disk, you'd only have to press the UpArrow and Return keys.

The Shell

Another CLI enhancement offered by Workbench 1.3 is a slightly "smarter" command shell. While the normal CLI only executes the command whose name appears as the first word of the command line, the Shell knows a few additional tricks. Since the Shell is not (as of Workbench 1.3) the default command handler, however, it must be added to the system with a command. To get the system to load the Shell code in from the file *L:Shell-Seg*, in which it resides, you must use the command:

RESIDENT CLI L:Shell-Seg SYSTEM pure

Executing this command, however, will not convert the CLI from which the command was issued into a Shell CLI. Only CLI windows that are opened after the command is given will have the properties of a Shell. The default Startup-sequence file on Workbench 1.3 executes the necessary RESIDENT command, so all CLI windows that you open from the Workbench have the Shell characteristics. The command NEWSHELL not only opens a new Shell process (if the Shell-Seg has been loaded), but opens it with a NEWCON: window as well.

The first enhancement offered by the Shell is recognition of a new PROMPT argument. When you use the characters %S in a prompt string, they will be replaced the name of the current directory, whatever that happens to be at the time. For example, the command:

Prompt "%N.%S> "

will lead to a prompt string that looks like this:

1.Workbench 1.3>

Whenever you change your current directory (more about this in Chapter 3), the prompt will change to reflect the new location.

The second new feature of the Shell is much more substantial. This is the power to create *aliases* for commonly used AmigaDOS commands. An alias is an assumed name for an existing command, usually shorter than the actual filename of the command. For example, you could give the command Makedir the alias md, and then, whenever you wanted to create a new directory, you'd only

The CLI Environment

have to type `md`, instead of `Makedir`. To create an alias, you use the Alias command, which is recognized only by the Shell (it can be thought of as an instrinsic command, one the Shell knows about without reading in a command file). The format for this command is:

`ALIAS name command`

where *name* is the new name by which you wish the command to be known, and *command* is the command you want executed when that name is given. In the example above, you'd give the `Makedir` command its alias by saying:

`ALIAS md Makedir`

Alias is good for more than just changing a command's name, however. It can be used as a handy shortcut for an entire command line. For example, you could use it to condense the command `Format drive df0: name Empty noicons` down to the command `fmt` with the Alias command:

`ALIAS fmt Format drive df0: name Empty noicons`

Not only can you enter command parameters into an alias, but you can even enter in a partial list of parameters, and specify a place where substitutions will be made with a pair of square brackets [ ]. For example, if you wanted the above alias to be usable with any floppy drive, not just the internal one, you could give the command

`ALIAS fmt Format drive df[ ]: name Empty noicons`

When you give the `fmt` command, the square brackets are replaced by whatever number you type as a command parameter. For example, to format drive 1, you would type

`FMT 1`

There are a few more facts you should know about the ALIAS command. The command ALIAS entered by itself will list the current aliases. To remove an ALIAS, type `ALIAS name` with no command, where *name* is the alias you wish to remove. Finally, each set of aliases is known only to its own particular shell process. If you start a new Shell, it won't know about about the old Shell's aliases. The same is true for the enhanced prompt. If the old Shell had a prompt that contained the %S character, the new Shell will inherit a prompt that reflects the directory of the old Shell at the time the new one was created. This prompt will not automatically change to reflect the new Shell's path. Since it would be rather inconvenient to enter a new prompt string and a new set of aliases for each new Shell you create, AmigaDOS lets you use a startup file that automatically does it for you. If you start a Shell with the

The CLI Environment

NEWSHELL command, it will automatically execute all the commands in the file *S:Shell-Startup* at the time of its creation.

The last two features of the Shell will be covered in greater depth later on, since they concern subjects we haven't covered yet. We'll mention them here, just for the sake of completeness. The first involves sequence file execution. Normally, you use the EXECUTE command to execute a command sequence file. With the Shell, however, its possible to execute sequence files just by typing their names, if the file's S protection bit has been set. The second feature is a new kind of output redirection. Normally, when you redirect output to a file, it creates a new file that overwrites the old file of the same name. With the Shell redirection operator >>, new information is appended on to the end of the old file, if any.

> Throughout the rest of the book, you'll occasionally come across lines to be entered on the Amiga which, because of the book's formatting, are split on the page. A continued line is indented—do not press Return at the end of the first physical line, but simply continue typing with the indented characters.

Chapter 3

The Filing System

The Amiga personal computer comes with an internal double-sided, double-density 3½-inch disk drive. Each 3½-inch disk can hold 880K bytes—in other words, 901,120 characters of information. To use a disk for storage, AmigaDOS must first write some organizational information to the disk that will be used by the computer's filing system to find the information it stores on the disk. This is called *formatting* the disk and is performed by the FORMAT command. Its syntax is

`FORMAT DRIVE df0: NAME Volume name`

Volume Names

When you format a disk, the program notifies you as each of the 80 cylinders (tracks) on the disk is formatted (written), then verified (read) to make sure the formatting information is correct. If you want to format the disk on a drive other than the internal drive, just substitute the device name of that drive (for example, df1: refers to the first external 3½-inch drive). Notice that after the name of the drive, the command specifies NAME *Volume name*. AmigaDOS requires you to give each disk a name, known as the *volume name*. You must use the keyword NAME before entering the name. To name a disk as *Wordprocessing*, you'd use **NAME** Wordprocessing. It's a good idea to use a name that identifies the disk as precisely as possible. AmigaDOS is able to identify a disk by its volume name as well as the device name of the drive in which it resides. Therefore, if you remove the *Wordprocessing* disk from the drive and DOS wants to access something on that disk, it will prompt you to *Please insert volume Wordprocessing in any drive*. (The message is somewhat misleading—sometimes the disk *must* be placed in a specific drive, normally the one it was in earlier. If you put the disk in the wrong drive, the message will reappear.) You can change the volume label of a disk at any time with the RELABEL command program. To change the name of the disk in the above example to *Spreadsheet*, for instance, you'd type

`RELABEL df0: Spreadsheet`

The Filing System

Identification
Besides the volume name, AmigaDOS also writes an identification number on each disk. It tries to make each of these ID numbers unique, so even if two disks both have the same volume name, the disk operating system can tell them apart. The disk-duplication programs provided on your Workbench disk don't reproduce the old ID number on the new disk, so even exact copies can be distinguished from the original. Only if a disk is duplicated by a commercial mass-duplicating machine (or special copying programs) will the IDs on copies match that of the original.

Info
After a disk is formatted, the INFO command shows that it contains 1758 blocks of usable storage space, each containing 512 bytes. Note that this is two blocks short of 880K—the disk operating system reserves these for its own purposes. In addition, DOS uses two of these 1758 blocks, leaving you with 1756 free blocks (878K) on a newly formatted disk. If you want to verify this, you can use the command program INFO to display the amount of storage used on the disk and the amount of remaining free space. Type INFO, and you'll see a display that looks like this:

Unit	Size	Used	Free	Full	Errs	Status	Name
DF1:	880K	1317	441	74%	0	Read/Write	Workbench
DF0:	880K	2	1756	0%	0	Read/Write	Wordprocessing

Mounted disks:

Volumes available:
Wordprocessing [Mounted]
Workbench [Mounted]

This display tells you the size of the total storage space on each disk currently in each drive (mounted), how many blocks have been used, how many are free, the percentage of disk space that's used up, how many errors were encountered in reading from the disk, whether or not the disk is write-protected, and the volume name of each disk.

Installing
There are a couple of other things you should know about formatting a disk. First, it's not necessary to format a disk before you perform a DISKCOPY to it—the DISKCOPY program both formats the new disk and copies all the information from the source disk to this disk. Second, the system will not accept a newly formatted disk if

The Filing System

it's inserted at the prompt that tells you to put in the Workbench disk (it just keeps asking for a Workbench disk). In order to make a newly formatted disk bootable, you must use the INSTALL program. To install the boot information on drive df0:, for example, enter

`INSTALL df0:`

The INSTALL program doesn't prompt you to put the disk into the drive—it does the installation immediately. This makes it difficult to use INSTALL on a single-drive system because you must have the INSTALL program on the disk you want to install. If you don't want to copy that program to the disk, you can copy it to the RAM disk instead (we'll be talking about the RAM disk at greater length in the next chapter).

To do this, put your CLI disk in the drive, and type

`COPY c/install TO ram:`

Put the new disk you want to INSTALL to into the internal drive (it must be formatted first), and type

`RAM:INSTALL df0:`

Once the INSTALL process is completed, you may put that disk into the internal drive when the system prompt for the Workbench appears on the screen, and the disk will boot and show the CLI 1> prompt. Unless you put the DOS command files on that disk, of course, you cannot use the commands just by typing their names.

Version 1.3 of the Workbench added a new function for the INSTALL command. If you add the keyword CHECK to the INSTALL command line, the program will check to see if the information on the boot block of the disk is the standard Commodore-Amiga code, or some nonstandard code which may indicate that the disk contains a virus (a hidden program that may adversely affect your computer's performance). Using the INSTALL program to rewrite the book block to the disk will destroy most virus programs, but it can also cause some copy-protected programs to cease functioning.

Files and Their Characteristics

The basic unit of information stored on a disk is called a *file*. A file is just a group of characters of information that are stored together on the disk under a common filename. A file can represent a computer program, or a collection of data used by that program, such as the text of a document created by a word processing program.

The Filing System

To see the contents of a file, use the TYPE command.

To print a text file called *document* on the screen, for example, enter the command TYPE document. You may remember from the previous chapter that you can pause output to the screen at any time by striking a key, such as the space bar, and restart output by using the BACK SPACE key to erase that keystroke. TYPE is really only helpful for seeing the contents of text files. If a file contains the numeric code for a computer program, the TYPE command will print out what seems like a jumble of nonsense characters.

Each file has a number of characteristics associated with it. These include the name of the file, the number of characters it contains, the number of disk blocks it uses, the protection level, the date and time of its creation, and comments (if any). If you just want to see a directory listing of the names of files on a disk, sorted into alphabetical order, use the DIR command program.

The LIST command displays a list of files and all of their characteristics. You can LIST all the files in a directory, a selected portion of the files, or even a single file. There are a number of variations on this command (see the "Command Reference" section for details). The simplest form is

LIST

which displays information about the files and directories in the current directory. As with other displays, you can pause it by pressing a key, such as the space bar, and resume it by pressing the BACK SPACE key.

In the sections below, we'll examine in detail each of the file characteristics displayed by the LIST command program.

Filenames

The most important characteristic of a file is its name, since you must know the name in order to access the information a file contains. A filename may be up to 30 characters long and may contain almost any character, with a few exceptions. A filename can't contain a slash (/) or colon (:); DOS uses these to identify the directory to which a file belongs (see the section below on directories for more information). A filename cannot use nonprinting characters (like TAB) or characters from the alternate character set (which appear when you hold down the ALT key and type a character).

If you want to use the special characters that the CLI recognizes as command modifiers in a filename, you'll have to jump through some hoops. To use the space ( ), plus (+) at the end of a name, equal (=), or semicolon (;) in a filename, you must put

The Filing System

the whole filename in double quotation marks. For instance,

COPY SOB TO "Son of a Blitter Object"
RENAME "3+3" TO Sixpack

If you include the device name and/or directory name as part of the file specification, the whole file specification must appear in quotation marks, like this:

"DF1:Programs/My Program"

Not like this:

DF1:Programs/"My Program"

By using the double quotation mark for this purpose, you've made it an exception to the naming rules. So what if you want to have a filename that includes quotation marks? You'll have to use an asterisk (*) in front of the double quotes as an escape character to tell DOS you want the quotation mark to appear in the name and not just set off a chunk of text that contains space characters. This means you would type the filename *"So-Called" Facts* like this:

"*"So-Called*" Facts"

Confused? It gets worse. Now you've made the asterisk an exception, too. This means in order to use the asterisk in a name, you must use another asterisk in front of it. The name **void where prohibited* must be typed as

"**void where prohibited"

To summarize:

- Filenames may be up to 30 characters long.
- They may not contain a colon (:), slash (/), nonprinting, or ALTernate character.
- If you want to use characters like the space, plus (+) at the end of a name, equal (=), and semicolon (;), all of which have special significance to CLI, you must put the entire filename in double quotation marks (*"A Special File"*).
- If you want to use double quotation marks (") or an asterisk in a filename, you must precede them with an asterisk (*"*"Confusion**10*""* for *"Confusion*10"*).

In the examples above, some of the filenames appear in lowercase characters, some in a combination of upper- and lowercase. Any combination can be used in naming a file. When you LIST the filenames, they'll be printed using the same combination of uppercase and lowercase used when the file was named. The CLI, however, does not distinguish between cases. You can refer to a file named CAPITAL as *capital* or *Capital* or even *CAPital*, and the CLI reads them all identically. Since you cannot have two files with the same name in the same directory, a single directory cannot contain files named *Test* and *TEST*, because to the CLI each name looks the same.

Filenotes

Though the name of a file is your chief source of information about its contents, AmigaDOS provides another source as well. Using the command program FILENOTE, you can attach a comment of up to 80 characters to a file. This comment can be used to note what's in the file or show how this file differs from other files with similar names. When you use the LIST command to obtain information about the files on a disk, the FILENOTE comment is displayed right beneath the name of the file.

Not all files have filenotes attached. (No filenote is automatically attached to the file when it's created.) You must enter it yourself with the command FILENOTE, which uses this format:

FILENOTE *filename* COMMENT *"This comment tells you about the file"*

The use of the keyword COMMENT before the comment is optional. The rules for using special characters (such as spaces) within comments are the same as those for using such characters within filenames. If you use spaces within the text of the comment, the entire comment must be enclosed within quotation marks, and if you want to include quotation marks or an asterisk in the comment, you must precede them with an asterisk.

An interesting characteristic of filenotes is that they remain firmly attached to the file to which they're appended. The comment does not change or disappear when you rename the file. If you copy the contents of a file to one that has a filenote, the filenote stays attached, even though its contents have changed. If, however, you copy a file with a filenote to a new file, the filenote is *not* copied along with the contents. It sticks like glue to the original. There is no way to delete a filenote alone. If you want to get rid of it, you have to change the comment to something innocuous, like blank spaces, or copy the whole file and delete the original.

File Size

The LIST command displays a number after the filename. This number represents the size of the file in bytes (characters). This number should not be confused with the number of disk blocks that the file uses. Even though each block can hold 512 bytes of information, every file uses a *minimum* of two disk blocks. This

The Filing System

means a file only one character long uses up 1024 characters of disk space.

To test this, type INFO to see the number of free blocks on your disk. Now type

COPY * TO test

Press the Return key, and then the CTRL key and the backslash key (\) at the same time.

This copies from the keyboard of your console device (represented by the asterisk) to a disk file named *test*. The CTRL-\ key combination is the end-of-file character, which signals the end of output from the console device and stops the copying process. You end up with a file that contains only one character.

If you enter LIST test, you'll see that the file length is really one character. But if you type INFO again, the number of free blocks has decreased by two. Keep this in mind—numerous small disk files may take up more space than if the same information were stored as one long file. Even an empty file uses up one block of storage.

Protection Level

On the display provided by LIST, there's space for eight characters next to the size of the file. Seven of these characters—*sparwed*—represent the seven protection status flags associated with each file. These flags determine whether or not you can read, execute the file as a script without using the EXECUTE command, make it resident with the RESIDENT command, and write, execute, or delete the file. *Read, write,* and *delete* are fairly self-explanatory—if set, these flags allow you to read from the file, write new information to it, and delete the file completely. The *Execute* bit operates only on program files—it allows DOS to execute (run) the program. If you set the execute flag on a nonprogram file (a text file, for instance), you cannot expect DOS to load and run the file. It's important to note that in all releases of AmigaDOS to date, the read, write, and execute bits do not perform their intended function. You can set these flags, but DOS does not act on those settings.

The final three flags were added under AmigaDOS 1.3. The S (or Script) bit is used to tell the Shell that a file is a script file that would normally be run with the EXECUTE command. If you type in the name of a script file at a Shell prompt, the Shell will execute the script even though you don't type in the EXECUTE command name.

The P (or Pure) flag is used in conjunction with the RESIDENT command, which loads a CLI command into memory and uses it as

The Filing System

if it were a "built-in" AmigaDOS command. Since only certain types of programs can be made RESIDENT (those that can be run from multiple CLI's at the same time, using only one copy of the program), the pure bit is used to tell the RESIDENT whether the file in question is a suitable candidate.

The *A* (or Archive) flag doesn't have any intrinsic meaning to AmigaDOS, but is provided for the use of backup programs which are used to create archival copies of data. When the backup program copies a file, it sets the A bit to show it has been archived. If the user later changes that file, the A flag will be removed, so the next time a backup is performed, the backup program will know this file has been changed, and must be saved again.

When a file is created, the *RWED* flags are set. As indicators, the four characters (*rwed*) appear in the LISTing of the file name (along with four dashes, representing unset flag bits). To change the protection status of a file, use the PROTECT command program. The form of this command is

PROTECT *filename* FLAGS *rwed*

where *filename* is the name of the file whose status you wish to alter, and *rwed* are the letters for the flags you wish to enable. For example, if you want to remove just the deletion flag from a file called *LifesWork*, you'd enter

PROTECT LifesWork FLAGS rwe

This would allow you to read, write, or execute the file, but not to delete it. As of Workbench 1.3, the PROTECT command allows you to use the + and − characters to add or subtract one or more protection flags. For example, to set the Script flag on a file called *Execute.Me*, you'd enter

PROTECT Execute.Me FLAGS +s

File Dating

The final item displayed by the LIST command program is the date and time the file was created. The Amiga 2000 and 2500 come equipped with a battery-powered clock/calendar module, from which the time and date is read at power-on, using the SETCLOCK command. The Amiga 1000 doesn't come with such a clock module. And on the Amiga 500 the clock module is optional. If your computer does not have a clock/calendar, it's up to you to set the correct time and date each time you turn on the machine, or reset the computer. You can find out what time and date the Amiga is currently using by checking the time setting in the Preferences program or by entering the command filename DATE. You can set the

The Filing System

time from the Preferences program that comes with the Workbench disk or by using the DATE command program.

To set the time using the DATE command, use the form

DATE *HH:MM:SS*

where *HH* is a two-digit number for the hour, *MM* is a two-digit number for the minute, and *SS* is a an optional two-digit number for the second. If you don't specify the seconds, the Amiga uses 00 for you (if you don't specify seconds, you don't need to include the final colon). Note that hours are expressed in a 24-hour format, in which 1:00 p.m. is referred to as 13:00, and midnight as 00:00.

The DATE program expects the date in the format *DD-MMM-YY*, where *DD* is a two-digit number representing the day of the month, *MMM* is the first three letters of the name of the month, and *YY* is the last two digits of the year. For example, to set the date to September 29, 1989, you'd type

DATE 29-Sep-89

It's possible to set both the date and time with one command:

DATE 16-May-89 14:56

Besides the *DD-MMM-YY* format, AmigaDOS also understands some common ways of expressing the date, such as Yesterday, Today, Tomorrow, and the days of the week, such as Monday, Tuesday, Wednesday, and so on. You can use these expressions in place of the *DD-MMM-YY* format anytime you want to change the current date to one *within the coming week*. For example, let's say you just turned on the Amiga and used the DATE command to find out the current time and date setting. If today is Sunday, November 26, 1989, and you last wrote a file to the disk the day before, you may find that the setting is *Saturday 25-Nov-89-20:20:02*. To make the date current, you need only type

DATE tomorrow

or

DATE Sunday 10:00

Either form advances the setting one day.

Remember that using the name of a day of the week (you can't use abbreviations here—you must use the full name of the day) will always set the date *forward* to that day. In the example above, if you'd typed DATE Friday, it would have set the date to Friday 01-Dec-89 instead of Friday 27-Nov-89. The only date word that sets the date backward is *Yesterday*. The *DATE Yesterday* command moves the date back by one day.

The Filing System

AmigaDOS also uses these words in its LIST display, so don't be surprised if you see recent files with dates like Yesterday or Today. The meaning of such terms in the LIST display is somewhat different with the DATE command, however. DATE expects that the new date you're setting will be later than the current date that's shown, so if you use day names like Tuesday, it sets the date to the Tuesday following the current date. LIST, however, assumes that files on an existing disk must have been created previously, so when LIST says Tuesday, it means the Tuesday *before* the current date. If you put in a disk that wasn't in the drive when you booted up the Amiga, and there's a file on the disk with a date later than the current date, LIST will show its date merely as Future. To see the actual date of such a file, you'd have to change the current date far enough to the future so it's *later* than that of the file.

If you've set the correct date, expressions like Today or Wednesday can be helpful in quickly picking out new files from old ones. But what date does the Amiga use if you haven't set the correct date? AmigaDOS sets aside a place on each disk where it records the latest date and time that a file was created. This latest date is updated with the current date and time every time you write to a file (provided that the current date is later than the latest date). When you boot up the computer, AmigaDOS checks the latest date recorded on the boot disk (and on the disk in the external drive as well, if one's inserted). It sets the current date and time just a little later than the latest date found (AmigaDOS appears to advance it by 11 seconds). That way, even if you forget to set a new time and date when you boot up, your files will still appear in correct chronological order. You won't be able to tell the exact date and time a file was created, but you *will* be able to tell which was created most recently.

This time-stamping feature of AmigaDOS can be a great aid when you're trying to identify one file among several. In fact, it's so convenient that if your computer doesn't have a clock/calendar, you may want to alter the startup command file so it prompts you to enter the correct date and time whenever you turn the computer on. An example of such a file can be found in Chapter 5, which explains command sequence files.

Directories and Subdirectories

With 880K of space, it's quite possible to have over a hundred files on one disk. That many files in a single directory makes disk operations very clumsy—just scanning a directory listing becomes a chore. This problem becomes much worse when you start to work

The Filing System

with a hard disk that has 20 or 60 million bytes of available storage space.

AmigaDOS's answer to this is to provide multiple directory levels, which branch out from the highest directory on down. This allows you to place several related files into their own directory, where you can work with them in an environment isolated from the other, unrelated files on the disk. Your Workbench disk, for example, contains directories like *c*, which contains command program files, and *devs*, which contains files for device drivers like the one that makes your printer work. Some of these subdirectories, such as *Utilities*, have icon files associated with them which make them appear on the Workbench screen as drawers.

Root and MAKEDIR

When you create a new file structure by formatting a disk, there's only one directory on the disk. This is the highest level, or *root*, directory. When you write files to this disk, these files go into the root directory. If you wish, however, you can create new directories, known as *subdirectories*, within the root directory. Let's say you're going to use part of the disk for storing word processing files and part of the disk for telecommunications files. You could create separate subdirectories for each kind of file by using the MAKEDIR (make directory) command program. Just type `MAKEDIR`, followed by the name of the directory. The rules for naming directories are the same as for naming files (see above for more information). Using the names in the example above, you'd type

`MAKEDIR Wordprocessing`
`MAKEDIR Telecommunications`

After you put a few files into each of the directories, your directory structure might look like this:

A Typical Directory Structure

This structure is similar to what you might see if you draw a family tree. At the top level is the *root directory*, which contains a file (a data file called *Textfile*) and two subdirectories (*Wordprocessing* and *Telecommunications*). These subdirectories in turn

The Filing System

contain their own files. The *Wordprocessing* directory contains the files *Textfile* and *Moretext*, and the *Telecommunications* directory contains the files *Terminal* and *Downloads*.

You'll notice that the root directory and the *Wordprocessing* directory both contain a file named *Textfile*. You can't have two files of the same name in the *same* directory. If you tried to create a new file with the same name as an existing one, the new file would overwrite and replace the existing one. But, there's no problem having two files of the same name in *different* directories. Each directory can be thought of as its own small disk except that a directory doesn't have a fixed size limit (within the space considerations of the disk itself). A directory takes up as much space as required to hold its files and subdirectories.

Just as the root directory can contain either files or subdirectories, the subdirectories themselves may contain files or subdirectories. For instance, if you have a large number of document files in the *Wordprocessing* directory, you may wish to group them into subdirectories, such as *Personal Letters, Business Letters, Proposals,* and *Speeches*. There's no limit to the number of directory levels you can create—again other than the space available on the disk. Most people will find, however, that about four or five levels down is as far as they care to go.

If you want to see the complete contents of a disk, including files within subdirectories, you can do so by adding the phrase OPT A (for *all*) to the DIR command. If you examine the sample disk illustrated above with the command DIR OPT A, you'll see the following display:

```
Telecommunications (dir)
    Downloads                    Terminal
Wordprocessing (dir)
    Moretext                     Textfile
Textfile
```

Gaining Access

You can gain access to files within subdirectories in one of two ways. If you wish, you can specify complete information about the file, including each of the directory levels between it and the root directory (this is known as the *full pathname*). Do this by naming each of the directories, in order, from the root down, separating the name of each directory with a slash (/). If the disk described above is in the internal drive, you could refer to the file *Textfile* in

The Filing System

the *Wordprocessing* directory as *DF0:Wordprocessing/Textfile*. Specifying the entire path from the top down always works, but it can be a bit tiresome (particularly with a file like *DF0:Wordprocessing/Personal Letters/Aunt Charlotte—Thank You*).

A less burdensome alternative involves the concept of the current, or default, directory. If you refer to a file without specifying a device or directory path, AmigaDOS looks for that file in whichever directory is currently the default directory. When you first start up the computer, AmigaDOS sets the root directory of your boot disk (the one in the internal drive) as the current directory. You're free to assign a new current directory at any time. Just type CD (for the Current Directory command program), followed by the name of the directory (or directory path, if you're going down more than one level). Using the same example, you could make the *Wordprocessing* directory the current one by typing

CD Wordprocessing

From then on, if you want to use the file *Textfile*, you could refer to it by name, instead of as *Wordprocessing/Textfile*. If you use the command DIR after changing the current directory to *Wordprocessing*, you'd see only a list of the files in that directory.

Up and Down

It's even possible to skip down more than one level at a time. If you want to change the current directory from the root directory to the *Business Letters* subdirectory of the *Wordprocessing* directory, enter

CD "Wordprocessing/Business Letters"   (*quotes needed for names with spaces*)

The CD command always assumes the name you give it is of a directory or path that lies *below* the level of the current directory. To move up to a higher level, you must use one of two special characters. The first is the familiar slash (/). A slash in front of a directory name is the signal to move *up* a level to the directory that contains the current directory. The backslash alone works—you don't have to specify the name of the higher directory—since each directory has only one directory immediately above it. To change the current directory to the one immediately above, just type

CD /

You're not limited to a single slash. You can use as many slashes as there are directories above the current one. Thus,

CD //

moves you up two directories.

The Filing System

Nor are you limited to going in one direction at a time with CD. Assume your current directory is the *Letters* subdirectory of the *Wordprocessing* directory, and you want to change to the *Telecommunications* subdirectory of the root directory. You could use the command form

CD //Telecommunications

The first slash takes you up to *Wordprocessing*, the second slash takes you up to the root directory, and *Telecommunications* takes you down one level to make that directory current.

If your goal is to return to the root directory, however, it's not necessary to enter a slash for each level. You can use the colon (:) to indicate a move directly up to root level. For instance,

CD :

makes the root directory the current directory, while

CD :Telecommunications

assigns the *Telecommunications* directory as the current directory, no matter how far down you were when you entered the command.

CD is not the only command that takes the initial slash as a signal to move up one directory level, and you can use the colon to refer to the root directory at any time. Commands such as

DIR :
DIR :Wordprocessing
DIR /
DIR /Wordprocessing

all work, as long as the directories referred to really exist.

If you wish to change the default directory to one located on another disk, you must specify the device name or volume name when using CD. To switch to the root directory on the disk in the external 3½-inch drive, for example, you'd use

CD df1:

Note that when you switch the current directory to another disk, AmigaDOS internally refers to that disk by its volume name and not by the device name of the disk drive in which it's mounted. This means when you put a disk with volume name CLI in drive df1: and type CD DF1:, AmigaDOS changes the current directory to the root directory of volume CLI. If you take that disk out of the external drive and replace it with another, AmigaDOS will be very unhappy. Use DIR with the new disk in the drive, and DOS won't comply. It will put up a requester box asking you to replace volume CLI in any drive. That's because to AmigaDOS, the current directory is the root of the specific disk named CLI, not just

The Filing System

any disk that happens to be in the external drive. When you wish to replace that disk with another, you should change the current directory to one of the disks you'll use. In the example above, once you replace the CLI volume with another disk, you could issue the command CD DF1: once again, making the root directory of that volume the new current directory. Then if you issue the DIR command, you would not be prompted to swap disks. If you're ever unsure which is the current directory, simply use the command CD (and that's all) to display the current directory name. For more information on device names, logical devices, and volume names, see Chapter 4.

File Manipulation Commands

Some of the most commonly used CLI commands are those that copy, delete, rename, and join (combine) files.

COPY

The COPY command is used to create a duplicate of a file in the same directory, in another directory, or even on another disk.

COPY vitalstuff TO vitalstuff.backup

This creates a backup copy of the file in the same directory with another name.

COPY programfile Programs/programfile

While this command line creates a copy of the file with the same name in the subdirectory named *Programs*.

COPY *filename* df1:

And this command makes a copy of the file (with the same name) in the root directory of the disk in drive df1:.

RENAME

The RENAME command program changes the name of a file or a directory. When you RENAME a directory, you change its position in the directory structure:

RENAME program TO program.old

This changes the name of the file *program* to *program.old*.

RENAME df1:c/delete TO df1:c/erase

While this command line changes the name of the command program *delete* on disk drive df1: to *erase*, also on disk df1:.

RENAME Wordprocessing/Letters TO :WordWiz/Textfiles

The Filing System

And this example moves the directory *Wordprocessing/Letters* and all of its contents to the directory *WordWiz/Textfiles*.

DELETE
DELETE removes a file from the disk. Once you delete a file, the information contained in it is lost forever. DELETE lets you name up to ten files to delete at a time. Separate each filename with a space.

DELETE oldfile

This permanently erases the file *oldfile*.

DELETE oldfile1 oldfile2 oldfile3

And this sample erases all three of the named files.
    DELETE can also be used to erase a directory, but *only* if it does not contain any files or subdirectories. You can use the same DELETE command first to erase the files in the directory, then to delete the directory, or you can use the keyword ALL.

DELETE Wordprocessing/lonefile Wordprocessing

This first deletes the only file in the *Wordprocessing* directory, then deletes the directory. Or you can use

DELETE Wordprocessing ALL

which deletes the directory and all files it contains.

JOIN
The JOIN command file takes the contents of from 2 to 15 files and combines them into a new and larger file. The original files are unchanged.

JOIN firsthalf secondhalf AS bothparts

This creates a new file called *bothparts* which contains all the information of both *firsthalf* and *secondhalf*.

Pattern Matching (Wildcards)

Sometimes it's possible to specify one or more filenames that have a common characteristic without typing the entire filename. This technique, called *pattern matching*, lets you do such things as list all files with names ending in the characters *.bas* or delete every file in a directory at one time.
    AmigaDOS pattern matching is similar to the concept of *wildcard* characters used in MS/PC-DOS, but there are important differences. In PC-DOS, the asterisk (*) can be used to substitute

The Filing System

for any string of characters in a filename. In AmigaDOS, the asterisk is used as an escape character, to allow quotation marks (and other asterisks) in a filename. Also, as you'll see in the next chapter, the asterisk is used to refer to the currently active console device.

PC wildcards can be used with more commands than AmigaDOS pattern matching, which is mostly confined to COPY, DELETE, DIR, and LIST. AmigaDOS patterns, however, are much more flexible. They allow you to match names starting with the same group of characters, end with the same group of characters, or have the same characters in the middle, preceded by any number of characters and followed by any number of characters. Such flexibility makes the system somewhat complex to learn, but well worth the time and effort required.

? and

The most important pattern-matching characters are the question mark (?) and the pound sign (#). The pound sign followed by a single character matches any number of repetitions of that character (including none). For example, #STUTTER matches STUTTER (#S substitutes for one S), SSSSTUTTER (#S substitutes for four consecutive S's), and TUTTER (#S can also substitute for zero occurrences of the letter S). The question mark is used to replace any single character (but not the null string, or no character). Thus, ?LA?S matches FLATS (first ? replaces F, second replaces T) or 2LAPS (first ? replaces 2, second replaces P), but not LAPS (first ? must replace an actual character).

When you put these two special characters together (#?), they become a powerful pattern that can match any number of any characters (or no characters at all). For example, you could use PART#? if you wanted a pattern to match all filenames starting with the letters PART. If you wanted to LIST all of the icon information files (whose names always end in .info), you could use the pattern #?.INFO to find them. You could also use a pattern like PART#?.INFO to match any file starting with PART and ending with .INFO, with anything (or nothing) in between (like PARTICLE.INFO, PARTYANIMAL. INFO, PART47ZYC-332.INFO, and even PART.INFO). Likewise, you could use a pattern like #?CAT#? to match a filename that had the letters CAT anywhere in it (like CATAPULT, SCAT, SCATTER, or "I SNEEZE AT CAT HAIR").

The Filing System

( )

In addition to the pound sign and question mark, there are three other characters that have special meaning when used for pattern matching. Parentheses ( ) may be used to group a number of characters together into a single pattern element. If you follow a pound sign with a group of characters within parentheses, for instance, it will match any number of repetitions of that pattern group (including none). Thus, *#(YO)* matches the filenames *YO, YOYO, YOYOYOYO*, and so on. If you didn't use the parentheses, *#YO* would match *YO* and *YYYYO*, but not *YOYO*, because the *#Y* could substitute only for repetitions of the single letter *Y*. Parentheses let you become creative, doing things like using *#(P?NG)* to match the filename *PINGPONG*.

|

The vertical bar (|), entered by pressing the SHIFTed backslash key, is used when you want one of two or more patterns to match the characters in the filename. *A | B* matches either the letter *A* or the letter *B*. The pattern *GOOD | BAD* matches either a file named *GOOD* or one named *BAD*. And pattern *MO(B | N)STER* matches both *MONSTER* and *MOBSTER* (note how the parentheses were used to set off the *B | N* as a distinct pattern). AmigaDOS understands the vertical bar as applying only to one part of the pathname. For example, the command

    COPY df0:c/COPY|DIR|LIST to ram:

would be understood to mean copy any file named COPY, DIR, or LIST from the C directory on df0: to the root directory of the RAM disk, and not copy the file named COPY from the C directory of df0:, or DIR or LIST from the current directory to the RAM disk. This aspect of the vertical bar can be very handy when dealing with several files in a complicated path at one time. Note that prior to Workbench 1.3, there was a limit of 31 characters in any one wildcard expression, which limited the number of files you could join with the vertical bar. This limit was removed in 1.3.

%

The percentage sign (%) represents the null string (no character). You've already seen how a pattern starting with the pound sign matches any number of repetitions of the following character, including none at all. The pattern *S#HIN*, for example, matches *SHIN, SHHHIN*, and *SIN*. But if you want to match only a single appearance of the character or none at all, you can use the form *(H | %)*, which stands for either *H* or the null character (no character

The Filing System

at all). Therefore, *S(H | %)IN* would still match *SHIN* and *SIN*, but would not match *SHHHIN*, which repeats the *H* character more than once.

Combining the percentage sign with the question mark in the form *(? | %)* creates an expression that will match *any* character or no character at all. Using a previous example, you could substitute the pattern *(? | %)LA?S* to match either *2LAPS* or just plain *LAPS*.

There's one final character used to address a problem created by the other special characters. Since those characters have special meanings in the language of pattern matching, it makes it difficult when you want to match a name that contains one of those special characters as part of the filename. In order to match a filename that contains a question mark, for example, you must precede the question mark with an apostrophe (') to let the pattern matching mechanism know that you want to match an actual question mark, without using the question mark as a substitute for any other character. For instance, you could use the pattern *?OW'?* to match filenames like *HOW?* and *COW?*.

Naturally, since the apostrophe is now a special character, you must use two apostrophes to represent an apostrophe that might be part of a filename. A pattern like *?ON''T* is needed to match filenames like *DON'T* and *WON'T*. If these rules remind you of the rules for naming files, all the better. The same rules apply to pattern substitution, too. If you're using a pattern containing space characters, for example, you must enclose the entire pattern with double quotation marks.

Pattern Matching Summary

#c   Matches any number of repetitions of the character *c* (including none)
N#O matches *N, NO, NOO,* and *NOOOOOOOOOOO*

#(group)   Matches any number of repetitions of *group* (including none)
#(TOM) matches *TOM* and *TOMTOM*

?   Matches any single character (but not the null character)
K?NG matches *KING* and *KONG* (but not *KNG*)

#?   Matches any number of repetitions of any character (including none)
#?.BAS matches any *filename* ending in *.BAS*

P1 | P2   Matches either pattern *P1* or *P2*
B(A | O)Y matches *BAY* and *BOY*
df0:c/LIST|DIR matches *df0:c/LIST* or *df0:c/DIR*

%   Matches the null string (no character)
(S | %)TOP matches *STOP* or *TOP*

The Filing System

(? | %) Matches any character or no character
         (? | %)LOT matches *SLOT, CLOT,* and *LOT*
( )   Used to set off a group of characters as its own distinct pattern
         (M | P)A matches *MA* or *PA*
         M | PA matches *M* or *PA*
'   Used in front of one of the special characters to show that you want to match it, not invoke its special meaning
         ?ON"T matches *WON'T* and *DON'T*

Chapter 4

Devices

The main function of a disk operating system like AmigaDOS is to let you control disk devices. But there are several other kinds of devices that the Amiga is capable of accessing, and the CLI provides ways of interacting with them also. Some of these devices are physical devices, like the console screen and keyboard, hard disks, printers, and modems. Others are "software" devices like the RAM disks and pipe handler. As you'll discover later, AmigaDOS even treats some disk directories as *logical* devices.

Some of these devices are *built-in*, and AmigaDOS recognizes them automatically. Others must have their driver or handler software added to the system by use of the MOUNT or BINDDRIVERS command.

Disk Drives

Every Amiga comes with an internal disk drive. This device is known as DF0: (for Disk Floppy). Optionally, you can connect an external 3½-inch drive (or in the case of the 2000 or 2500, a second internal drive), known as DF1:.

Although the Amiga supports up to four floppy drives, the power supply that comes with the Amiga 500 really only provides enough power for one external drive. If you want to run more drives than that, you'll have to find a drive with an independent power supply, or buy one of the larger replacement power supplies available for the 500.

The Amiga 2000's power supply is quite sufficient for four floppies, and even the 1000 should be able to handle three or four of the newer drives, which consume much less power than previous models.

The 5¼-inch drive Commodore offers for use with MS-DOS is self-powered, but is not automatically recognized by AmigaDOS. The MOUNT command must be used to add this device to the system (a sample entry can be found in the DEVS:Mountlist file that comes with the Workbench for this device, under the name DF2:). When used this way by AmigaDOS, however, the 5¼-inch drive can only store 440K, half of the amount stored on a 3½-inch drive.

A disk drive is not a single, indivisible device like a printer. Rather, its storage area is divided into a number of different directories and files. Therefore, you'll most often use the device name DF0: or DF1: only as part of a file or a directory description.

A Complete Description

The most complete kind of file description contains the disk device name, followed by the names of each succeeding directory level (separated by slashes), then finally the name of the file. The name *DF1:WordWiz/Letters/Formletter* is a good example. The filename is *Formletter*, which is in the directory *Letters*, which in turn is in the directory *WordWiz*. All are found on device *DF1:*, the external (or second internal) disk drive.

If you refer to a device as simply DF1:, however, AmigaDOS interprets this as a reference to the root directory of the disk mounted in that drive. *WordWiz* may not be the current directory, and getting to it may take some keystrokes.

Fortunately, you don't always have to give a complete description of a file. AmigaDOS also recognizes references to a file that are relative to the *current* directory. One directory is always recognized as the current directory. When you first start the Amiga, it uses the root directory of the disk in the internal drive as the default directory. Therefore, when you refer to a file like *Myprogram*, AmigaDOS interprets this as *DF0:Myprogram*. If you change the current directory to *C*, for example, using the CD command, a reference to the file *Dir* will be taken to mean *DF0:C/Dir*.

You can also use the colon (:) to indicate the root directory of the disk on which the current directory is located. Therefore, even when *C* is the current directory, you can specify a file in the *S* directory with the description *:s/startup-sequence*, which is equivalent to *DF0:s/startup-sequence* (as long as DF0: is the drive holding the disk on which the current directory is located). Note that AmigaDOS ignores case in these names. Any combination of uppercase and lowercase can be used, as long as the letters themselves match.

You may also use the volume name of the disk itself in place of the device name of the drive in which it's mounted. For example, if you have a file called *program.bas* located on a disk whose volume name is *Extras*, you could describe the file as *Extras:program.bas*. In fact, such a description may be preferable to using the device name of the drive, since it's valid regardless of which drive is used for the *Extras* disk.

In some cases, it's necessary to refer to a disk by its volume name. Let's say you have only one disk drive and want to list a directory of a disk that doesn't contain the DIR command program.

Devices

The volume name of this disk is *Stuff*. When you insert the *Stuff* disk into the drive and type DIR, the system prompts you to put the disk containing the commands into the drive. When you do, the Amiga lists a directory of *that* disk, not *Stuff*. But if you enter DIR Stuff:, you'll be prompted first to put in the disk with the commands, then to put in *Stuff*. Now you'll get a listing of the *Stuff* disk. Of course, there are other solutions to this problem—you could copy the DIR file to *Stuff*, or you could copy your commands to the RAM: disk device (see below). But if you want to specify operations on a particular disk, using the volume name assures you of the correct result. In fact, AmigaDOS keeps track of the disk with the current directory in just this way. If you take the disk out and type in a command, DOS prompts you with the volume name of the disk it wants you to insert.

Hard Disks

Hard disks are fixed (nonremovable) drives that either fit inside the computer itself, or in a box that sits next to the computer. Although hard drives are more expensive that floppy drives, they can read and write information much more quickly, and can store a lot of information in one place. These advantages are particularly important to Amiga owners, since the Amiga floppy drives are relatively slow, and some of the Amiga system software (such as text fonts) must be read in from disk. As we'll see in the section on logical devices, software may require files to be read in from the Workbench disk at any time, so it can be quite handy to have that disk constantly available. With the 1.3 Kickstart ROM, Commodore introduced autobooting to the Amiga, which means it's possible for the computer to start up from the hard drive, without having to read a Workbench disk in the floppy drive.

Although hard drives were not well supported by AmigaDOS until version 1.2, there are now a number of different interfaces that can be used to add a hard disk to your system. The device driver software that gives AmigaDOS access to these hard drives is added to the system through the use of the MOUNT or BIND-DRIVERS command, or by means of a special mounting program like *SupraMount* (for hard drives manufactured by Supra Corporation) or *DJMount* (for drives connected to the A2000 via the IBM compatibility option, or Bridge Board).

In most cases the hard disk device is addressed as DH0: (for Hard Drive 0), although SCSI (Small Computer System Interface) drives connected to Commodore's own hard drive controller are numbered starting at DH2:. AmigaDOS partitions on a hard drive that's connected to a PC Bridge Board on the Amiga 2000 are known to AmigaDOS by names such as JH0: and JH1: (which stands for Janus Hard drive, after the Janus software that allows the Amiga and IBM-compatible sides of the computer to work together).

Hard drives are much larger storage devices than floppy disks, holding as much information as dozens of the smaller disks. For this reason, most hard drive interface software allows the user to partition the drive into smaller, logical drives. A 40 megabyte drive, for example, might be divided into a 10 megabyte partition called DH0:, a 13 megabyte partition called DH1:, and a 17 megabyte partition called DH2:. The details of partitioning depend on how the device driver software is added to the system. Hard drives that use the MOUNT command usually have an entry describing each partition in the devs:MountList file. Hard drives that use BIND-DRIVERS or custom software may have special software that writes partition information to the hard drive itself. In the case of IBM compatible hard drives interfaced through the Bridge Board, there is a program on the IBM side called ADISK which creates Amiga-DOS partitions on the MS-DOS hard drive.

Using a hard drive on the Amiga is very similar to having a large floppy disk drive, so the information found above concerning floppies (DF0: and DF1:) generally applies to hard disks as well. If you wish to use a hard disk for loading system files, assign all the logical devices to the proper directory of DH0: (see below for more information about the assignment of logical devices). You may wish to make such assignments part of your *startup-sequence* file so they occur automatically whenever the computer is turned on (see Chapter 5 for more information about command sequence files). You may also find that some programs may require some logical device name assignments to be made if they are to be run from a subdirectory on a hard drive. The instruction manuals for most programs contain hard drive installation instructions.

Commodore introduced a new piece of system software in Workbench 1.3, called the Fast File System (FFS). This is a new AmigaDOS disk software interface that provides much quicker disk access than the old filing system. The FFS won't work on normal floppies, because it stores data on disk in a different manner than the normal AmigaDOS file system. This means if 3½-inch drives used the new system, they wouldn't be able to read current AmigaDOS disks. Nonremovable media, however, like hard disks and RAM disks, don't face this problem. Most hard drives can be formatted using the new layout, resulting in speed increases of 500 percent or more. The new filing system software is located in a file called *FastFileSystem*, located in the *L* directory of the Workbench disk. Details of using the Fast File System vary from drive to drive, so you'll have to consult your hard disk interface manual for instructions on installing it on your hard drive.

The RAM: Disk

There's another disk drive available to all Amiga users. AmigaDOS allows you to reserve a section of memory for use as a super-fast electronic disk drive, known as the RAM: device. The RAM: device does not exist when you first start up the computer. You create it simply by referring to it. For example, when you COPY a file to RAM:, the device is automatically created. But you don't have to move any information to RAM: to create the device. Typing a command like CD RAM:, which changes the current directory to the root directory of RAM:, works as well.

Though AmigaDOS understands references to RAM:, the actual device handler for RAM: (the program that routes information to the device) must be loaded in from disk before the device can be used. This handler is located in a file called *Ram-Handler* in the *l* directory of the system disk. If this file is not available when the first reference to RAM: is made, the device cannot be created. Once it's loaded, however, the system doesn't have to refer to this file again when using the RAM: device. The startup-sequence file on Workbench 1.2 and 1.3 disks refer to RAM: in their command sequence, so the RAM disk is automatically created when one of these Workbench disks are used.

You can read, write, execute, and delete files from RAM: just as from any other disk device. There are, however, a few important differences. The most significant is that RAM: is a *temporary* storage device. Its files disappear when you turn off the power or when you warm-start the computer with the CTRL-Amiga-Amiga key combination. *If you store files to RAM:, remember to copy them to a physical disk device before you turn the power off or reset the computer.*

Another difference between RAM: and the physical disk drives is capacity. The 3½-inch disks have a fixed storage capacity of 880K, but RAM: is limited to available free memory. Unless you have substantial expansion memory, you won't be able to store as much in the RAM: disk as on the physical drives. In fact, you should avoid storing too much information in the RAM: disk. First of all, it's possible to crash the system if you take up all available memory. Even if things don't reach that stage, however, you may not have enough room to run application programs if your RAM: disk is too full.

Devices

One of the best ways to put the RAM: disk to use is to copy all or some of your CLI command programs to it and use the ASSIGN command (explained below) to make it the new command directory. The simplest way to do this is

```
COPY C: RAM: ALL
ASSIGN C: RAM:
```

This is discussed at greater length in the section "Logical Devices," later in the chapter.

Communications Ports

The Amiga personal computer comes with two communications ports—one serial and one parallel. The serial port can be used for transferring information to or from a modem (or another computer), a MIDI musical device (with the proper interface), or to a serial printer. The communication speed for this serial interface can be set from the Preferences program at speeds ranging from 110 to 19,200 bits per second (bps). The parallel port is initially set up by the system as a Centronics-type printer interface, which can be used only to send information to a printer. Application programs (but not AmigaDOS) can configure this parallel port so it can be used to input information as well. For example, external devices like audio digitizers, video digitizers, and clock/calendars, all use the parallel port for input rather than output.

AmigaDOS allows you to write information to either of these devices just as you would to a disk file. For example, if you wish to transfer the contents of a disk file named *wordfile* to a parallel printer, you could use the command TYPE wordfile TO PAR: or COPY wordfile TO PAR:. You could send the contents of the file to a serial printer or modem with the same commands by substituting the device name SER: for PAR:. You may also use the redirection operator (>) to cause the output from one of the disk commands to be sent to the parallel or serial devices (see the section on redirection below).

You should note that the handlers which actually know how to direct output to the communications ports are not an integral part of AmigaDOS. They reside on disk files named *serial.device* and *parallel.device* in the *devs* directory of the Workbench disk. The first time AmigaDOS tries to open these devices, it must read the proper handler file from disk. If it can't find the file, it can't open the device. Once the handler is loaded, DOS doesn't need to access the file again.

Devices

Using PRT:

Although you can control a serial printer directly through the SER: device and a parallel printer via the PAR: device, there's a better way. The device called *PRT:* can be used to send output to the printer, regardless of whether you have a serial or parallel printer connected. The PRT: device gets its information about which type of printer is connected from the *system-configuration* file in the *devs* directory. This is the file the Preferences program uses to store the preference settings. In order to route information through the printer device, DOS must first load a handler stored in the disk file *printer.device* in the *devs* directory of the Workbench disk. This handler itself must refer to a specific printer-driver file in the *printers* subdirectory of the same *devs* directory. The PRT: device uses the information stored there to translate control codes (such as those used to start and stop underlining) to equivalent codes used by your printer. In addition, the PRT: device translates the linefeed character (CTRL-J or ASCII 10) to a carriage-return character (CTRL-M or ASCII 13), plus a linefeed character. If you wish to use PRT:, but don't want a carriage return added to the linefeed, you may specify the device PRT:RAW.

Diagnosing problems with the PRT: device can be difficult, because there is both a hardware and software component to the device. Printer problems may be due to the hardware connection between the printer and the computer, or they could be due to problems with the printer driver software. When testing a printer, it's helpful to first try sending output to the PAR: or SER: device first (depending on whether the printer is connected to the parallel or serial port). A command like COPY s:Startup-Sequence to PAR: should print the file to the device. If this procedure doesn't work, the problem is with the hardware connection between your printer and computer (either the printer isn't ready to print, or you've got a bad cable). If it does work, however, you know the problem lies with the printer driver software.

To summarize the AmigaDOS device names that can be used to send information to the printer:

Device Name	Function
PAR: or SER:	Sends data directly to the printer, with no translation.
PRT:RAW	Sends data to the printer, translating printer codes, but does not add a carriage return to each linefeed.
PRT:	Sends data to the printer, translating printer codes, and adds a carriage return to each linefeed.

Console and Others

The console device is used to accept input from the keyboard and the mouse, and to print the characters on the screen. Output goes to a window on the screen, known as the *console window*. The console device accepts input from the keyboard a line at a time. At any point before you press the RETURN key, you may edit the line using CTRL-H or the BACK SPACE key to delete characters, and CTRL-X to delete the entire line (see Chapter 2 for more information about the editing capabilities of the console device). When the console receives a line of text, it translates the keystrokes into ASCII and extended ANSI codes. As noted in Chapter 2, the console device itself responds like an ANSI terminal to many escape codes that control things like cursor positioning, screen scrolling, line insertion and deletion, and the like.

Workbench 1.3 comes with an enhanced console device called NEWCON:, which introduces new features like line editing and command history. Since this device is not automatically recognized by AmigaDOS, but must be added with the MOUNT command, we'll cover it more fully in the treatment of MOUNTable devices, below.

Each CLI comes with its own console window (it's the window in which the >n prompt appears). When you use the NEWCLI command to start a new CLI process, you may specify the starting position, size, and title of its console window (see Chapter 2 for more information on starting a new CLI process). If you don't specify these characteristics, a default console window is used.

It's possible, however, to create your own console windows that aren't related to any existing CLI process. To do so, you refer to the device as

CON:*hpos*/*vpos*/*width*/*height*/*windowtitle*

where *hpos* is the horizontal position of the top left corner of the window (expressed as the number of pixels in from the left edge of the screen), *vpos* is the vertical position of the top left corner of the window (expressed as the number of pixels down from the top edge of the screen), and *width* and *height* give the size of the window in pixels. The maximum size for a console window is the screen size, normally 640 × 200 pixels. The minimum is 81 × 25 pixels. The last entry, *windowtitle*, is optional and allows you to enter a title that will appear in the title bar. If you don't enter a title, the title bar is left blank. Note that the final slash is required, even when you don't specify a title.

Each console window comes with a sizing gadget to change its size, but the window doesn't redisplay the current data after you

Devices

change the window size. This means if you make the window smaller, the text in the area the window previously occupied is wiped out. If you later make the window larger again, the new area of the window will be blank, rather than holding its old contents. Besides the sizing gadget, each console window has the depth arrangement gadgets in the upper right corner, which let you send the window to the back of the screen or bring it forward on top of another window. Console windows also have a drag gadget (which coincides with the title bar) that lets you change the position of the window on the screen.

Like the RAM: device, you create a new console window by referring to its device name. For instance, to LIST the directory to a new console window, you could type

LIST TO CON:0/0/640/100/

Try this, and you'll see that although a new console window is created and the listing prints within it, it disappears as soon as the command is completed. Though you can pause the display before it disappears by hitting any key (use the BACK SPACE key to restart), the short-lived nature of such a window limits its usefulness as an output device.

Console as Input

The console window can also be used as an input device. In this role, it can act as a mini text editor, which can be used to create small text files or printed documents. For example, you can create a text file on the RAM: disk by typing

COPY "CON:40/40/200/100/File Creator" TO RAM:text

The new console window appears and is the active window. Start typing text, using the BACK SPACE key to delete errors. When you've finished a line, press the RETURN key and that line is sent to the file. When you finish, enter a CTRL-\ character to signal AmigaDOS that you're at the end of the file. Enter this character by holding down the CTRL key and pressing the backslash (\) key, located next to the left of the BACK SPACE key. When you end the file, the window disappears and the disk file is closed. To see the contents of that file, enter

TYPE RAM:text

The console device gives you a handy way to create a small file (like the command sequence files discussed later). You can also send input from a console device to any other device (even another console window). For example, type

COPY CON:40/40/200/100/Typewriter TO PRT:

and each line that you type in the window is sent to the system printer (as soon as you press RETURN). Again, use CTRL- \ to end the session.

In addition to the new console windows you create, you can also use the existing console windows belonging to your CLIs. Do this by referring to the active console device, named * (asterisk). This use of the asterisk should not be confused with the universal wildcard character used by MS-DOS or the asterisk used as an escape character before quotation marks in a filename. As an output device, * is more durable than CON: since the window doesn't vanish after each command. Unfortunately, it's not much more useful, since most commands output to the current console window anyway. It, too, can be used as an input device, and as such, it's even handier to type

```
COPY * TO textfile
```

than specifying a long CON: device name. This is a quick and easy way to create a short text file.

RAW

There's one more window device available to AmigaDOS, but it's really only suitable for application programs and not for general use by the CLI command programs. This device is called *RAW:*, and it's an apt name. A normal console window heavily filters what comes through it. You'll notice, for example, that the cursor keys have no effect when you're typing in a console window. The RAW: device, on the other hand, doesn't filter anything. Thus, it would be nice to use if you wanted to create a file that contains characters other than the standard letters, numbers, and punctuation marks—such as cursor movement codes. But, alas, RAW: passes through the CTRL- \ without interpreting it as an end-of-file character. So while a CON: disappears before you're through with it, there's no way to close a RAW: window from CLI and therefore no way to close the file to which it's writing. If you really want to play with RAW:, remember that once you create the window, the only way to get rid of it is to warm-start the computer by pressing the CTRL-Amiga-Amiga key combination. A fairly safe experiment for the incurably curious is to type

```
COPY RAW:0/0/100/50/Input TO RAW:0/50/640/100/
  Output
```

Click in the Input window to activate it and start typing. Everything you type shows up in the Output window, including cursor movement keys. You can now warm-start the computer, se-

Devices

cure in the knowledge that you've tried everything at least once and that RAW: is as useless for ordinary purposes as we say it is.

It's NIL
Speaking of useless, the last device to investigate does absolutely nothing. True to the British origins of AmigaDOS, it's called *NIL:*. When used as an input device, NIL: just sends the end-of-file character. When used as an output device, NIL: accepts the output, and *does nothing with it*. Still, it's not as useless as it may seem at first. Programmers sometimes have a use for such devices in testing I/O routines. And even for the casual user, there are occasions where it's useful to get rid of output without showing it to anybody. For example, if you examine the command file called *startup-sequence* in the *s* directory, which is normally used to load and run the Workbench, you'll find that the last line of the file reads *endcli > nil:*. (You can look at this file by warm-starting the Amiga, then putting the Workbench disk in the drive [the Workbench disk, *not* the CLI disk you've probably created], opening the System drawer, double-clicking on the CLI icon, and typing TYPE s/startup-sequence.) The ENDCLI command usually prints the message *CLI task n ending* (where *n* is the task number), just before the window disappears. Apparently, the developers didn't want that message to print when the Workbench loaded and so used output redirection (which is discussed at the end of this chapter) to send the offending character string to limbo. Another practical example of using the NIL: device is shown in Chapter 5, which deals with command files, where the output from DATE ? is sent to NIL: as a way of allowing you to enter the date without seeing the command template as a prompt.

Logical Devices
In addition to physical devices like the disk drive and printer, AmigaDOS also supports a variety of pseudodevices known as *logical devices*. Logical devices provide a way of giving a short devicelike name (ending in a colon) to a particular disk directory. For example, if you assign the logical device name *let:* to the directory *df0:Wordprocessing/personal/letters*, you could refer to a file in that directory as *let:AuntMartha* rather than as *df0:Wordprocessing/personal/letters/AuntMartha*. This makes it easier to shorten the reference to a directory, without having to make that directory the current one.

Logical devices also allow a program to have access to a file without knowing its exact physical pathname. For example, a word

Devices

processing program may need to read a dictionary file in order to perform spell checking functions. It can assume that the dictionary is in the current directory, but that makes it difficult to store the dictionary in RAM: for faster access, or to place it in a directory of your choosing on your hard drive. If the program looks for the dictionary in a logical device called DT:, however, you can store the file wherever you want. By assigning the logical device name DT: to whatever directory you use to store the file, you can make it accessible to the word processing program, regardless of its actual physical location.

You can use the ASSIGN command program to assign logical devices to directories. When used for this purpose, the command format is ASSIGN *devicename directory*. The assignment given in the first example above could be accomplished by the command

```
ASSIGN let: df0:Wordprocessing/personal/letters
```

Assigning for Itself

User-created logical devices aren't the only kind found on the Amiga. AmigaDOS itself makes use of these devices to alleviate a potential problem of the operating system. Much of the Amiga's operating system doesn't reside in memory all the time. From time to time, the operating system must bring in data necessary to support certain of its features from disk files. You've already seen several examples. The most basic is that of the CLI commands, which all reside on disk and must be loaded before they can be used. The handlers for the RAM: disk, the parallel, serial, and printer devices, all must be brought in from disk. As you'll soon see, the list of disk files that contain information significant to the operating system is quite long. AmigaDOS recognizes that it would be foolish to assume that each of these files is always in the current directory. Therefore, it uses logical devices as a means of providing an alternate place to search for these important files. When you start up the Amiga, DOS assigns a number of logical device names to certain directories. When DOS needs to find one of the system files, it first looks in the current directory, but if it doesn't find the file there, it searches one of the logical devices.

To see a list of the logical devices that DOS creates, use the ASSIGN command name by itself. This command program displays a list of all logical devices, both the ones assigned by the system and those assigned by you. If you've not assigned any logical devices, the display produced by ASSIGN looks like this (assuming

Devices

a dual-drive system and disks in the drives with volume names of *Extras* and *Workbench*):

```
Volumes:
Extras [Mounted]
Workbench [Mounted]
Directories:
S         Volume: Workbench  Dir:  s
L         Volume: Workbench  Dir:  l
C         Volume: Workbench  Dir:  c
FONTS     Volume: Workbench  Dir:  fonts
DEVS      Volume: Workbench  Dir:  devs
LIBS      Volume: Workbench  Dir:  libs
SYS       Volume: Workbench  Dir:  Workbench

Devices:
DF1  DF0  PRT  PAR  SER
RAW  CON  RAM
```

S:
There are seven directories to which DOS assigns logical device names. S:, the first logical device, is a directory used to hold command sequence files (batch files). When the EXECUTE command is told to execute a sequence file, it first looks for the sequence file in the current directory. If it doesn't find the file, it tries the directory to which the logical device name S: has been assigned. The Workbench disk contains a file called startup-sequence in this directory. This sequence file is automatically executed when the Workbench disk is inserted, and it in turn loads the Workbench program and runs it.

If the Workbench 1.3 Shell has been installed, script files can be run directly, without using the EXECUTE command, if the S bit of the file protection flag is set. When you run them that way, however, AmigaDOS searches for them as if they were commands, and not scripts. See the description of the logical device named C:, below, for more information on command searches.

L:
AmigaDOS looks for its own library functions in this file. These are extensions to AmigaDOS itself, such as the *Ram-Handler* file which controls the RAM: device. The most necessary of these is the *Disk-Validator*, which is used to check if disks are in the proper AmigaDOS format. Many of the MOUNTable devices such as NEWCON: and SPEAK: have their device handlers stored in the L: directory also.

Devices

C:

The command directory, this is one of the most significant logical devices, especially to CLI users. Whenever you issue a command to the CLI, DOS first looks in the current directory for a filename matching the first word of the command line. If it doesn't find the command in the current directory, it then searches the C: device directory. Although C: is in the default search path for commands, you can extend this search path with the PATH command. For example, the command *PATH RAM: Sys:System ADD* will cause the two directories named to be searched for commands after the current directory, and before the C: directory.

Since the C: directory is always in the command search path, if you don't keep the disk that contains it in one of your drives, you may be in for a lot of disk swapping. Every time you issue a CLI command not found in the current directory, you'll be prompted to insert the volume that contains the C: directory. One way around this dilemma (if you have sufficient RAM) is to transfer the command files to the RAM: disk and assign the C: device to it. The easiest way to do this is

COPY C: RAM:
ASSIGN C: RAM:

This copies all the command files to the root directory of the RAM: device. If you'll be using the RAM: device for other files as well, you may wish to create a *c* subdirectory first, move the files to this directory, and then assign C: to it with

MAKEDIR RAM:c
COPY C: RAM:c
ASSIGN C: RAM:c

You may find it convenient to place this sequence of commands in the batch file *startup-sequence* on your boot disk. (Remember that this file automatically executes every time you turn the computer on.) Notice, however, that there are 64 command files in the *c* directory of the Workbench 1.3 disk. If you copy all of them, the RAM: disk takes up well over 240K of memory. That's most of the free memory available on a 512 Amiga system.

This doesn't mean you can't have AmigaDOS search for commands in RAM: if you only have 512K in your Amiga. It just means you'll have to be a little more selective. Move only the most frequently used command files, like COPY, DELETE, DIR, and LIST to RAM:, and use the PATH command to add RAM: to the search path, so AmigaDOS will look there before assigning the C: device name. This way, you can create a custom-tailored list of intrinsic commands that are always available.

Devices

If you have Workbench 1.3, you may want to make some of the commands RAM-resident, using the RESIDENT command. This command only works in the Shell, so make sure you're working from a Shell window, and not a normal CLI window. To make the DIR command resident, type RESIDENT DIR. This loads the DIR command into memory, and keeps it there. Then, any time you give the DIR command, the Shell executes that command from the copy already in memory. This eliminates the need to read the command in from disk, eliminates the duplication that can occur when you keep a command in the RAM disk (where the "disk" copy in RAM: is loaded into memory a second time in order for the program to execute), and causes the command program to run instantly.

There are, of course, some drawbacks to making commands resident. First, just as with storing commands on RAM:, each command you make resident reduces the amount of free memory you have. Secondly, not every program can be made resident. Each time the program is executed, it's run from the same copy that was initially loaded into memory. Therefore, only programs that are reexecutable (can be run a second time without being unloaded and loaded again) and reentrant (can be executed from separate Shell windows at the same time) qualify as resident programs. Because of this, the RESIDENT command will only load programs with the *P* bit set on the their file protection flag. You will find that most of the CLI commands in the C directory of the Workbench disk have the pure bit set, and can be made resident.

FONTS:

This device contains the files for the various text fonts for the Amiga. These are the disk-loaded fonts that can be used from programs like Notepad, painting programs, and desktop publishing programs. When a program calls the system routine *OpenFonts*, which must be done whenever a new font is used, the operating system tries to find the new font in this directory if it's not already loaded into memory.

DEVS:

This device directory holds handlers for the various devices already discussed—the serial device, the parallel device, and the printer device, and the recoverable RAM disk device we'll cover a bit later. It also contains drivers for devices the CLI commands don't use directly, like the narrator (speech synthesizer) and the clipboard. A call to the system routine *OpenDevice*, made the first time any device is used, looks in the DEVS: device directory for the device driver if it's not already loaded. In addition to device drivers,

Devices

DEVS: also contains the *system-configuration* file containing the preference settings, the *Mountlist* file used by the MOUNT command, and the printer drivers for the various printers supported by the system (these latter files are within the *printers* subdirectory).

LIBS:
This is the logical device where system library files can be found. These are used for operating system extensions implemented as a library of functions. The LIBS: directory contains library files that support features such as text-to-speech conversion (the *translator.library* file), disk-loaded text fonts (*diskfont.library*), and floating-point math calculations (*mathtrans.library, mathieeedoubbas.library, and so on*). Whenever a program calls the *OpenLibrary* routine, the operating system looks to this device for the library file, if the library is not already resident.

SYS:
The final assignment DOS makes is the SYS: device. This is assigned to the root directory of the disk that was used to boot up the system. Since it's a reasonable assumption that you'll use a disk which includes all the system files when you boot up, it gives you a handy way of referring to that system disk. In the example above, after you'd transferred only some of the CLI command files, and then assigned C: to RAM:, you used the volume name of the Workbench disk to access a command located in *Workbench/c*. You could also have specified the command directory as *SYS:c*, without having to know the volume name of the boot disk. Even if you did know the volume name of the boot disk, the device name of SYS: is shorter. The assignment of SYS: has some impact on the Workbench, since the program run when one disk icon is dragged over the other has the default path *SYS:System/Diskcopy*.

In summary, here are the logical device assignments made by AmigaDOS:

Device Name	Assignment
S	Assigned to directory *s* of the boot disk. AmigaDOS looks for sequence files to EXECUTE here if not found in the current directory.
L	Assigned to directory *l* of the boot disk. AmigaDOS looks here for its own extensions, like the *Ram-Handler*, if they're not already loaded.
C	Assigned to directory *c* of the boot disk. AmigaDOS looks for CLI command files here if not found in the current directory.
FONTS	Assigned to directory *fonts* of the boot disk. The *OpenFonts* operating system routine looks here for fonts if they're not already loaded.

Devices

DEVS   Assigned to directory *devs* of the boot disk. The *OpenDevice* operating system routine looks here for device drivers if they're not already loaded.

LIBS   Assigned to directory *libs* of the boot disk. The *OpenLibrary* operating system routine looks here for system library extensions if not already loaded.

SYS   Assigned to the root directory of the boot disk. Can be used as a short way of referring to the system disk.

File Assignments

Not only can you ASSIGN a device name to volumes and directories, but you can also ASSIGN a device name to program files. This allows you to create short "aliases" for program names, without using the 1.3 Shell. While names like *EXECUTE* and *DELETE* may not seem so hard to type, it's more convenient to type names like X: and D:. If you ASSIGN X: EXECUTE:, you can type

X: *program*

instead of

EXECUTE *program*

    It may seem like a small savings in keystrokes, but time saved by ASSIGNs and Shell ALIASes can add up (particularly if you're not a crack typist). If you place these ASSIGN statements in the *s/startup-sequence* file, the logical device names you ASSIGN will always be available to you.

Notes

Before leaving the subject of logical devices, there are a few final points to note:

- The logical device assignments apply to *all* CLIs, regardless of which was used to make the assignment (as opposed to Shell ALIASes, which apply only to one Shell).
- The ASSIGN command can be used to *remove* an assignment. The form for this is ASSIGN *devicename*. Note that it's possible to delete the assignments the system makes. ASSIGN C:, for example, removes the command directory assignment so commands must be located in the current directory in order to be executed. Obviously, some caution should be exercised in removing the assignments that AmigaDOS has made.
- It's not possible to use the ASSIGN command to change the names of physical devices like SER:.
- Finally, you should note that the *T* directory, though not a logical device, is significant to many programs. For instance, the system screen editor, ED, uses this directory to store a backup of the original text file being edited.

MOUNTable Device Drivers and Handlers

One of the most important features added to the 1.2 version of the Workbench was the MOUNT command. Used in conjunction with a text file in the DEVS: directory called *Mountlist*, which describes various device attributes, and specifies the file that contains the device driver or handler software, the MOUNT command allows almost any type of hardware or software device imaginable to be added to the system (see the MOUNT entry in the reference section for more information on the Mountlist file). Mountable device drivers can be used to let AmigaDOS interact with external hardware devices like a hard drive. "Devices" may also consist merely of software drivers that use existing system resources in a new way, as with the RAM disk device.

The 1.2 Workbench contains only one Mountlist entry for adding the A1020 5¼-inch drive as an AmigaDOS device. Workbench 1.3 adds many more new standard devices to the system.

RAD:

Perhaps the most interesting of the new devices is one called RAD:. RAD: is a RAM disk device, which, like the familiar RAM: device, uses part of the computer's working memory as an electronic disk drive. RAD: is an additional device, not a replacement for RAM:, as there are many important differences between the two.

RAM: is an integral part of the AmigaDOS system; you create the RAM: device merely by referring to it in an AmigaDOS command. RAD:, on the other hand, must be added to the system with the MOUNT command, and its device driver, which is contained in a file called RAMDRIVE.DEVICE, must be present in the DEVS: directory.

RAM: automatically adjusts its size according to its contents. As you add more files to it, it grows in size, and that size is limited only by the amount of memory available. RAD: has a fixed size, determined by the Mountlist entry used to MOUNT it.

Because it's of a fixed size, RAD: acts more the Amiga's floppy disks than its RAM disk. Like the standard 3½-inch floppies, RAD: is set up as a double-sided drive, with 512 bytes per sector, and 11 sectors per track. This means it uses 11k memory per track (512 × 2 × 11). The number of tracks used for RAD: is determined by the LowCyl and HighCyl entries in the mountlist. An entry of LowCyl = 0 ; HighCyl = 21, for example, allocates 22 tracks, at 11K per track, for a total memory usage of 242K. This is enough to store all of the files in the C directory on the Workbench. If you have a couple of megabytes of fast memory on your Amiga, you might even set the HighCyl value to 79, for an 880K RAD: drive, the exact

Devices

same size and layout as a floppy disk. When the RAD: drive is the same size as a floppy, it's possible to use the Diskcopy command to copy an entire floppy to RAD:, or vice versa. It's even possible to format the RAD: drive, something that can't be done with RAM:.

The most important difference between RAD: and RAM:, however, is their duration. Since both use the computer's memory to simulate disk storage, the contents of both devices is lost when the computer is turned off. A warm boot situation is a different story, however. While RAM: loses its contents whenever you press the Ctrl-Amiga-Amiga key combination, or your computer takes a trip to the Guru, RAD: is what's known as a recoverable RAM: disk. As long as the error that caused the Guru Meditation didn't scramble the contents of memory as well, with the 1.2 Kickstart ROM you can MOUNT RAD: again, and it will reappear with its contents intact. Not only can you recover the contents of the RAD: drive after rebooting, but you can even reboot from the RAD: device itself, using Kickstart 1.3.

Along with the ability to boot from devices like hard disks and network, the 1.3 ROM adds the ability to reboot from RAD:, provided that it has been mounted, and no bootable disk is found in drive df0: at warmstart time. Even if a boot disk is used for a warm-start, Kickstart 1.3 automatically restores RAD: upon warm boot, with no need to reMOUNT it. Of course, 500 and 2000 owners will have to change Kickstart ROMs to gain this ability, but 1000 owners need only to use the new Kickstart disk. Sometimes, RAD: can be a little too persistent. Since it doesn't disappear when you warm boot, like RAM: does, the only way to remove it short of turning off the power is to use the REMRAD command. This deletes the contents of RAD:, shrinks it down to the smallest possible size, and makes it nonrecoverable, so it disappears at the next warm boot.

Since RAD: is a MOUNTable device that can be formatted, it can also take advantage of the new Fast File System (FFS). To use the FFS on RAD:, you must add two items to the RAD: entry in the DEVS:MOUNTLIST file. These two lines are:

```
GlobVec = -1
FileSystem = l:FastFileSystem
```

These lines can be added anywhere after RAD: and before the # that ends the entry. In addition, the FastFileSystem file mentioned in the second line must appear in the l: directory on your Workbench disk. After you've changed the Mountlist entry, you may use the command MOUNT RAD: to mount the drive. Because you're using a different filesystem than the default one, you must format the drive before you use it. You can, however, use the new QUICK option of the FORMAT command, which shortens the process:

:SYSTEM/FORMAT drive RAD: name Speedy QUICK

Using the FFS on the recoverable RAM disk does speed up operations somewhat, though since it is a RAM drive, those operations are fairly quick without it. But with the 1.3 Kickstart, you lose the ability to reboot from the RAM drive if you format it with the FFS (you should add the line BootPri = −129 to the RAD: entry in the Mountlist file to tell AmigaDOS not to try rebooting from this device). In fact, with the 1.3 ROM, you can't even recover the contents of the RAM drive when you reboot if you have it formatted with the FFS, since the drive is automatically mounted on warmstart as a normal DOS filesystem device. Since Kickstart is expecting the RAM drive to be in the old AmigaDOS format, it thinks it's not a DOS disk. Using the 1.2 Kickstart, however, you must MOUNT the drive again after a warmstart, and so even though you can't reboot from the RAM drive, you can recover its contents even if it is formatted with FFS.

PIPE:

Next on the list of device handlers added by Workbench 1.3 is one called PIPE: This device emulates the pipes feature of UNIX and MS-DOS, which allows the user to transfer the output of one program directly to the input of another. Let's say, for example, that you wish to display a large disk directory on screen. The DIR command may not be suitable, since it outputs file names in a continuous stream, and doesn't pause when the screen fill up. By piping the output of DIR to the MORE program, which displays text a screen full at a time, you get the information you want, in the format you prefer. In UNIX or MS-DOS, this can be accomplished with a command like DIR | MORE. Unfortunately, the Amiga command shell doesn't recognize the | operator, so it's necessary to simulate pipes to achieve the same result.

Amiga owners have always been able to get similar results by using file redirection to a temporary storage area on the RAM: disk. In the case of the example discussed above, you could use the command sequence

DIR >ram:temp
MORE ram:temp
DELETE ram:temp

to achieve the same result. Still, there are instances in which you may not have enough room on the RAM: disk to create the intermediate file. For example, if you create a hex dump of a 25K program file using the TYPE OPT H command, you may end up with

Devices

a text file that's 100K or longer. In such a case, you may wish to MOUNT PIPE:, whose handler is found in the file l:pipe-handler.

The PIPE: devices acts as a conduit, directing the output of one program to the input of another. One process writes to the pipe, assigning it an arbitrary file name (such as pipe:temp). Each pipe name uses a 4K buffer, which means only that much may be written to the pipe before the writing process is blocked. When the second program reads that 4K buffer (by accessing the same file name as was written), the first program can write 4K more of data, until all of the output is transferred. In the example above, you could pipe the output of DIR to more using the command sequence

```
RUN DIR >pipe:temp
MORE pipe:temp
```

assuming, of course, that you had first used the MOUNT PIPE: command (the normal Startup-Sequence file on Workbench 1.3 mounts this device automatically). Note that in the above example we used RUN to spin off a separate process for DIR. Both commands can't use the same CLI process because if the directory output is larger than 4K, DIR won't terminate and give back the CLI prompt until MORE has read all of its output.

The roundabout method that PIPE: uses to simulate pipes may not be as simple as that available on other systems, but it does have some unique advantages. In addition to the traditional pipe situation described above, PIPE: can be used for its buffering capabilities alone. Many terminal programs, for example, download files in a synchronous fashion. This means they receive a block of data, send it to the disk, wait until the disk write is finished, and then ask to receive the next block. Each intermediate disk write causes a slight delay in the transmission. You can always avoid this delay by downloading to a file in RAM:, but in doing so you run the risk of filling up the RAM disk before the file transfer is completed, or of forgetting to copy the file to a floppy before turning off your computer. A better solution is to use the command:

```
COPY pipe:temp TO df0:downfile
```

before running your terminal program, and then downloading to the file pipe:temp. That way, large amounts of data are buffered before any writes actually take place, which means fewer delays. At the same time, you avoid the risks associated with downloading to RAM:, since when the download process is terminated, your file is stored safely on disk.

AUX:

Another new device handler that duplicates the function of existing public domain software is the one called AUX:. The AUX: device, whose handler is located in the file L:Aux-Handler, transfers data through the serial port, much like the SER: device. While SER: buffers its output, however, sending it out only after a 512-byte block has accumulated, AUX: provides unbuffered communication with the serial port. The main use for an unbuffered serial device is to create a CLI window that uses the serial port for its input and output. Such a window can be set up by MOUNTING the AUX: device (this is normally done automatically by the Startup-Sequence file), and typing the command:

NEWCLI AUX:

This procedure lets you hook up another computer or terminal to the Amiga, and give AmigaDOS commands from that machine over the serial port, or even over a modem. While you cannot, of course, run Intuition-based windowing programs on your remote terminal (at least not yet), you can use CLI commands like DIR and INFO to gain information about the Amiga disks, and the TYPE command to send files to the remote screen (where they can be captured to a buffer file).

There is even a public domain program called CANCEL! which automatically hits the Cancel button whenever a system requester pops up. While serial-port CLI's don't exactly make the Amiga a multiuser system, they do come pretty close.

SPEAK:

In an effort to make the built-in speech synthesis feature of the Amiga even more accessible, Commodore has added the SPEAK: device handler to the 1.3 Workbench. SPEAK: is similar to the SAY program in the Utilities drawer, in that it converts text input into speech which is output through the audio channels. Like SAY, it uses the *translator.library* file from the LIBS: directory to convert the text to phonemes, and the *narrator.device* from DEVS: to output the phonetic speech. While SAY takes input only from the keyboard, however, SPEAK: is mounted as a device, which means it can take its input from any source that can write to a disk file. For example, you can COPY a file to SPEAK: from the CLI, save a file to SPEAK: from a text editor or word processing program like *MicroEMACS* or Notepad, or even open SPEAK: as a capture file for a terminal program, so output coming in over the modem is spoken.

As with the SAY program, it's possible to adjust SPEAK: in order to vary the spoken output. You may change the pitch and

Devices

speed of the speech, choose male or female voice characteristics, and select natural or robot (monotone) speech inflection. To add a voice setting, you include it as part of a SPEAK:opt/ path name when you access the device. For example, to listen to a file with a female voice at a pitch setting of 200, you could use the command:

COPY *filename* to SPEAK:opt/f/p200

The full list of voice options that can be added to the SPEAK:opt/ pathname is shown below:

P### Set Pitch. (### is a number from 65 to 320)
S### Set Speed. (### is a number from 30 to 400)
M   Use male voice characteristics
F   User female voice characteristics
R   Robot speech (uninflected monotone)
N   Natural speech (natural inflection)
O0   Do not allow option settings in input stream
O1   Allow option settings in input stream
A0   Turn off phoneme input mode
A1   Turn on phoneme input mode
D0   Determine sentence breaks by punctuation alone
D1   Determine sentence breaks from Carriage Return and Line Feed, as well as punctuation

When option settings are allowed in the input stream, you can change the voice characteristics with commands given in the data sent to the device. For example, if you give the command

COPY * to Speak:opt/O1

and then type *This is a test*, the phrase is pronounced in the default voice. If you then type the lines

opt/f/p200
This is a test

the phrase is pronounced in a high female voice.

NEWCON:

One of the major complaints about the CLI command environment has always been that the console window it uses doesn't support command line-editing. If you make a typing mistake in the first word of a command line, you have to erase the whole line and start over again. A new 1.3 device called NEWCON: finally provides a console window that not only allows editing with the cursor keys, but also adds a 2K command history buffer. After you mount the NEWCON: device, (whose handler is located in the file L:newcon-handler), you may open a CLI window that uses this new console device with the command:

NEWCLI NEWCON:*x*/*y*/*w*/*h*/*name*

where *x* and *y* specify the position of the upper left corner of the window, *w* and *h* specify its width and height in pixels, and *name* designates an optional window name. With a NEWCON: window, you can edit a command line by using the left- and right-arrow keys to move the cursor back and forth across the line one space at a time, or in combination with the Shift key to take you to the beginning or end of the line. The up- and down-arrow keys implement a command history feature. Each time you enter a command line, that line is stored in a 2K circular buffer. Pressing the up-arrow key retrieves the previous entry in the buffer, which appears at the command prompt. Pressing the down-arrow key moves you forward through the buffer (Shift-down arrow takes you to the bottom of the buffer). If you don't want to cursor through each previous command, you can use the command history's search feature. Typing a partial command line, and then pressing Shift-cursor up, initiates a search for the last command line that matches the partial string.

Redirection of Input and Output

Ordinarily, AmigaDOS accepts input from the keyboard and outputs it to the current console window. These are known as the *standard input* and *standard output* devices. In some cases, you may redirect input to a program so it comes from a device other than the console keyboard, and you may redirect output from the program so it goes to a device other than the console display. Redirection of command input/output (I/O) is accomplished through the use of the redirection operators < and > (the angle brackets—you may be more familiar with them as the *less than* and *greater than* signs—which are entered by pressing a SHIFTed comma and SHIFTed period, respectively). The left angle bracket (<) is used to redirect input, and the right angle bracket (>), to redirect output. You can easily remember which is which, because the direction in which the angle bracket is pointing indicates the direction in which the information is going (*from* is left, *to* is right).

You use a redirection operator, followed by the name of the device or file you wish to use for input or output, directly after the command name. For example, if you wish to send a directory listing to the printer, you could type

DIR > PRT:

Devices

You can use one redirection operator or both for a particular command, but the operator(s) must come right after the command name, not after the command parameters:

DIR > PRT: OPT A

is correct, but

DIR OPT A >PRT:

is incorrect because DIR will interpret >PRT: as the root directory of a volume named >PRT.

Note that several commands, such as COPY and LIST, allow you to specify a destination device to which output is directed. Therefore, you don't have to use the redirection operator to specify the output for those commands.

Redirection of input is a little trickier than redirection of output, since the CLI commands generally take all their input from the command line rather than waiting for it. One way of getting around this is to use the question mark (?) as a command parameter. When you put a question mark after the command name as its only parameter, AmigaDOS prints out a command template and waits for you to enter the command parameters. For example, if you first redirected the output of ECHO to a file named *textfile*:

ECHO >textfile "*"This is a test*""

you'd end up with a one-line text file that starts and ends with double quotation marks. Then, you could use ECHO to print the contents of the file by typing

ECHO <textfile ?

ECHO first prints out a colon (:)—its command template—and then gets the input to print from *textfile*. Notice that this works only with short files, since ECHO can only take a character string shorter than 256 characters. Another handy use for input redirection is with commands that require a carriage return to continue. If you wish to use the DISKCOPY command to automatically copy your boot disk to the recoverable RAM disk on startup, you'll find that DISKCOPY prompts you to hit Return to start the copy. To avoid having to manually enter a Return (and thus defeating the automatic nature of the script), you could use the command:

DISKCOPY <NIL: DF0: to RAD:

The input from NIL: will satisfy DISKCOPY's desire for a carriage return.

Devices

Redirection applies only to the command in which the operators are used. Subsequent CLI commands will use standard input and output.

The 1.3 Workbench Shell provides an additional output redirection operation, which uses two angle brackets (>>) instead of one. If you use the standard operator to direct output to a file that already exists, the existing file will be replaced by a file consisting of the new output. If you use the new redirection operator on an existing file, however, the new material will be added to the end of the current file.

Chapter 5

Command Sequence Files

Running individual command programs from the CLI is easy—you just enter the name of the command. You may find, however, that to accomplish certain tasks, you must enter several CLI commands, one after the other. You may find that you even use a particular sequence of commands again and again. AmigaDOS offers a way to simplify this process—it allows you to enter each of the commands into a text file and to use the EXECUTE command whenever you wish to execute that sequence of commands. Such a text file is known as a sequence file, a batch file, or a script file. When EXECUTEd, a batch file will run a sequence of commands, one after the other, just as if it had been typed at the console keyboard. The sequence will continue to run until all of the commands have been carried out, or until a command fails, or the user manually breaks out of the sequence by pressing the CTRL-D key combination.

Sequence files can do more than just execute a fixed series of commands. There are provisions for testing certain conditions and for issuing alternative commands depending on the outcome of those tests. They also allow you to substitute text within the command file so the commands operate with options you specify in the EXECUTE command, not just with a fixed set. Finally, the special command file named *startup-sequence* lets you automatically execute a number of commands whenever you turn on the computer.

Batching Simple Commands

In order to use the EXECUTE command, you must first create a text file containing the command statements you want to execute. You may use either of the system editors, ED or EDIT, to create the command file (see Chapters 6 and 7, which explain the use of the editors). You may also use any word processor or text editor which can save a text-only file, one without embedded command characters in the text. (To create such a file using *WordPerfect*, for instance, you must choose the Save Text File option on the Project

Command Sequence Files

menu.) Another handy method of creating short command sequence files is to use a console window as a mini text editor. Chapter 4 shows you how to do this.

The file you create should contain one or more lines of CLI commands, one command to a line, with a RETURN character at the end of each line. The format should look like this:

```
ECHO "The current date and time settings are:"
DATE
ECHO "*N*E[3mThe current device assignments are:*E[0m"
ASSIGN
SAY All, done.
```

Notice that you've just used a new command, ECHO. ECHO prints out the text string enclosed in quotes. It's really only useful when included in command sequence files. By placing ECHO statements in command files, you can let the user know what the command file is doing. Note that ECHO uses the asterisk (*) as a special escape character. The asterisk causes ECHO to treat subsequent characters as formatting commands, rather than as text that it should print. In the example above, the *N combination causes ECHO to skip a line. The *E combination is used for the ESC character, so console escape sequences, like the one that changes to italic print, can be used (see Chapter 2 for more on console escape sequences).

The SAY command, found in the last line above, is similar to the ECHO command except that it uses the Amiga Narrator device and Translator library to actually speak the words typed on the command line. Notice that with the SAY command, no quotation marks enclose the text—if you included quotation marks, your Amiga would try to speak them. Also, notice that punctuation marks like the comma and period can change the inflection of the speech.

Let's assume you've created a disk file in the current directory named *Report*, which contains the lines of text listed above. You could then type EXECUTE Report, and each of the commands in the file would be executed in sequence, producing the following screen output:

Command Sequence Files

> *The current date and time settings are:*
> Saturday 15-Nov-86 18:27:01
>
> The current device assignments are:
> Volumes:
> Extras [Mounted]
> Workbench [Mounted]
>
> Directories:
> S   Volume: Workbench Dir: s
> L   Volume: Workbench Dir: l
> C   Volume: Workbench Dir: c
> FONTS Volume: Workbench Dir: fonts
> DEVS   Volume: Workbench Dir: devs
> LIBS   Volume: Workbench Dir: libs
> SYS   Volume: Workbench Dir: Workbench
>
> Devices:
> DF1 DF0 PRT PAR SER
> RAW CON RAM

    In the above example, it's assumed that the file *Report* is in the current directory. If it were in another directory, you could use the full pathname to identify its location (*EXECUTE df1:Utilities/Report*). But there's another way to make the EXECUTE command execute a sequence file that isn't located in the current directory. As you may remember from the previous chapter, the system assigns the logical device name S: to the the *s* directory on the boot disk when you turn on the computer. The EXECUTE command first looks for the command file in the current directory, but if it doesn't find it there, it looks in the S: directory. By saving your command files to the S: device, therefore, you can be sure that EXECUTE will always be able to find it, regardless of which directory is current. directory is current.

    If you are using the 1.3 Shell window instead of an ordinary CLI, its possible to execute script files without using the EXECUTE command. If the script file has the S protection bit set, you may execute the sequence just by typing the name of the file. To do this with the file in the example above, you would first set the file's S bit with the command:

PROTECT Report +S

Afterwards, you could execute the sequence just by typing **Report**. Since the Shell executes script files as if they were CLI commands, it doesn't use the normal sequence file search path to find them.

Command Sequence Files

Instead, it looks for them in the normal command file search path. If you use a lot of script files from the shell, and these scripts are stored in the S: directory, you may want to add S: to your command search path.

Startup-Sequence: The Autoexecuting Command File

As has been mentioned several times already, AmigaDOS recognizes a special command sequence file located in the S: directory called *startup-sequence*. The sequence of commands contained in the *startup-sequence* file is executed whenever you turn on the machine or reset it by holding down CTRL and both Amiga keys. To see the standard command file that comes on the Workbench disk, enter `TYPE S:startup-sequence`. For Workbench 1.3, the displayed file should look like this:

```
Addbuffers df0: 10
c:SetPatch >NIL: ;patch system functions
cd c:
echo "A500/A2000 Workbench disk. Release 1.3 version 34.20*N"
Sys:System/FastMemFirst ; move C00000 memory to last in list
BindDrivers
SetClock load ;load system time from real time clock (A1000 owners should
              ;replace the SetClock load with Date
FF >NIL: -0 ;speed up Text
resident CLI L:Shell-Seg SYSTEM pure add; activate Shell
resident c:Execute pure
mount newcon:
;
failat 11
run execute s:StartupII ;This lets resident be used for rest of script
wait >NIL: 5 mins ;wait for StartupII to complete (will signal when done)
;
SYS:System/SetMap usa1 ;Activate the ( )/* on keypad
path ram: c: sys:utilities sys:system s: sys:prefs add ;set path for Workbench
LoadWB delay ;wait for inhibit to end before continuing
endcli >NIL:
```

The first command allocates additional disk buffers to speed up floppy disk access. The second installs software fixes for Kernel ROM bugs, and the third makes C: the default directory. The next command uses the ECHO program to send a message to the screen. The *FastMemFirst* command is run to give priority to external expansion memory if any is present.

Next, the *BindDrivers* command adds in any device drivers in the expansion drawer, such as the one needed to integrate the PC

Command Sequence Files

Bridgeboard into the system. The *SetClock* is used to set Amiga-DOS' system clock from the hardware clock in the 2000 and 500's equipped with the clock option. Next, the FF command is used to speed up text printing. The first Resident command loads the program needed for the 1.3 Shell, and the next makes the Execute command resident, after which the Newcon: device is mounted to add enhanced console functions to Shell windows.

The *Failat* command is used to set the failure level higher, so the script won't end abruptly if one of the subsequent commands should fail. Next, Run is used to Execute a separate batch file that does some Assigns and other startup tasks. A *Wait* command is used after this to stop the current script until the other script is done. This prevents the two scripts from trying to access the same disk at the same time, a situation which slows down disk access, and causes a lot of unecessary disk seeks. This Wait command will wait for five minutes, or until the other script sends it a Break, whichever comes first. After the other script has signalled that it's done, the *Setmap* command is used to install a new keymap, one which recognizes the extra keypad keys on the 500/2000 that weren't on the 1000. The *Path* command is used to set some extra default search paths for commands. LoadWB is used to start the up the Workbench environment, and *EndCLI* is used to terminate the initial CLI window.

The *startup-sequence* command file is a powerful tool because it lets you specify what happens every time you turn on your Amiga. For instance, you can choose to load the Workbench every time or stay in CLI mode, or have both interfaces available at the same time. You've already seen that to stay in CLI mode, all you have to do is leave out the last two lines of the standard file. But if you want to load the Workbench *and* keep a CLI window, you can insert the line

NEWCLI con:20/20/200/100/

or for 1.3 users

NEWSHELL Newcon:20/20/200/100/

right before the *LoadWb* line. This starts up a smaller CLI window that will stay on the Workbench screen after the Workbench is loaded. (See Chapter 6 for details on how to edit a file such as *startup-sequence*. Briefly, though, to add this line, type ED s/startup-sequence, which puts you in the screen editor. Use the cursor keys to move to the *LoadWb* line, press RETURN, cursor up to the empty line, and enter what you see above. Press ESC, then enter X, and press RETURN. The new *startup-sequence* file will

Command Sequence Files

overwrite the old. Wait until all disk activity has ceased; then warm-start your Amiga by pressing the CTRL key and both Amiga keys at the same time. The Workbench should appear, along with a CLI window.

There are a number of other things you may want to do automatically at startup time. If you're using a hard disk or other other external peripheral device, you may need to run a program to integrate these resources into the system. One of the most useful sequences of commands to include in the *startup-sequence* file is one that sets up a RAM disk directory containing a collection of your most frequently used commands and ASSIGNs it as the default command directory. The simplest sequence to use is

```
MAKEDIR RAM:c
COPY SYS:c ram:c ALL
ASSIGN c: RAM:c
```

This is faster than copying each individual file since DOS doesn't have to read the COPY program from disk each time. The disadvantage is that you end up using a lot of RAM to hold command programs you seldom, if ever, use. Taking up over 128K of RAM for command programs is wasteful on a 512K system and prohibitive on a 256K system. The alternative is to copy files selectively. You can do this one of two ways.

First, you can move all of the files from C: which you want to go to the RAM disk to a new directory called *D*. Then, replace the *SYS:c* reference in the above example to *SYS:d*. The other choice is to copy specific files individually. Something like this may be what you use:

```
C:CD C:
MAKEDIR ASSIGN D: RAM:c
COPY C:copy RAM:c
D:/copy assign|cd|delete|dir|diskcopy D:
D:/copy echo|ed|endcli|info|join|list D:
D:/copy Makedir|newcli|run|type D:
PATH D: Add
```

This first copies the COPY program to RAM:, then uses that version to copy the rest of the files. This reduces the time spent reading the COPY program from disk. Some other steps are taken to shorten the time required to execute this script. First, we change the current directory to C:, to make the CLI look there first for each command, instead of wasting time looking in some other default directory. When a command in another directory is needed, we use complete path name. Also, the or wildcard (|) is used to allow each

77

Command Sequence Files

COPY command to copy several files, without having to load the copy program each time. When all the required files are copied, we add the RAM:c directory to the default command search path with the PATH command.

Users of the 1.3 Workbench Shell may find it more beneficial to make often-used commands resident by using the RESIDENT command instead of copying those files to the RAM disk. A resident program is always loaded in memory, ready to go, and Shell windows search the Resident list before looking in any of default search paths. Resident commands may also be given new, shorter names, like DEL for Delete, and MD for Makedir.

Another common task you can perform at startup time is setting the system clock and calendar. If you've purchased an optional hardware clock/calendar for the 1000, it probably came with a program for setting the system clock from the hardware clock. The command to run this program should be part of your *startup-sequence* file (A SetClock command for 500 and 2000 owners is already in the default startup file). If you don't have a hardware clock, you should set the time and date manually each time you start the system. The original *startup-sequence* file on your Workbench disk prints a message telling you to set the date and time from the Preferences program. If you prefer, you can give yourself the opportunity to set the time and date as part of your *startup-sequence* file. The following example demonstrates one technique for doing this:

```
ECHO " "
ECHO "The current setting of the date and time is:"
DATE
ECHO " "
ECHO "Enter the correct date and/or time now."
ECHO "Use the form DD-MMM-YY for the date (format
   as 09-Sep-86)."
ECHO "Use the form HH:MM:SS or HH:MM for the time
   (format as 14:55)."
ECHO " "
```

The next command is tricky. It uses the question mark form of DATE to prompt you with the command template and wait for input. It uses redirection to send the prompt text down a black hole. The result is that it accepts input and sends it to DATE.

```
DATE > nil: ?
ECHO " "
ECHO "The new date and time settings are:"
DATE
DATE >now
```

Command Sequence Files

As the comments in italics explain, this example uses the question mark form of DATE. Normally, when you type DATE ?, the DATE command prints out its command template and waits for you to enter input in that format. By redirecting the output of the command to NIL:, which does nothing with it, you suppress the command template and instead provide more detailed instructions as reminders to yourself. Redirecting the output to NIL: performs an additional function as well. If you decide that you don't want to change the date and just press RETURN, the DATE command doesn't get any instructions about what date or time is to be set. In such a case, the command normally prints out the *current* date or time. Here, that would be inappropriate and would confuse the display. Luckily, the redirection to NIL: prevents this text from being displayed so if you just press RETURN, nothing happens.

Notice that the last command in the new *startup-sequence* file redirects the output from DATE to the file *now*. This kind of date stamping can be helpful, for the Amiga looks to the most recently modified or created file to set the time (if you don't do it yourself manually). Thus, if you haven't altered or created any files since the last time you booted up the computer, it looks to *now* for the current date.

Passing Instructions to Commands

As convenient as it may be to EXECUTE a sequence of fixed commands stored in a file, it limits you to working with the same specific files and directories every time. That's why AmigaDOS has a mechanism for passing words from the EXECUTE command line to the command file and substituting them in the commands. This lets you create command files which do different things, depending on what you type in the EXECUTE command line.

Since this concept is much easier to demonstrate than to explain, let's take a very simple example. Suppose you want to create a command file that makes a backup copy of a file. You need some way of specifying the name of the file so you won't be continually backing up the same file. The following short command file, named *Backup*, does just this:

```
.KEY   filename     (.K filename is also acceptable)
COPY   <filename>   TO :Backups
```

To use this command file, type EXECUTE Backup Mydata. The result is that the file named *Mydata* is copied to the *Backups* directory (this assumes that the *Backups* directory already exists in the root directory of the current disk). If you typed EXECUTE Backup Program, the file named *Program* would be copied to *Backups*. The

Command Sequence Files

key to this process is in the first line of the file. The line starts with the word .KEY, which is not a normal CLI command, but rather a sequence file directive which tells the EXECUTE command how to operate. The .KEY directive tells EXECUTE that the command template which follows should be used to determine what commands can be passed to this command file. In this case, .KEY tells EXECUTE that if a word is entered on the EXECUTE command line after *Backup*, that word is to be referred to as *filename*. Anytime <filename> appears in the *Backup* file, the word appearing on the command line after *Backup* is substituted. Thus, when you type EXECUTE Backup Mydata, EXECUTE takes the command line *COPY <filename> to :Backups* and substitutes *Mydata* everywhere <filename> appears. The result is the command line *COPY Mydata TO :Backups*.

If you don't enter any command words after the name of the command sequence file, there's nothing to substitute for the keyword specified by the .KEY (or .K) directive. In the above example, the command *EXECUTE Backup* translates to the command line *COPY TO :Backups*, which copies everything in the current directory to the *Backups* directory. This may not be the result you wanted. Fortunately, AmigaDOS provides a way to prevent this. It allows you to specify a default value to be substituted for the keyword if the user (yourself, more than likely) doesn't enter a substitution value. There are two ways of specifying the default value.

You can use the .DEF directive, followed by the substitution value. When you use this directive, the default value is substituted wherever the keyword appears in the absence of a normal substitution. Let's change the *Backup* command file to look like this:

```
.KEY filename
.DEF filename #?.bas
ECHO "Copying <filename> to the Backups directory"
COPY <filename> TO :Backups
```

Now, if you type EXECUTE Backup, the pattern expression *#?.bas* is substituted for the keyword, and the command becomes *COPY #?.bas TO :Backups*. The pattern matches any file whose name ends in the characters *.bas*, so any file fitting that description is copied to *Backups*. An ECHO command was added to tell you what's happening. The default value is substituted in that command as well, so ECHO prints the message *Copying #?.bas to the Backups directory*.

The .DEF directive can also be used to substitute every instance of the keyword in the file with the default value. Another directive, the dollar sign ($), can be used to substitute each occurrence on a case-by-case basis. Using this directive, the *Backup* file now looks like this:

```
.K name
ECHO "Copying <name$all BASIC program files> to the
   Backups directory"
COPY <name$#?.bas> to :Backups
```

Using this version of the *Backup* command file, the command *EXECUTE Backup* still copies all files ending in *.bas* to the *Backups* directory. This time, however, the default value is only substituted in the COPY command. A different value is substituted in the ECHO command. The message printed by ECHO is *Copying all BASIC program files to the Backups directory*. Notice that you didn't have to put quotation marks around the phrase *all BASIC program files*, even though it contains spaces. The substitution value replaces the keyword with the exact string of characters which appears in its definition. The 1.3 version of the Execute command recognizes one additional substitution directive. Two dollars signs together ($$) within brackets are substituted by the number of the current CLI. For example, the string file_number<$$> would be interpreted as "filenumber1" in a batch file that was executed from CLI 1. This substitution is useful for creating temporary files with unique names, that won't be overwritten if the same batch file is run from two separate CLIs at the same time.

The EXECUTE command doesn't limit you to substituting a single word on the command line. The .KEY directive can specify a template that contains as many keywords as you like (up to a total of 255 characters). The only restriction is that the template must be in the same format as the command template that prints when you type a command name followed by a question mark (see the beginning of the "AmigaDOS Command Reference" section for more information on command templates). This means, among other things, that the keywords must be separated by a comma, with no spaces between them. It also means you can use /A after the name to show that this argument is required. For example, let's say you wanted to be able to back up two named files each time you executed *Backup*. The following command file shows how you can substitute both filenames:

```
.K name1/a,name2/a
COPY <name1> to :Backups
COPY <name2> to :Backups
```

Using this *Backup* command file, if you type EXECUTE Backup document letter, both the document and letter files will be copied to the *Backups* directory. If you don't specify at least two files

Command Sequence Files

on the command line, however, the command will fail.

As you've seen from earlier discussions of filenames and pattern matching, naming conventions can cause some problems. The execute directives are no exception. What if you want to use the default message *Copying files -> thisaway* in the above example? EXECUTE will look at the entered command ECHO "Copying <name$files -> thisaway> to the Backups Directory, and print *Copying files - thisaway> to the Backups Directory*, not *Copying files -> thisaway to the Backups Directory*, as you wanted. Since the angle brackets have a special meaning for EXECUTE, substituting a string containing these characters is going to pose a problem. A similar problem occurs when you try to use the redirection operators (< for input redirection and > for output redirection) in a script file that contains keyword substitutions. To avoid these problems, AmigaDOS provides directives that let you redefine the directive characters. For example, you can change the left angle bracket character to a left square bracket character with the directive *.BRA [.* (the final period after the bracket character is necessary). Likewise, to change the right angle bracket to a right square bracket, use the directive *.KET].* (again, the period after the bracket is mandatory). The *.DOLLAR* or *.DOL* directive is used to change the character that introduces the default substitution value. The directive *.DOL #* changes the dollar character to a pound sign, for example. And finally, the *.DOT* directive allows you to redefine the period character that appears in front of most of the directives.

To summarize, the EXECUTE command recognizes the following directives:

Directive	Function
.KEY *value1,value2* or **.K** *value1,value2*	Uses the command template (value1,value2) for substituting command values
<*value1*>	Substitutes the first command value here
<*value1$default*>	Substitutes the first command value here, but if none is given, substitutes *default*
<$$>	Substitutes the current CLI number (Workbench 1.3)
.DEF *value1 default*	If the command value was not entered, substitutes *default* for <*value1*> everywhere
.space	Comment line (must be a space after the period)
.newline	Blank comment line
.BRA *character*	Replaces the left angle bracket (<) with *character*
.KET *character*	Replaces the right angle bracket (>) with *character*
.DOLLAR *character* or	Replaces the dollar sign ($) with *character*

Command Sequence Files

Directive
.DOL *character*
.DOT *character*

Function

Replaces the dot (.) with *character*

Testing Conditions with IF

A command sequence file that always does the same thing is not very intelligent. For example, the *Backup* file described above assumes that a directory named *Backups* exists in the root directory of the current disk. If it doesn't exist, the COPY command will fail. One solution is to insert a MAKEDIR command to create the directory. But if the directory already exists, the MAKEDIR command will fail.

The solution to this is to let the command sequence file test whether or not the directory exists, and then act accordingly. If the directory does exist, the copy can take place. If it doesn't exist, the MAKEDIR command can first be used to create it. EXECUTE uses the mechanism IF command to make such decisions. IF can be used to test a number of conditions. If the condition it tests is true, the subsequent commands will be executed. If the condition is not true, none of the subsequent commands in the file will be executed (until the ENDIF command is given).

One of the conditions you can test with IF is whether or not a disk volume, directory, or file exists (although the EXISTS option of the 1.3 version of the ASSIGN command is better for testing volumes, since no Insert Volume xxx in any drive requester appears if the volume doesn't exit). The form of this command is

```
IF EXISTS name
```

You can also use the keyword NOT to reverse the test. While *EXISTS name* is true if the object called *name* exists, *NOT EXISTS name* is true only if it doesn't exist. Applying these facts to the problem raised at the beginning of this section, you can come up with this new, improved *Backup* command file:

```
.KEY filename
IF NOT EXISTS :Backups
MAKEDIR :Backups
ENDIF
COPY <filename$#?.bas> to :Backups
```

Now when you EXECUTE *Backup* (by typing EXECUTE Backup *filename*), the command file first checks whether the *:Backups* directory exists. If not, it creates the directory. But if it does exist, the command file skips the MAKEDIR command and copies the file. Workbench 1.3 users should note that this process isn't necessary using the newer Copy command; it creates the target directory automatically if it doesn't exist.

Command Sequence Files

The IF-ENDIF sequence also allows for an ELSE clause. Commands that come after the ELSE command will be executed *only* when the IF clause is *not* true. Let's look at the following sample command file:

```
.Key from/a,to/a
IF NOT EXISTS <to>
COPY <from> AS <to>
ELSE
ECHO "Sorry, there's already a file named <to>."
ECHO "If I copy <from> to <to>, it will wipe out
   <to>."
ENDIF
```

Call this command file *safecopy*. It's a cautious version of the COPY command. The COPY command is pretty reckless—if you tell it to copy the file *ordinary* to another file called *important*, and there's already a file *important*, the contents of *ordinary* replace the *important* file. You've just lost *important*'s contents. This version first checks to see if there's a file with the target. If not, it executes the COPY command and then skips from ELSE to ENDIF. But if the file already exists, it skips the COPY command and instead executes the command sequence starting with ELSE, which politely explains why it can't make the copy. Note the use of the command template characters /a after the keywords. These characters indicate that both keywords are required. If you try EXECUTEing the file without specifying a *from* and a *to* file on the command line, the sequence will fail.

Another condition IF can test is whether two text strings are the same. The keyword used for this test is EQ. The format of the test is *IF string1 EQ string2*. One use for this test is to determine what string was substituted for a word designated by the .KEY directive. You can even test it to see whether any substitution was made. Let's look at an example:

```
.KEY name
IF <name>q NOT EQ "q"           ;if name1 was entered, this is true
IF EXISTS <name>                ;check to see if the file exists
RUN EXECUTE Backup <name>       ;you can nest EXECUTEs
ELSE                            ;matches IF EXISTS <name>
ECHO "I can't find a file called <name> "
ENDIF                           ;matches IF EXISTS <name>
ELSE                            ;matches IF <name>q NOT EQ "q"
ECHO "You did not enter the name of a source file"
ENDIF                           ;matches IF <name>q NOT EQ "q"
```

Command Sequence Files

As you can see, this is a bit more complicated than the previous examples. There are two IF statements, one nested within the other. The first IF tests whether any value was entered on the command line to be substituted for the keyword *name*. It does this by seeing if what was substituted for *name*, plus the letter *q*, is equivalent to the letter *q* alone. If any substitution was made, the two strings will not be equal, and the condition is true. If no substitution was made, the EXECUTE command branches to the ELSE clause, which prints *You did not enter the name of a source file.*

After the command file has tested to see whether the name of a source file was entered, it must still test to see whether that file exists. The second IF statement takes care of that, using the EXISTS keyword as the test. If the file exists, the *EXECUTE Backup* command is run as a background process to back up the file. This demonstrates that you can both run an EXECUTE sequence as a background process and that you can use one command file to EXECUTE another. If the file doesn't exist, execution skips to the ELSE clause, which prints the message *I can't find a file called <name>.*

The Workbench 1.3 version of the IF command has several new capabilities. First, it can test for all possible string comparison cases, with the addition of GT (greater than) and GE (greater than or equal) keywords. To test for less than or and less than or equal conditions, use NOT GE and NOT GT. These string comparisons normally use alphabetical order to test whether the value of one string is greater than or less than another. Using the new VAL keyword, however, it's possible to test the strings by numeric order instead. For example, when you execute the script

```
IF "044" GT "14"
ECHO "044 is greater"
ELSE
ECHO "14 is greater"
ENDIF
```

it prints *14 is greater*. If you change the script to read

```
IF VAL "044" GT "14"
ECHO "044 is greater"
ELSE
ECHO "14 is greater"
ENDIF
```

however, you come up with the correct answer. Another change to the IF command in Workbench 1.3 is the use of the dollar sign ($) as a substituion character. A string that starts with a dollar sign will

Command Sequence Files

be replaced by an environment variable of the same name. An environment variable is a string that's stored with the SETENV command, and can be retrieved with the GETENV command. For example, the command SETENV name Fred stores the value Fred in an environment variable called name. If this is the case, the statement

`IF $name EQ "Fred"`

will be true.

The last condition that IF tests is the return code left by the previous command. The return code is a number passed to the CLI by a program when it finishes. The code indicates whether the program was successfully completed or whether an error occurred. Programs normally use a return code of 5, 10, or 20 to indicate that an error happened. The higher the return code, the more serious the error. IF lets you test for each of these codes with the keywords WARN, ERROR, and FAIL. IF WARN is true if the last return code was 5 or greater, IF ERROR is true if the code was 10 or greater, and IF FAIL is true if a code of 20 or greater was returned.

Normally, if a serious error occurs during a command sequence, the entire sequence is immediately terminated. The default cutoff point for this is a return code of 10 or higher. Using this default setting, it's impossible to test for a FAIL or ERROR condition, since the sequence terminates before the test can take place. It's possible to change the point at which a command sequence fails, however, using the FAILAT command. Entering the command FAILAT 25, for instance, insures that the sequence doesn't terminate unless a program returns an error code of 25 or higher. The new failure threshold applies only to the current command sequence. Once it has finished executing, the default value is restored.

In most circumstances, you'll want to terminate the command sequence if a serious error is encountered. Changing the FAILAT threshold and testing for the error yourself gives you an opportunity to present the user with a message that clearly explains what happened. For example, you could change the command file allowing the user to input the date and time to read:

```
ECHO " "
ECHO "The current setting of the date and time is:"
DATE
ECHO " "
ECHO "Enter the correct date and/or time now."
ECHO "Use the form DD-MMM-YY for the date (09-Sep-
   89)."
```

```
ECHO "Use the form HH:MM:SS or HH:MM for the time
   (14:55)."
ECHO " "
FAILAT 25
DATE > nil: ?
IF ERROR
ECHO "You did not enter a correct date and/or time
   setting."
ECHO "The current settings remain in effect."
ELSE
ECHO "The new date and time setting are:"
DATE
DATE >now
ENDIF
```

If this example were part of a larger *startup-sequence* file, there's a good chance you wouldn't want the entire sequence to terminate if the user didn't enter the date or time correctly. Using FAILAT to reset the failure threshold and IF ERROR to test for errors, you can tell the user that the attempt was not successful and continue with the rest of the sequence.

Even if you've used FAILAT to change the failure threshold, you may exit from a command sequence at any time by using the QUIT command. QUIT also allows you to leave a specific return code. The command QUIT 20, for example, terminates the command sequence immediately and leaves a return code of 20.

To summarize, the IF command uses the following keywords for making its test:

Keyword	Function
EXISTS *name*	Is true if the volume, directory, or file exists
string1 EQ *string2*	Is true if the text of the two strings is the same (ignoring uppercase and lowercase)
string1 GT *string2*	Is true if the ASCII value of string1 is greater than the ASCII value of string2 (Workbench 1.3)
string1 GE *string2*	Is true if the ASCII value of string1 is greater than or equal to the ASCII value of string2 (Workbench 1.3)
VAL *string1* GT *string2*	Is true if the numeric value of numeric string1 is greater than that of numeric string2 (Workbench 1.3)
WARN	Is true if the previous program left a return code of 5 or greater
ERROR	Is true if the previous program left a return code of 10 or greater
FAIL	Is true if the previous program left a return code of 20 or greater
NOT	Reverses the result of the test

Note: Under Workbench 1.3, IF evaluates $VAR as the string contained within the environment variable named VAR.

Command Sequence Files

Branching with SKIP
For most simple cases, IF-ELSE branching is sufficient. But if you're making a number of tests, the SKIP command can make things easier. It allows you to use the results of the IF test to jump to a subsequent command line. The LAB command is used to designate the line at which you wish execution to resume. This is the general format:

```
IF test        ;If the results of test are true,
SKIP Next      ;Execution jumps ─┐
ENDIF          ;                 │
command        ;                 │
command        ;                 │
command        ;                 │
LAB Next       ; to here ◄───────┘
command
```

SKIP is particularly useful where you may wish the same thing to happen after a number of tests. Rather than writing the commands over and over in the body of the IF-ELSE-ENDIF clause, you can have each command jump to the same labeled line. The following command file demonstrates this principle. It copies both a file and its associated icon file to another volume or directory:

```
.Key from,to
IF <from>q EQ "q"
SKIP Missing
ENDIF
.
IF <to>q EQ "q"
SKIP Missing
ENDIF
.
IF NOT EXISTS <from>
SKIP Missing
ENDIF
.
COPY <from> <to>
IF EXISTS <from>.info
COPY <from>.info <to>
ENDIF
SKIP Done
.
LAB Missing
ECHO "You must enter the name of an existing file to
    copy,"
ECHO "and the volume or directory to copy it to."
LAB Done
```
88

Prior to Workbench 1.3, it was not possible to use SKIP to move backward within the command file. With version 1.3, a new option, BACK, was added. When the BACK option is used, SKIP starts searching for the LABEL at the beginning of the file, instead of at the current line. Even so, you can't use BACK to SKIP past a prior EXECUTE command.

EXECUTEing from a Command Sequence File

It is possible, and sometimes quite useful, to use the EXECUTE command from within a command sequence file. A command file can even EXECUTE itself. This permits a limited form of looping. For example, let's say you have a number of disks to copy, and you want to write a command sequence file that continuously prompts you to insert source and destination disks, and then copies one to the other. To avoid having to swap the Workbench disk when DOS wants to read the commands, let's copy them to RAM:

```
COPY c:DiskCopy to RAM:
COPY c:Execute to RAM:
MAKEDIR RAM:T
CD RAM:
```

Now let's create a file called *RAM:ConCopy* that continuously executes the DiskCopy command:

```
DiskCopy df0: to df1:
Execute ConCopy
```

When we EXECUTE *ConCopy*, it runs DiskCopy once, then EXECUTEs itself. Note that we created a directory :T in RAM:. The EXECUTE command often needs to create a temporary file, and tries to store this file in the :T directory. If there is no :T directory, the error message *EXECUTE: Can't open work file ":T/Command-0-T01"* appears and the command fails. As of Workbench 1.3, however, EXECUTE will first try to create its temporary files in T: if it is assigned, and if not, will then go to :T.

Chapter 6

ED, the System Screen Editor

The screen editor program, ED, found in the *c* directory of the Workbench disk, can be used like any CLI command program. But ED is not really a DOS file-management command program. Rather, it's a full-screen text editor which can be used to create a text file or edit an existing one. It differs from the other text editor program included on the Workbench disk, EDIT, in a variety of ways. EDIT is a line-oriented editor, which means that you must first select the line you want to change. ED, however, is a *screen-oriented* editor, which displays a whole screen of text at a time and lets you move the cursor around the screen, adding or deleting text as you see fit. While EDIT can be used to alter files which contain binary code, ED is designed to edit text-only files. And, finally, ED files always end with a linefeed character, which ED adds if it doesn't find one already present.

To start ED, type ED, followed by the name of the file you wish to edit. If the filename doesn't describe an existing file, ED assumes that you want to create a new file. To exit the ED program, type ESC-Q simply to quit or ESC-X to save the current file and exit.

ED starts with a maximum workspace of 40,000 characters. Unless you change the size of the workspace, you're limited to editing files of that size. To change the size of the workspace, use the keyword SIZE on the command line which you use to run ED, followed by the number of characters you want in the workspace. For example, entering the command ED Windbag SIZE 100000 lets you edit a file called *Windbag* which can contain up to 100,000 characters. It's a good idea always to specify a size somewhat greater than the exact size of the file.

There are two ways of issuing commands to ED—*immediate mode* and *command mode*. In immediate mode, you give ED its commands by pressing nonprinting key combinations. In extended command mode, you first type the ESC character, which places your cursor on the command line at the bottom of the screen. You may then type in one or more command strings. The command is not executed until you press RETURN.

ED, the System Screen Editor

Immediate Mode

The ED program starts in immediate mode. Here, the characters you type are inserted into the text document. To edit, just move the cursor to the appropriate place and either erase existing text or add new text. In addition, there are a number of control commands which help in editing. These commands are executed by holding down the CTRL key, then pressing another key. (The notation CTRL-x will be used to refer to these commands. This indicates that you're to hold down CTRL, and press the key specified by x.) All CTRL character commands are executed as soon as you press the key combination.

Cursor Commands

The cursor is a colored block which indicates the position where additional characters will enter the text buffer. If you're using the default set of colors, it appears as an orange block highlighting the current character. You can move the cursor in any direction by pressing one of the cursor arrow keys to the right of the RETURN key. If there's more text in the buffer than appears on the screen, moving the cursor to any edge of the screen and pressing the corresponding cursor arrow key shifts all text (scrolls) to show part of the hidden text. For example, if you move the cursor to the bottom line of the first screen of a long document, then press the down-arrow key, the cursor moves down to the next line and reveals the hidden first line of the next screen. What was formerly the top line scrolls up and out of sight. By using the down and up arrows, you can move forward and backward through the text file.

Other immediate commands allow you to move the cursor in larger increments. The **CTRL-T** combination moves the cursor right to the first character of the next word. **CTRL-R** moves the cursor back to the space at the end of the previous word. **CTRL-]** moves the cursor to the end of the current line, scrolling the screen if the line is longer than the screen width. If the cursor is already at the end of the line, CTRL-] moves it back to the beginning of the line. If you press CTRL-] a number of times, the cursor alternates between the first and last characters of the line. Likewise, **CTRL-E** moves the cursor to the beginning of the first line on the screen. If, however, the cursor is already at the start of the first line, CTRL-E moves it to the end of the last line on the screen.

The scroll commands don't change the absolute position of the cursor, but rather move the text itself. **CTRL-U** scrolls the screen up, which appears to make the cursor move down toward the end of the document. **CTRL-D** scrolls the screen down, which in effect moves the cursor toward the beginning of the document. Either

ED, the System Screen Editor

command causes the whole screen to be redrawn from the top, making the scrolling action rather slow.

Note that in ED, the TAB key is strictly a cursor movement key. When you press TAB (or CTRL-I), the cursor moves to the next TAB position, which is one greater than an even multiple of the TAB setting. For example, if you're using the default TAB setting 3, the TAB key moves the cursor from column 1 (the left edge of the screen) to column 4, then column 7, column 10, column 13, and so on. You can change the size of the TAB stops with the extended command ST (see below). Unlike some editors, ED doesn't insert characters into the text when you press TAB. The TAB key leaves neither a TAB character nor spaces in the text, though if it passes over a blank portion of the line, the space characters it bypasses remain in the text. Note also that if you enter a text file which contains TAB characters into ED, ED replaces each with a number of spaces.

Character Deletion/Insertion

When you've moved the cursor to the text location you want to edit, there are several immediate mode commands which you can use to delete or insert text. The BACK SPACE key (or CTRL-H) moves the cursor one character to the left, deleting the character. The DEL key deletes the character under the cursor and moves the text to the right one position to the left.

You can also delete characters in larger chunks. The **CTRL-O** command's actions depend on whether the cursor rests on a character or a space. If the cursor is on a space, CTRL-O deletes all spaces it finds until the first character of the next word. Otherwise, CTRL-O deletes the current character and all characters it finds until the next space between words. Thus, CTRL-O can be used alternatively to delete whole words or the spaces between words. **CTRL-Y** deletes everything from the current character position to the end of the line. **CTRL-B** deletes the entire current line, regardless of the cursor position.

Unlike most screen editors, ED doesn't let you delete the RETURN character at the end of a line. This means that once you've split a line with a RETURN, the only way to join it together again is with the extended command J (see below).

The ED editor is always in *insert mode*. This means that any characters typed in push text to the right rather than overwriting characters. Thus, no special character insertion commands are needed. ED *does* have an immediate mode command, **CTRL-A**, which allows you to insert a blank line below the current line and moves the cursor to the beginning of that line.

ED supports lines wider than the screen display. To see different parts of such lines, scroll the text horizontally by moving the cursor left or right. Each line has a maximum of 255 characters—ED won't let you insert characters in a line of maximum length.

Another interesting characteristic of ED is that it supports a form of word-wrap. This means that if a right margin is set, and you're typing a word which extends past that margin, ED automatically ends the current line with a RETURN character at the space before that word and moves the start of the word down to the next line. This wordwrap feature applies only when you're typing at the end of a line. If you insert characters into the middle of the line, forcing the line over the margin, ED won't break the line. You can also disable this feature by using the extended command EX, which acts like the margin release on a typewriter (see extended commands below). You may also use extended commands to change the left and right margins from their default positions of 1 and 77 respectively.

Miscellaneous Immediate Commands

The **CTRL-F** command flips the case of the current character and moves the cursor one position to the right. This means that if the current character is in uppercase, it changes to lowercase and vice versa. If the current character is not a letter, it doesn't change, but the cursor still moves to the right. If the cursor is positioned at the first letter of the word *this*, and you press CTRL-F four times, the word changes to *THIS*.

CTRL-V redraws the screen. Since ED itself refreshes the display if you size the window or move it or scroll it in any direction, this command will be useful only on rare occasions.

CTRL-G is used in conjunction with the extended mode commands. It repeats the last extended mode command you issued. The usefulness of this command will soon become apparent, as the discussion turns to the extended commands.

Extended Mode Commands

Although immediate mode commands are faster and more convenient to use, the extended mode commands are more powerful. Generally, you may use extended commands to execute any of the cursor movement and deletion functions of the immediate commands. In addition, you may use extended mode commands to delete, copy, or move whole blocks of text, to save and load text files, to find and replace text strings, and to perform various other functions. You can even issue a number of commands at one time or

ED, the System Screen Editor

indicate that one or more of these commands is to be executed a number of times.

To issue an extended command, you first press the ESC key (or CTRL-[). When you do, an asterisk appears on the bottom line of the screen, and the cursor moves to the space following the asterisk. This indicates that you've moved to the command line, and any text you enter is to be interpreted as an editor command, not as text to be inserted into the document. After entering the command(s), pressing the RETURN key executes the command. If you just press RETURN without entering a command, no command is executed and you return to immediate mode.

For instance, let's say you want to use the T command (explained below) to go to the top of the file. You first press ESC, and the line at the bottom of the screen shows an asterisk:

*

You then type T and press RETURN:

*T <CR>

The command line disappears, and the display moves to show the top of the file.

Extended mode commands are made up of one or two letters. Case is not important, and you can put more than one command on a line by separating them with semicolons.

Sometimes a command requires an *argument*, such as a number or a text string. A text string must be set off with characters known as *delimiters* so that it won't be confused with a command string. The delimiter character can be anything except letters, numbers, spaces, semicolons, or brackets. Double quotation marks are the most common delimiters, though if you want to type a string with double quotation marks in it, you must use something else (like the slash or exclamation point). Strings may appear properly in commands in the form "this is a string" or /this is a "string"/ or !c:sub/"so called"!.

Cursor Movement Commands

The **CL** (Cursor Left) and **CR** (Cursor Right) commands work just like the left- and right-arrow keys, moving the cursor one space to the left or right. As explained below, however, you can add a repeat count so that 4CL moves the cursor four spaces to the left. The **N** command (Next) moves the cursor to the start of the next line, while the **P** command (Previous) moves the cursor to the start of the previous line.

ED, the System Screen Editor

CS (Cursor Start) and **CE** (Cursor End) move the cursor to the start and end of the line respectively. **T** (Top) and **B** (Bottom) move the cursor to the top or bottom of the document, while **M** (Move) moves the cursor to an absolute line number. For example, M 662 moves the cursor to the start of line 662. This can be extremely helpful when used with compilers which identify the line numbers where errors occurred.

Deletion/Insertion Commands
The **DC** command works just like the DEL key, deleting the character under the cursor. The **D** command functions like the immediate mode command CTRL-B and deletes the entire current line.

I (Insert line) is used to insert a string of text as a new line *above* the current line. The string follows the I command, as in

*I"This goes above the current line"

The **A** (Add after) command is similar to the I command, but adds the new line *after* the current line.

S (Split) and **J** (Join) are used to split one line into two and join two lines into one. The S command acts just like a RETURN character, which ends the current line and moves the text to the right to a new line below. In effect, the J command deletes the RETURN character at the end of the current line, thus joining it with the next line.

Search and Replace (Find and Exchange)
Another way of scrolling the screen to a particular place in a document is with the **F** (Find) command. The F command is issued along with the text string you want to find:

*F"Intuition"

Once issued, F searches the document for the exact text specified, from the current cursor position forward to the end of the file. A complementary command, **BF** (Backwards Find), searches from the current cursor position to the beginning of the file. By default, both find commands are case-sensitive and will find a match only if both text strings contain exactly the same combination of uppercase and lowercase letters. You may, however, change this default so that searches ignore differences in case by using the **UC** command. Once you've issued this command, all searches ignore case differences until you reset the default with the **LC** command.

Sometimes you wish both to locate a phrase and replace it with another. The **E** (Exchange) command does just this. When

ED, the System Screen Editor

using E, you must first specify the phrase to find, then follow it with the replacement phrase, like this:

*E"Intuition"User Interface"

    This example looks for the word *Intuition* and replaces it with the phrase *User Interface*. The E command only looks forward, so if you want to catch all occurrences of the search phrase, you should first move the cursor to the top of the file with the T command.

    The **EQ** (Exchange with Query) command is a variation on E. Instead of making the substitution automatically, it prints the message *Exchange?* on the command line. If you press the Y key, the exchange takes place, but if you enter N, the cursor moves past the string.

    Both the find and exchange commands lend themselves well to the repeat features of ED. For example, once you've set up a search string with F, it's a simple matter to find the next occurrence of the string by using the immediate command CTRL-G. And it's just as simple to replace every occurrence of a search string with a command like

*RP EQ"me"myself"

which repeatedly replaces the word *me* with the word *myself* after verifying that you want to make each change. For more on repeating commands, see the section "Multiple and Repeat Commands" below.

Block Transfers

One of the most powerful groups of extended commands is that which manipulates an entire block of text at once. With these commands, you can delete, copy, or move an entire block of text.

    A *block* is made up of one or more adjacent lines of text. You use the **BS** (Block Start) and **BE** (Block End) to mark the beginning and ending of a block of text. When you issue the BS command, the block is marked as starting at the first character of the current line, regardless of where the cursor is presently positioned. In order to complete the marking of a block, you must cursor down to the last line of the block and issue the BE command. This marks the end of the block at the end of the current line. Both the BS and BE commands are needed to mark a block successfully, and the line you marked as the start of the block must be above the one you marked as the end. (In other words, you cannot mark the start of the block near the end of the file, then move the cursor up and mark the end of the block.) You can mark the start and end of the block on the same line, however, as with the command

*BS;BE

which marks the entire current line as a block.

You can only mark entire lines as blocks. BS always starts marking at the beginning of the current line, and BE always marks to the end of the current line. If you want to mark only parts of a line, you must first use the RETURN key to split the line. Also note that the block stays marked only so long as you don't make any changes to the text. Once you make any editing changes to *any* part of the text (not just the marked lines), the block markers disappear.

After you've marked a block, you can insert copies of the block by moving the cursor to where you want the block inserted, then using the **IB** (Insert Block) command. You can insert as many copies as you wish, as long as you perform the inserts immediately after marking the block and don't edit text in between insertions.

You can delete the entire block with the **DB** (Delete Block) command. Unlike some editors which retain a deleted block in a special buffer and allow you to retrieve it, ED simply discards a deleted block. Once you've deleted it, it's gone. You can move a block of text, however, by first duplicating it with the IB command, then deleting the original block with the DB command.

The **WB** (Write Block) command lets you save a marked portion of text to a named file. This allows you to split a large file into two smaller parts or generally manipulate portions of a file. The WB command must be followed with the name of the file to which the marked portion is to be written. This filename must be enclosed by the normal string delimiters, such as quotation marks:

*WB"RAM:tempfile"

The final block command is **SB** (Show Block). This command helps you identify the currently marked block by moving its text to the top of the screen.

File Management (Save/Load/Exit)

ED really has no load command per se, since you must specify the file to edit when you start the program. However, it's possible to insert text from a disk file within the current text file with the **IF** (Insert File) command. When you type

*IF "*filename*"

filename is inserted under the current line, and the rest of the text in the document is moved down.

ED, the System Screen Editor

ED won't let you start editing a file which contains binary (nontext) characters. If you try this, ED ends with the message *File contains binary*. It's interesting to note, however, that you may start by editing a blank file, then use IF to merge a file which *does* contain such characters. This isn't recommended, however, as such characters don't appear correctly on the screen, making it hard to do accurate editing.

The **SA** command is used to save a current copy of the document to disk. If you don't add a filename, the document is saved to the file named when you started ED. It's recommended that you periodically save your work to disk (every half hour or so is best) to protect yourself against the perils of power outages. Speaking of backups, you should be aware that ED creates a backup of your original text file in the *T* directory of the document disk (if the directory exists), in a file called *ED-Backup*.

If you use the SA command with a filename, you can save a copy of the current document to a file other than the one named when you started the program. This allows you to keep several copies of the document, each varying slightly. The format for this command is

*SA"*filename*"

There are two ways to exit the ED program. The first is with the **Q** (Quit) command. Q just quits, without saving your text. If you try the Q command after you have changed the text of the document, however, without saving these changes, you'll receive a prompt saying *Edits will be lost - type Y to confirm:*. This gives you an opportunity to save the changes—press any key and the quit is stopped. If you press Y, however, the program ends without saving the changes.

The other way to exit ED is with **X** (eXit). X both saves the current document and exits the program. Think of it as first performing an SA, then a Q command.

Tabs and Margins

The **SL** (Set Left) and **SR** (Set Right) commands are used to set left and right margins. As explained above, the right margin is used for the purpose of wordwrapping. This means that as you add characters to the end of a line and force it over the right margin, a RETURN character is inserted and the word past the margin is moved to a new line below. Wordwrapping occurs only when you add characters to the end of a line. If you insert characters in the middle of a line, you can cause the end of the line to go past the margin without wrapping. If you wish to disable the wordwrapping

ED, the System Screen Editor

feature for the current line, use the **EX** (EXtend margin) command. This works like the margin release on a typewriter, allowing you to add characters to the end of the line past the right margin. The EX command extends the margin only for the current line, however. If you wish to extend the margin permanently, change the right margin setting from its default value of 77.

You can also set a left margin with the SL (Set Left margin) command. The default setting is 1 (the leftmost column). When you change this setting, each new line begins at the position indicated. The preceding character positions will be filled with space characters. This left margin is not a "hard" margin. You don't have to use the EX command to move past it. You may use the backspace character to move to the left of it. The CS command moves you back to column 1 as well.

The **ST** (Set Tabs) command is used to set the distance between tab stops. The default setting is a stop every three characters.

Miscellaneous Commands

The **U** command (Undo) gives you a very limited undo capability. When you start to edit a line, ED saves the original contents of the line. As long as you stay on that line, you can restore its contents by issuing the U command. However, once you move off that line, you cannot undo the changes. Moreover, U cannot restore a line once you remove it completely, either with the immediate command CTRL-B or with the D command.

The **SH** (SHow information) command displays information about the current editing session. When you use the SH command, a number of lines appear at the top of the editing screen, showing the name of the file you're editing, the tab setting, the left and right margins, the first and last few characters in the block (if any is marked), and the percentage of the edit buffer that's filled. This display disappears as soon as you type a character.

Multiple and Repeat Commands

When in extended command mode, you're not limited to issuing one command at a time. Several commands may be placed on the same command line, separated by semicolons. For example, if you want to search for the first occurrence of the word *Amiga* in a text file, you could use the command sequence

*T;F"Amiga"

which moves the cursor to the top of the document, then starts the search. In addition, you can specify that a command should be repeated a number of times by placing that number in front of the command. For instance, the command

*4D

deletes four lines in a row, starting with the current line. You can also use the special repetition command **RP** to specify that you want the command repeated until an error occurs. Let's say that you frequently misspell the word *separate* as *seperate*. If you want to change every occurrence of the word *seperate* to *separate*, you could use the following command series:

*T;RP E"seperate"separate"

The first command, T, moves the cursor to the top of the document. The next command, RP, specifies that you want to repeat the following sequence until an error occurs. Finally, the E command causes the second string to be exchanged for the first. The result of all this is that ED searches for *seperate* and replaces it with *separate* until it can't find the string any longer. When that happens, an *End of file* error is issued, which causes RP to stop. (Notice that you don't have to separate RP and the following command to be repeated with a semicolon.)

You can stop any command or series of commands by pressing any key. ED always exits the extended command mode as soon as you press a key and displays the message *Commands abandoned* on the command line.

Using a repetition count or the RP command only repeats the command immediately following. Let's say that you're editing a double-spaced file, in which every other line is blank, and you wish to delete all blank lines. One strategy would be to position the cursor at the top of the file (assuming it's not a blank line), then repeatedly move the cursor to the next line and delete it. You might try the command

*T;RP N;D

but this wouldn't work. The cursor first moves to the top, but only the N command repeats so that the command just moves the cursor to the last line of the file where it encounters an *End of file* error.

To counter this problem, ED allows you to group commands together in parentheses. When you do this, the repetition count applies to all of the commands enclosed in the parentheses. Thus, the command

*T;RP (N;D)

does just what you want. It moves the cursor to the top of the document and then repeats both the N and D commands, again and again.

ED Command Summary

Keyboard Commands
Cursor Movement

Cursor keys	Move cursor one character up, down, right, or left
TAB, CTRL-I	Move cursor right to next TAB position (don't insert any characters into text)
CTRL-T	Moves cursor to start of next word
CTRL-R	Moves cursor to end of previous word
CTRL-]	Moves cursor to end or start of line (alternates)
CTRL-U	Scrolls text up (moves cursor down) a page
CTRL-D	Scrolls text down (moves cursor up) a page
CTRL-E	Moves cursor to top or bottom of screen (alternates)

Insert/Delete

BACK SPACE, CTRL-H	Delete character to left of cursor
DEL	Deletes character under cursor
CTRL-O	Deletes next word or spaces before next word (alternates)
CTRL-Y	Deletes to end of current line
CTRL-B	Deletes entire current line
CTRL-A	Inserts a new line below current line

Miscellaneous Commands

CTRL-F	Flips case of character under cursor (and moves cursor one character to the right)
CTRL-V	Verifies (redraws) the screen
ESC, CTRL-[	Enter extended command mode
CTRL-G	Repeats last extended command

ED, the System Screen Editor

Extended Mode Commands (Press ESC to Enter Command Mode)

Cursor Movement

CL	Moves cursor left one character
CR	Moves cursor right one character
N	Moves cursor to start of next line
P	Moves cursor to start of previous line
CS	Moves cursor to start of line
CE	Moves cursor to end of line
T	Moves cursor to top of file
B	Moves cursor to bottom of file
M*linenum*	Moves cursor to line number *linenum*

Insert/Delete

DC	Deletes character under cursor
D	Deletes entire current line
I/*string*/	Inserts *string* as a new line above current one
A/*string*/	Inserts *string* as a new line below current one
S	Splits current line at cursor position (same as RETURN)
J	Joins current line with next line (deletes RETURN at end of current line)

Find and Exchange (Search and Replace)

F/*string*/	Finds *string* in following text (forward search)
BF/*string*/	Backward find (searches previous text for *string*)
E/*string1*/*string2*/	Exchanges (replaces) *string1* with *string2*
EQ/*string1*/*string2*/	Exchanges (replaces) after query *string1* with *string2*
LC	Requires searches to match both uppercase and lowercase
UC	Ignores case differences in searches

Block Transfers

BS	Marks a block starting at start of current line
BE	Marks a block ending at end of current line
DB	Deletes current block
IB	Inserts copy of the block below current line
WB/*filename*/	Writes the block to file *filename*
SB	Shows the block onscreen

Save/Load/Exit

IF/*filename*/	Inserts file *filename* at the cursor (and moves rest of file down)
SA/*filename*/	Saves file to disk (to *filename* if given; if not, to current file)
X	Exits, saving text file to disk
Q	Quits without saving text

Tabs and Margins

SL*colnum*	Sets left margin to column number *colnum*
SR*colnum*	Sets right margin to column number *colnum*
EX	Extends right margin
ST	Sets distance between tab stops

Miscellaneous

SH	Shows information on filename, tab stops, margins, block markers, and buffer usage
U	Undoes changes to current line
;	Executes another command on same command line
number	Repeats following command *number* times
( )	Groups commands for purposes of repetition
RP	Repeats following command until an error occurs

Chapter 7

EDIT, the Line Editor

EDIT, AmigaDOS's line editor, can be used to change and inspect just about any kind of AmigaDOS file, including text, source language, and program files. Individual lines of text may be edited, inserted, or displayed. EDIT can also search for, delete, or replace selected text within one or more lines.

We often take for granted programs capable of manipulating text a screenful at a time. Full-screen editors with built-in functions optimized for producing source text are used everyday by professional programmers. Word processors that handle multiple windows of text and include integrated spelling checkers and thesauruses make writing reports and manuscripts a breeze. In the face of all this "gee-whiz" text processing power, it's easy to look down one's nose at the lowly line editor, with its seemingly crude user interface.

Line Editors—A Brief History
In the early 1970s, the most common medium used to get a program or other information read into a computer was the *punched card*, created on a mechanical device called a *keypunch*. A separate punched card was required for every line of information to be read into the computer. The cards themselves were read with a device called a *card reader*. If a single character was mistyped on a card, the entire card had to be retyped. Add to this the fact that keypunches were slow and prone to jams that invariably ate the one card that had finally been typed correctly on the fifteenth attempt. It's easy to understand why programmers who have been around for a while break out in a cold sweat when some careless associate evokes the memory of writing a thousand-line program on punched cards.

The very first programs which allowed programmers to type in and modify programs electronically were called *line editors*. Line editors freed a generation of computer programmers from the drudgery of keypunch machines. Text could be entered one line at a time at a cathode ray tube (CRT) equipped with a keyboard. If you made a mistake, you could actually back up and correct it. Pro-

EDIT, the Line Editor

grams could be saved, recalled, and modified at will. Simple as the first line editors were, it was like handing a gas-powered tractor to a farmer who had been tilling fields with a hand plow.

The Bottom Line

So why use EDIT? AmigaDOS comes with a fairly powerful full-screen editor (ED), and reasonably priced word processors for the Amiga are also available. While most Amiga owners will prefer either of the latter, some users will find using EDIT comfortable. AmigaDOS EDIT falls into the "quick and dirty" program category, much like EDLIN, the line editor of MS-DOS. It's handy, it's already resident in the *c* directory, and if you just need to change a couple of lines in a command file, EDIT is probably as good as anything else. EDIT's limited number of commands also makes it relatively easy to master.

EDIT does have two features which ED, its more powerful sibling, does not—EDIT can execute a series of prestored subcommands, and it is also marginally suitable for displaying and modifying compiled programs as well as text.

How EDIT Works

EDIT processes the contents of a source file (we'll call this EDIT's *From* file) sequentially—a line at a time—using editing commands specified by the user.

EDIT keeps track of its place within the material being edited. When EDIT is first invoked, the *current line* is the first line of the *From* file. As editing commands are executed, the current line changes. EDIT keeps tabs on the current line by maintaining an internal pointer called the *current line marker*.

As the current line marker is moved past a line, the line is moved into a special area called the *output buffer*. The output buffer has a fixed size for the duration of an EDIT session.

When the output buffer becomes filled, data is written to the file specified as the destination (EDIT's *To* file), on a first-in, first-out basis.

During an EDIT session, various informative messages and displays of the contents of lines are sent to EDIT's *verification device* (your Amiga's screen, unless another device is specified when EDIT is started up).

If EDIT's *To* file is different than its *From* file, the contents of the file used as input to the editor will not be altered. If the *To* file is the same as the *From* file, the original contents of the file will be moved to a temporary file called *:t/edit.backup*.

EDIT, the Line Editor

Invoking EDIT

An EDIT session is usually started from an active CLI by using AmigaDOS's EDIT command. What follows is a summary of the EDIT command's syntax. See the EDIT command section in the "AmigaDOS Command Reference" for a more detailed explanation.

EDIT [**FROM**] *fromname* [**TO**] *toname* [**WITH**] *withname* [**VER**] *vername* [**OPT** *option*]

EDIT's Parameters and Keywords:

FROM *fromname*—The name of the file whose contents will be edited. Throughout the rest of this chapter this is referred to as EDIT's *From* file.

TO *toname*—The name of the file which will contain the edited text after the EDIT session is ended. Throughout the rest of this chapter, this file is referred to as EDIT's *To* file.

WITH *withname*—Lets you specify a file that may optionally be used as input to the line editor's command processor.

VER *vername*—Lets you specify where you want messages from EDIT to be displayed.

OPT Pn or **OPT W**n or **OPT P**n**W**n—These options let you set the maximum line length (Wn) and/or number of lines (Pn) that EDIT will keep in its output buffer.

While you can edit files with more lines than the value of n, you'll only be able to move backward n lines. If the file to be edited is not unreasonably large, it's usually a good idea to specify an n greater than the number of lines in the file to be edited.

Starting an EDIT Session—Examples

Example 1—Edit a file called *mysource* in the current directory, using EDIT. The edited data is to be stored under the same filename. The number of lines is to be set to 40 and line width to 120 (EDIT's default values):

EDIT mysource

Example 2—Edit a file called *bigsource*. The edited data will be stored in the file called *edited bigsource*. The output buffer size is set to 1000 lines, with a maximum line width of 120:

EDIT bigsource "edited bigsource" OPT P1000

Example 3—Edit a file called *universe*. When EDIT starts up, execute the list of EDIT subcommands contained in the file *autocommands* located in the *myprocess/nebula* directory on drive df1:. The edited data is to be stored under the same filename. Send

EDIT, the Line Editor

all messages and verification displays from the line editor to the system printer. The number of lines in EDIT's output buffer is to be set to 40 and the maximum line width to 250:

```
EDIT universe WITH dfl:myprocess/nebula/auto
   commands VER PRT: OPT W250
```

Note: EDIT expects the *From* file to exist already. Issuing an edit for a file called *newfile* which doesn't exist, as in

```
EDIT FROM newfile
```

generates the error message *Can't open newfile*. However, you can use EDIT to type in a file by creating an empty file first and then editing the new file:

```
COPY * newfile    Press CTRL-\ after entering this command
EDIT newfile
```

Example 4—Let's create a sample file which you can type in, then experiment with using EDIT during the rest of this chapter. Type:

```
COPY * testfile
The door slammed and she stormed
out of the house. Meanwhile, the
toast burned and the eggs hardened.
He stared after her, wondering what
to say. Fortunately, he kept his mouth
shut. Better to say nothing than to
say something now.
```

Once you've typed this in, press CTRL- \ (end-of-file marker), which will close the file; *testfile* is now on your disk. You can access it by entering

```
EDIT testfile
```

Getting Out of EDIT

There are several ways to exit an EDIT session.

The **STOP** command exits EDIT, leaving the *From* file intact. The contents of the *To* file, if a separate one was specified, are unpredictable since STOP will not write the contents of the output buffer to the *To* file as it exits EDIT.

The **W** command (Windup) advances the current line marker to the *From* file's end-of-file (EOF) marker, moving lines into the output buffer as it goes. When the EOF is reached, EDIT saves the contents of the output buffer to EDIT's *To* file, and the editing session terminates.

EDIT, the Line Editor

The **Q** command (Quit) is used within EDIT command files to return control to the process which invoked the file's execution. If Q is issued from EDIT's primary command level, it has the same effect as W. (See the section "EDIT Command Files" later in this chapter for more information about the use of command files.)

The Current Line
EDIT keeps track of its place within the data and/or text being edited. When EDIT is first invoked, the *current line* is the first line of the *From* file. As EDIT subcommands are executed, this current line changes. EDIT keeps tabs on the current line by maintaining the *current line marker*, an internal pointer.

At the beginning of each session, EDIT associates sequential line numbers with all of the original lines of the *From* file. When EDIT begins, the current line is line number 1.

Verifying the Current Line
The **?** and **!** commands allow you to display the line number (if any) and contents of the current line.

?

displays the line number and contents of the current line.

Characters which cannot be displayed can be represented by a question mark. For instance, if issuing a ? command results in a display of

?
5.
Whom do you trust???

the question marks which appear to be a part of line 5 may not be question marks at all. In these cases, the ! command will display the hexadecimal value of the characters in question:

!
Whom do you trust?11
-                   03

The exclamation mark (!) revealed that there's only one genuine question mark in the line, followed by characters whose ASCII values are 10 and 13. The ! also displays a dash (–) under any uppercase letters contained in the current line.

Turning Verification On and Off
EDIT often displays a *verification* of the line number and contents of the current line in response to many EDIT commands. If the current line has no line number, +++ will be displayed instead. Ver-

ification displays may be turned on and off with the **V** (Verify) command.

V−

turns off automatic line verification, while

V+

turns verification on. Verification is always set to *on* by EDIT when an editing session begins.

Trailing Spaces
EDIT normally suppresses all trailing spaces.

TR+

turns EDIT's trailing spaces switch on, allowing trailing spaces on both input and output lines.

TR−

reinvokes suppression of trailing spaces (EDIT's default).

Operational Windows
When a command is executed which instructs EDIT to operate on the current line, EDIT normally scans all the characters in the line from left to right, beginning with the first character.

It's possible to instruct EDIT to begin its scan at a character other than the first in the line. The current line's *operational window* consists of only that portion of the line which will be operated on. The beginning of the current line's operational window is pointed to by the *operational window pointer*.

> moves the operational window pointer of the current line one character to the right.

< moves the operational window pointer of the current line one character to the left.

PR (Pointer Reset) sets the operational window pointer line back to the start of the line.

Whenever EDIT is instructed to display verification of the current line (by ?, !, or any other command which normally ends with a verification of the current line), a greater than (>) character may be displayed under the contents of the current line. Everything to the right of the > is within the current line's operational window. For instance,

3.
Well this is another fine mess
            >

indicates that the operational window pointer of the current line

109

EDIT, the Line Editor

has been moved so that the operational window of the line consists of the text *another fine mess*. If you told EDIT to search for the word *this*, it would not be found, since only the contents of the current line's operational window are scanned by the search operation.

Character Operations on the Current Line

EDIT supports four intraline commands which can change the case of characters, replace characters with a blank, and delete characters:

$ (dollar sign) forces the case of the first character in the current line's operational window to lowercase. After a $ command is executed, the operational window pointer is moved one character to the right.

% (percentage sign) forces the case of the first character in the current line's operational window to uppercase. After a % command is executed, the operational window pointer is moved one character to the right.

_ (underscore) forces the first character in the current line's operational window to be replaced by a blank. After an _ command is executed, the operational window pointer is moved one character to the right.

(pound sign) deletes the first character in the current line's operational window. The text remaining in the operational window is shifted one character to the left.

The intraline commands may be strung together on a single EDIT command line. Take a look at the following example.

Assume you start with the current line as *All the young dudes, carry the NEWS*. Several operations can be carried out on this line to change its appearance:

```
1.
All the young dudes, carry the NEWS
%%%####
1.
ALL young dudes, carry the NEWS
    >
>>>>>>>%%%%>>
1.
ALL young DUDES, carry the NEWS
                         >
>>>>>>_____>$$
1.
All young DUDES, carry    NewS
                            >
```

EDIT, the Line Editor

You could have strung all the commands in the previous example together on one command line. Several command lines were used to keep things from getting totally confusing.

Moving from One Line to Another

N (Next line). The current line marker can be moved forward by using the N command. If you attempt to move the current line marker past EDIT's end-of-file flag, the message *Input exhausted* displays, and the current line marker is set at the end-of-file flag.

N

moves the current line marker to the next line of the current *From* file. If line verification is on, the line number and text of the new current line is displayed. The current line marker may be moved ahead multiple lines by stringing multiple N commands on a single line or by preceding the command with a number:

N;N;N;N

is the same as

4N

P (Previous line). The current line marker may be moved backward with the P command. If you attempt to move the current line marker past the first line contained in EDIT's output buffer, the message *No more previous lines* displays, and the current line marker is set to the first line in the output buffer.

Remember, the default capacity of EDIT's output buffer is only 40 lines. For example, if you EDIT an 80-line file and the current line marker is pointing to line 60, EDIT's output buffer contains only lines 20 through 59 of the *From* file. Attempting to back up 40 or more lines results in the current line marker pointing to line 20.

P

moves the current line marker back one line. If verification is on, the line number and text of the new current line is displayed. The current line marker may be moved back multiple lines by stringing multiple P commands on a single line or by preceding the command with a number.

P;P;P;P;P;P

is the same as

6P

Both move the current line marker back six lines.

Ma (Move to line *a*). The current line marker may be moved backward or forward to a specific line number by using the M com-

EDIT, the Line Editor

mand. Using a period (.) in the *a* location, the current line marker is moved to the end-of-file flag of the *From* file.

If you attempt to move the current line marker back to a line number not in EDIT's output buffer, the message *Line number a too small* displays. If the line number specified is greater than the highest line number of the *From* file, the message *Input exhausted* displays, and the current line marker is set to the end-of-file flag.

M17

moves the current line marker to line number 17 (*not* the seventeenth line). If verification is on, the line number and text of the new current line is displayed.

M.

moves the current line marker to the end-of-file flag of the *From* file.

Displaying Your Text

It's often handy to examine the contents of more than one line at a time. EDIT has four commands which allow you to display multiple lines of the file being edited.

T*n* (Type *n* lines). The T command displays *n* lines on the screen (or verification device, if one other than the screen has been selected), beginning with the current line. The current line marker is set to the line following the last one typed by the T command. If *n* is not specified, all lines following the current line are displayed, and the current line marker is set to the end-of-file flag.

Assume that the sixth line of a file being edited is the current line. The command

T5

displays the sixth through tenth lines of the file, and the current line marker is changed to point to the eleventh line. The line number and text of the new current line are displayed.

If the current line marker of a 100-line file is pointing to the thirty-eighth line, and the current line marker is set to the end-of-file flag,

T

displays lines 39 through 100, and the current line marker is set to the end-of-file flag.

TP (Type Previous). The TP command displays the current contents of EDIT's output buffer. If the buffer is full, the current line marker remains unchanged. If the output buffer is *not* full, the TP command advances the current line marker to the point which fills the buffer and then displays the contents of the buffer, followed by verification of the new current line.

For example, assume that EDIT has been invoked with the default buffer length of 40 lines and that you're editing a 70-line file. If the current line is the tenth line of the file (which means there are only nine lines currently in the output buffer) and you issue

TP

EDIT changes the current line marker to point to the forty-first line, moving lines 10 through 40 into the input buffer (along with the file's first 9 lines). All 40 lines now residing in the output buffer are displayed, followed by a verification display of the file's forty-first line. Any TP commands issued immediately thereafter will have no effect on the current line marker, since the output buffer has been filled.

TN (Type Next). The TN command acts exactly like a **T**a command in which the value of a is determined by the number of lines that the output buffer has been set to hold (OPT Pn). The default value for a is 40 if no Pn is specified in the EDIT command which started the current session.

TLn (Type with Line numbers). The TL command displays n lines preceded by their line numbers, beginning with the current line. Lines that have been inserted or that are created by splitting a numbered line in two may have no numbers. If a line has no number, EDIT displays three asterisks (***) in its place. The current line marker is set to the line following the last one typed by the T command. If n is not specified, all the lines following the current line are displayed, and the current line marker is set to the end-of-file flag.

Inserting New Text

EDIT allows text to be inserted before the current line or any line that may be referenced by a line number. The text to be inserted may be typed in via the keyboard or may be read directly from another AmigaDOS file.

The **I** command, when used in conjunction with a specific or relative line number, allows text to be inserted in EDIT's output stream.

- **I** or **I.** is used to insert text before the current line.
- **I*** inserts text after the last line of text in the *From* file.
- **I**a, where a is the line number that EDIT associates with a given line of the file being edited. An Ia command may search backward into EDIT's output buffer or forward, past the current line,

EDIT, the Line Editor

in search of the specified line number. Once the line number is found, the line associated with it is made the current line.

Insert commands all throw EDIT into *insert mode*. Any text typed at the keyboard will be inserted before the current line (into EDIT's output buffer). Insert mode is terminated by typing a line containing *only* the letter *z* (lowercase or uppercase) in the first column and hitting the RETURN key. The inserted text will have no line number. Upon exiting insert mode, the current line will be displayed—it will be the same line as when the I command was invoked.

Let's try it out. Insert several lines before the current line:

I
Well this is a silly little example
of how to insert a couple of lines
and then get out of Input's insert mode.
z

Insert several lines before line number 17:

I17
Had enough folks?
EDIT can be a barrel of laughs.
z

Note: You may change the input mode terminator to any string of up to 16 characters by using the Z command. For example,

Z/fin/

changes the input mode terminator from *z* to *fin*; *fin* will remain the input terminator through the end of the current EDIT session or until another Z command is issued.

• **I**/*filename*/ (Insert before current line from a file)

or

• **I***a*/*filename*/ (Insert before line *a* from a file)

Insert also lets you specify an AmigaDOS file as the source for lines to be inserted. Filenames used in conjunction with insert and replace commands are normally delimited by slashes (/), although the colon (:), period (.), comma (,) and asterisk (*) may also be used. Lines inserted from an AmigaDOS file into EDIT will have no line numbers associated with them. Here are some examples.

Insert the contents of the file *mytext* before the current line:

I /mytext/

Insert the contents of the file *Wow/What a Party* on the external disk drive before line 66:

I66 /"DF1:Wow/What a Party"/

EDIT, the Line Editor

Replacing Lines with Inserted Text

EDIT also allows lines of text to be replaced by inserted text typed in via the keyboard or read directly from an AmigaDOS file.

The **R** (Replace) commands' syntax is almost identical to that of the I (Insert) commands.

- **R** or **R.** is used to replace the current line with inserted text.
- **R*** inserts text after the last line of text in the *From* file.

R*a b* replaces a range of lines with inserted text; *a* and *b* are line numbers which EDIT associates with specific lines of the file being edited. An I*a b* command may search backward for the specified range of lines into EDIT's output buffer, or forward, past the current line, in search of the specified line numbers. Once the lines are found, the line associated with it is made the current line. If *b* is omitted, only line *a* will be replaced by the inserted text.

Replace commands all throw EDIT into insert mode. Any text typed at the keyboard replaces the line(s) specified. Replace's insert mode is terminated by typing a line that contains only the letter *z* in the first column and hitting the RETURN key. The inserted text will have no line numbers associated with them. Upon exiting insert mode, the current line will be displayed—it will be the first line following the last replaced line.

As with the I command, you may also replace text from an AmigaDOS file.

Replace the current line with the phrase *One for the Money*:

```
R
One for the Money
z
```

Replace line 13 with several lines of text entered from the keyboard:

```
R13
I am Gosar, the Gosarian, keymaster
of Zuuul.
And many were those who knew what it
was to roast in the depths of the Slor
that day, I tell you
z
```

Replace lines 3–67 with the text contained in the AmigaDOS file *morestuff/edit*:

```
R3 67.morestuff/edit.
```

EDIT, the Line Editor

Renumbering Lines

As has been pointed out, EDIT normally assigns line numbers only when a *From* file is opened. Inserted text has no automatically associated line numbers. The renumber command (=) may be used to assign a line number to the current line and each line that follows it when the renumber is issued.

=10

renumbers the current line and all lines following. The current line is assigned a line number of 10.

If the file being edited contained three lines, numbered 1 through 3, and line 1 was the current line, =10 would change the line numbers to 10 through 12. Any line numbers associated with lines in EDIT's output buffer are lost.

Searching for Text

F/*string*/ (Find text). The find command searches for a specified text string beginning with the current line and proceeds forward through the lines of the *From* file until the text is found or until the end of the *From* file is reached. The search operation stops at the first occurrence of *string*, and the current line marker is updated to make the line containing the found string the current line. If verification is on, and the line containing the match is other than the original current line, the line number and contents of the new current line are displayed. If the search string is *not* found, the message *Input exhausted* displays, and the current line marker is set to the end-of-file flag.

If no search string is specified in an F command, EDIT attempts to use the search argument of the last find command issued. If no previous find command has been issued, the error message *Nothing to repeat* appears.

String expressions used for search (and replace) operations within EDIT are normally delimited by slashes (/), although the colon (:), period (.), comma (,) and asterisk (*) may also be used. EDIT searches are case sensitive. The search string *AmigaDOS* does *not* match the text *amigados*.

Here's an example—find the string *disk*. Begin the search with the current line and move forward through the *From* file:

F/disk/

BF/*string*/ (Backward Find text). The BF command searches for a specified text string beginning with the current line and proceeds backward through the previous lines contained in EDIT's output buffer until the text is found or until the front end of the output buffer is reached with no match. The search operation stops at the first occurrence of *string*, and the current line marker is updated to make the line containing the found string the current line. If verification is on, and the line containing the match is other than the original current line, the line number and contents of the new current line are displayed. If the search string is not found, the message *No more previous lines* appears, and the current line marker is set to the line which was at the head of the output buffer.

If no search string is specified in a BF command, EDIT tries to use the search argument of the last find command issued. If no previous find command has been issued, the error message *Nothing to repeat* displays.

Let's try one. Find the string *disk*. Begin the search with the current line and move backward through the output buffer:

BF/disk/

Find Command Qualifiers

There are five *qualifiers*, or options, which may be used in conjunction with the find and backward find commands to further restrict the conditions that will result in a search match.

The F and BF commands normally don't care where in a line the search string is found. The **B** and **E** qualifiers let you specify whether the text must begin a line (B) or end a line (E).

The **P** qualifier allows you to restrict matches to those lines which consist of nothing but the precise (P) text specified by the search string.

EDIT's searches normally proceed rightward from the first character of each line. The **L** qualifier instructs EDIT to search each line leftward (L) beginning with the last character of each line.

The B, E, P, and L qualifiers are *mutually exclusive*. EDIT does not allow any of these four qualifiers to be specified together in an F or BF command.

The **U** qualifier may be used by itself or in conjunction with any of the other four. U renders the search string case insensitive—it causes EDIT to treat both the search string and searched text as if everything were in uppercase (U). A few examples follow.

Search forward, beginning with the current line, for the line which ends with the words *Natasha Fatale*:

F E/Natasha Fatale/

Search backward, beginning with the current line, for the line that begins with *WayBack*

BF B/WayBack/

EDIT, the Line Editor

Search forward, beginning with the current line, for the line that is precisely *Into the valley of death, rode the six hundred.*

`F P/Into the valley of death, rode the six hundred./`

Search backward for the phrase *I can play CenterField.* Each line is to be searched leftward, beginning with the last character of each line. The case of the search text is to be ignored:

`BF LU/i can play centerfield/`

You can also find an empty line (one containing nothing) by specifying a null string as a search argument:

`F P//`

Remember, the current line marker is updated to point at the line containing a found string.

Replacing Text

One of the reasons you may want to find a specific text string is so that you can make changes to it. EDIT has three commands which can be used to replace and/or insert text in the current line.

E/*string1*/*string2*/ (Exchange text). The E command lets you exchange a string of text contained in the current line with another string of text. E searches rightward for *string1* in the current line, beginning with the first character of the line. If found, *string1* is replaced by *string2*, and the entire modified line is displayed. If *string1* is not found in the current line, the message *No match* displays. In either case, the current line marker remains unchanged.

More examples—change the phrase *too strange to be believed* in the current line to *too strange to have happened*:

`E/too strange to be believed/too strange to have`
`   happened/`

B/*string1*/*string2*/ (insert Before text). The B command inserts a string of text *before* a specified string contained in the current line. B searches rightward for *string1* in the current line, beginning with the first character of the line. If found, *string2* is inserted immediately before *string1*, and the entire modified line is displayed. If *string1* is not found in the current line, the message *No match* appears. In either case, the current line marker remains unchanged.

A/*string1*/*string2*/ (insert After text). The A command inserts a string of text *after* a specified string contained in the current line. In all other respects, A functions identically to B.

EDIT, the Line Editor

The Current String Alteration Command
The previous A, B, or E command executed is known to EDIT as the *current string alteration command*. Typing a single quotation mark (') repeats the current string alteration command.

Checking on the Last-Used Search Expression
The **SHD** (SHow Data) command displays EDIT's current saved information values, including the last search expression.

Pointing Variants of Replace Commands
There's a secondary form of the E, B, and A commands which performs text replacement/insertion, and one additional one. This secondary form of each command is referred to as the *pointing variant* of each, and they are respectively **EP**, **BP**, and **AP**.

If the current line is successfully modified, EDIT's character pointer is left pointing to the first character in the line which follows *string2* in the case of EP or AP, or in the case of a BP command, the first character in the line that follows *string1*.

Using Qualifiers with Replace Commands
The B, E, P, L, and U qualifiers which may be used in conjunction with find commands may also be used with the replace commands and their pointing variants. The effect of using the qualifiers and rules for their use is the same as described in the section entitled "Find Command Qualifiers."

Deleting Text
D (Delete line). The D command can be used to delete the current line, a multiple number of lines (beginning with the current line), a specific line number, or a range of lines delimited by lines having line numbers. After the requested deletion has taken place, the current line marker is advanced to the line immediately following the last line deleted by the operation, and the line number and contents of the new current line are displayed. If D does not find a specified line between the current line and the *From* file's last line, the message *Input exhausted* appears, and the current line marker moves to the end-of-file flag. The D command does not affect the contents of EDIT's output buffer. An example or two might help.

Delete only the current line. The current line marker is moved to the next line in the *From* file:

D

EDIT, the Line Editor

Delete the current line and the next three lines. The current line marker is moved to the line which was four lines after the original current line:

4D

Delete line 17. If line 17 is found, the current line marker is moved to the line which follows it after line 17 is deleted. If a line numbered 17 is not found, no deletion will take place, and the current line marker will be updated to point at the end-of-file flag:

D17

Delete the lines numbered 22, 28, and all lines between them. If line 28 is found, the current line marker is moved to the line which follows it after the requested lines are deleted. If line 22 is found, but a line numbered 28 is not, line 22 and all the lines that follow are deleted. The current line marker is updated to point at the end-of-file flag:

D22 28

Delete the current line and all the lines that follow. The current line marker is updated to point at the end-of-file flag:

D*

Delete Commands That Use Search Expressions

DTB/*string1*/ (Delete Text Before)

and

DTA/*string1*/ (Delete Text After)

The DTB and DTA commands let you delete text within the current line that occurs before or after a search expression you specify. DTA and DTB operate *only* upon the current line. After execution, the line number and new contents of the current line are displayed. If the search expression is not found, the message *No match* is displayed and the current line remains unchanged.

DF/*string*/ (Delete lines until Find). The DF command searches each line, beginning with the current line, for the specified search expression. If the line searched does not contain the search string, it's deleted. The search-and-delete process continues until the search string is found. The line found to contain the search expression becomes the new current line. *If the search string is not found, a DF command deletes the current line and all lines that follow until it reaches the end of the* From *file.*

EDIT, the Line Editor

Using Qualifiers with DTB, DTA, and DF

The B, E, P, L, and U qualifiers used in conjunction with find and replace commands may also be used with the DTB and DTA commands. The effect of using the qualifiers and rules for their use are the same as those described in the previous section "Find Command Qualifiers." Here are some examples to help.

Delete all text that precedes the word *gremlins* in the line *There is no reason to suspect gremlins as the cause*:

DTB/gremlins/

Delete all text to the right of the second occurrence of *ragged* in the line *Around the ragged socks the ragged rascals ran*:

DTA L/ragged/

Delete all lines encountered, beginning with the current line, until a line beginning with the phrase *enough already!* is found. Ignore the case of the search argument:

DF BU/enough already!/

Splitting and Joining Lines

EDIT provides two commands which may be used to split the current line into two lines, and a command which combines two lines into one.

SB*/string/* (Split line Before string). The SB command searches the current line for the specified text string, and if found, splits the current line in two. The first of the two lines consists only of the text in the current line that preceded the found string. The second line begins with the found string and includes all text that followed it in the current line. After SB has executed, the second of the two new lines is made the current line.

SA*/string/* (Split line After string). The SB command searches the current line for the specified text string, and if found, splits the current line in two. The first of the two lines consists of the text in the current line that preceded the found string *and* the found string itself. The second line consists solely of the text that followed the found string in the current line. After SA has executed, the second of the two new lines is made the current line.

CL*/string/* (Combine Lines and string). The CL command combines the current line and the line which follows it into a single line; *string* is optional, and if specified, inserts the text string in the middle of the combined line. If the length of the combined line exceeds the current maximum line width allowed by EDIT, the rightmost characters of the line are truncated. Take a look at these examples.

Consider the line of text *I would gladly pay you Tuesday for a hamburger today.*

SB/ for/

or

SA/sday/

results in the line being split in two:

I would gladly pay you Tuesday
  for a hamburger today

If you started with a current line *Time for all good men*, followed by the line *to aid their lemon lobby*:

CL/ and clones /

the result is

Time for all good men and clones to aid their lemon lobby

Note: The SA, SB, and CL commands also accept string qualifiers (B, E, L, P, and U). See the previous section "Find Command Qualifiers" for further information on their uses.

Global Operations

EDIT's global operation commands let you automatically insert and replace text in lines which match specified search criteria. Global commands set up editing "phantoms" that constantly look over EDIT's shoulder as lines of the *From* file are processed. Multiple global commands may be in effect during the course of an EDIT session. The global commands are

- **GA**/*string1*/*string2*/ (Global insert *string2* After *string1*)
- **GB**/*string1*/*string2*/ (Global insert *string2* Before *string1*)
- **GE**/*string1*/*string2*/ (Global Exchange *string2* with *string1*)

Once a global command is issued, EDIT applies the associated A, B, or E command to every line as it passes the current line marker.

Canceling Global Operations

When a global command is issued, EDIT displays an identification number associated with that particular global phantom.

An individual global phantom may be canceled by issuing the **CG** (Cancel Global) command followed by the phantom's ID number. For instance, to cancel a global command that's been issued the ID number G4, type

CG4

To stop all current global operations, simply type

CG

If you can't remember what the active global operations are, the **SHG** (SHow Globals) command will refresh your memory.

Command Groups

EDIT commands that have been strung together on a single line, separated by semicolons, may be grouped together by enclosing the commands in parentheses. The resulting expression is called an *EDIT command group.* Command groups are normally used when you wish to repeat a group of commands several times. One command group may be nested within another, such as in

2(25(E /red/blue/;N);50N)

This replaces the text *red* with *blue* in the current line and all lines within 24 lines of the current line. The current line marker is then moved ahead 50 lines. Occurrences of the text *red* are replaced with *blue* in the new current line and in the following 24 lines. Finally, the current line marker is again moved ahead 50 lines.

If you instruct EDIT to execute a command or command group zero times, the command continues to execute until the end-of-file is encountered or until CTRL-C is used to issue a BREAK.

EDIT Command Files

When EDIT is invoked, it accepts commands from the keyboard or from an AmigaDOS file specified by the WITH keyword in the DOS command line which started the editing session.

You can also dynamically invoke the execution of EDIT commands stored in AmigaDOS files from within EDIT by using the **C** command.

C .:my/stored/commands.

starts execution of the EDIT commands contained in the file *my/stored/commands* in the root directory of the current drive. Command execution continues until a **Q** (Quit) command is encountered in the command file or until the command file's end-of-file is reached. The filename must be enclosed by a valid EDIT delimiter. (Notice that in the above examples, periods were used to delimit the filename.) Command files may call other command files.

Suppose you want to set up an AmigaDOS command sequence

EDIT, the Line Editor

file that will create a nicely sorted list of the contents of the current directory. The following command sequence file, when used in conjunction with a simple EDIT command file, does the trick:

```
LIST > mylist
EDIT mylist WITH df0:unwanted
SORT mylist TO finlist
TYPE finlist TO prt:
```

The contents of the filename *unwanted* are

```
D
M*
D
W
```

When the above AmigaDOS command sequence file is executed, an unsorted list of the contents of the current directory is directed to the file called *mylist*. EDIT is invoked using the WITH option to pull in the commands in the file *unwanted*. These commands remove the first and last lines of the LIST output (since they contain information about the current directory rather than the file or directory names in it). The edited file is saved and you're returned to the command sequence file. The edited file is then sorted and sent to the system's printer.

Merging Selected Parts of Files/Outputting Multiple Files

It's also possible to use EDIT to merge selected parts of different files together and to create multiple versions of the edited text. This is accomplished in a somewhat roundabout way, using facilities within EDIT that allow you to change the current *From* and *To* files on the fly from within EDIT.

FROM/*filename*/. The lines that follow the current line are replaced by the contents of the new *From* file. The original *From* file remains open and the lost lines may be accessed again by issuing a FROM command with no filename. A file opened by FROM may be closed by the **CF** (Close File) command, which has a format of **CF**/*filename*/.

The following sequence of EDIT commands merges the first 15 lines of three different files into one:

```
EDIT onefile TO myfile
14N
FROM ,twofile,
15N
FROM ,threefile,
16N
```

EDIT, the Line Editor

```
D*
CF onefile
CF twofile
W
```

TO/*filename*/. The TO command lets you dynamically switch EDIT's destination, or *To,* file. TO writes EDIT's existing output buffer to the *To* file before the switch is made and then clears the buffer. TO leaves the previous *To* file open. Issuing a subsequent TO command with no filename results in the original *To* file being reselected.

The following example outputs lines 1–100 of the file *bigfile* to a file called *firsthundred,* and lines 101–200 of *bigfile* to a file called *secondhundred.*

```
EDIT bigfile TO firsthundred
100N
TO .secondhundred.
100N
CF
D*
W
```

The Rewind Command
REWIND scans the remaining lines from the current line forward, executing any global commands in effect as it proceeds, until it reaches the last line of the *From* file. The contents of the output buffer are written, and the *To* and *From* files are closed. The *To* file is then reopened as a new *From* file.

The Halt Command
H (Halt) lets you set a line number as a brick wall which the current line marker cannot be moved past.

```
H134
```

prevents EDIT from moving past line 134 of the *From* file. If a command causes line 134 to be reached, the operation is halted and the message *Ceiling reached* displays.

Point Before and After
PB (Point Before) and **PA** (Point After) move the position operational window pointer in the current line.

PA/*string*/ moves the operational window pointer immediately after *string* in the current line.

PB/*string*/ moves the operational window pointer immediately before *string* in the current line.

EDIT, the Line Editor

EDIT Command Reference

Ending an EDIT Session

STOP   Quick bailout; *From* file remains intact
W   Windup; advance to EOF, save, and exit EDIT
Q   QUIT; return to previous process

Verification Commands

?   Verify current line
!   Verify current line; display codes of undisplayable characters
V+/V−   Turn auto verification on/off
TR+/TR− Display/suppress trailing spaces

Operational Window Commands

\>   Move operational window pointer right
<   Move operational window pointer left
PR   Reset operational window pointer
$ Change character at operational window pointer to lowercase
%   Change character at operational window pointer to uppercase
_   Change character at operational window pointer to a blank
Delete character at operational window pointer
PB/*string*/ Move operational window pointer before *string*
PA/*string*/ Move operational window pointer after *string*

Moving from One Line to Another

N   Next line
P   Previous line
M*a*   Move to line *a*

Displaying Text

T*n*   Type *n* lines
TP   Type previous lines
TN   Type next lines
TL   Type with line numbers

Inserting Text

I/I.   Insert before current line
I* or R*   Insert at end-of-file marker
I*a*   Insert before line *a*
Z/*string*/   Change input mode terminator
I/*filename*/ Insert file before current line
I*/*filename*/ Insert file at end-of-file marker
I*a*/*filename*/ Insert file before line *a*
R/R.   Replace current line with inserted text
R*a b*   Replace lines *a* through *b* with inserted text

EDIT, the Line Editor

Renumbering Lines

=n   Renumber; assign *n* to current line

Search and Replace Commands

F/*string*/	Find string
BF/*string*/	Backward find string
E/*string1*/*string2*/	Exchange *string2* with *string1*
B/*string1*/*string2*/	Insert *string2* before *string1*
A/*string1*/*string2*/	Insert *string2* after *string1*
'	Repeat string alteration command

String Qualifiers

B	Search string must begin line for match
E	Search string must end line for match
P	Entire line must match search string
L	Search from right to left for string
U	Ignore case of search string

Deleting Text

D *a b*	Delete lines *a* through *b*
DTB/*string*/	Delete text before *string*
DTA/*string*/	Delete text after *string*
DF/*string*/	Delete lines until *string* found

Splitting and Joining Lines

SB/*string*/	Split line before *string*
SA/*string*/	Split line after *string*
CL	Join line
CL/*string*/	Join lines with *string*

Global Operations

GA/*string1*/*string2*/	Global insert *string2* after *string1*
GB/*string1*/*string2*/	Global insert *string2* before *string1*
GE/*string1*/*string2*/	Global exchange *string2* with *string1*
CG*n*	Cancel global operation *n*
CG	Cancel all global operations
SHG	Show global info

External File Commands

C/*filename*/	Execute EDIT commands in *filename*
FROM/*filename*/	Change current *From* file
TO/*filename*/	Change current *To* file
CF/*filename*/	Close current *From* or *To* file

EDIT, the Line Editor

Miscellaneous

SHD	Show data
REWIND	Close *From* and *To* files; open previous *To* file as new *From* file
H*n*	Halt movement past line *n* of the *From* file

Part 2

AmigaDOS Command Reference

AmigaDOS Command Reference

The CLI accepts command lines up to 255 characters long. It's possible, therefore, that a single command line will occupy more than one line on the screen. When you reach 255 characters, the console will refuse to accept any keyboard input that would cause the line to expand to 256 characters.

When using the CLI, you cannot use the cursor keys to move up or down to another command line that appears on the screen, edit it, and use the revised line for your command. Each time you issue a new command, you have to enter the entire command line from scratch. You cannot use the cursor keys to edit the line you are on. If you make a mistake at the beginning of a line, you have to erase the whole line and start over.

The NEWCON handler of Workbench 1.3, discussed in detail in Chapter 2, adds several convenient editing features to the CLI, including command history.

CON: Editing Features

Key(s)	Function
BACKSPACE or CTRL-H	Erases character to left of cursor
CTRL-X	Erases entire current line (cancels line)
CTRL-L	Clears the screen (form feed)
RETURN or CTRL-M	Ends the line and executes the command
CTRL-J	Moves cursor to next line but doesn't execute the command
;	Marks start of a comment
CTRL-\	End-of-file indicator

Though not really an editing character, the semicolon (;) is significant to the CLI. The CLI interprets anything in a command line that follows a semicolon as a comment, ignoring the entire rest of the line.

AmigaDOS Command Reference

Other CON: Features

Key(s)	Function
TAB or CTRL-I	Moves cursor one space to the right (inserts a tab character)
CTRL-K	Moves cursor up one line (vertical tab)
CTRL-O	Switches to ALTernate character set (shifts out)
CTRL-N	Switches back to normal character set (shifts in)
ESC-[1m	Switches to bold characters
ESC-[2m	Switches character color (to black)
ESC-[3m	Italics on
ESC-[4m	Underline on
ESC-[7m	Reverse video on
ESC-[8m	Switches character color (to blue—invisible)
ESC-[0m	Switches to normal characters
ESC-C	Clears screen and switches to normal characters

AmigaDOS Filename Conventions

- AmigaDOS filenames may be up to 30 characters long.
- Filenames may not contain a colon (:), slash (/), or nonprinting or ALTernate characters.
- If a filename is to contain special characters, such as spaces, plus (+), equals (=), and semicolon (;), that have special significance to CLI, the entire filename must be enclosed in double quotation marks (").
- If a filename is to contain double quotation marks (") or an asterisk (*), each " and * must be preceded by an asterisk.
- Any combination of uppercase and lowercase can be used in naming a file. When you LIST the filenames, they'll be printed in the same combination of uppercase and lowercase used when the filename was created. The CLI, however, does not distinguish case. Since CLI ignores case and you cannot have two files with the same name in the same directory, two files named *Test* and *TEST* cannot reside in the same directory.

Pattern Matching (Wildcards)

Some AmigaDOS commands allow you to reference one or more files at a time using a technique called *pattern matching*. Pattern matching lets you do things like getting a listing of all files whose names end with the characters *.bas*, or deleting every file in a directory at one time. AmigaDOS pattern matching is similar to the concept of the *wildcard* characters used in MS/PC-DOS, but there are important differences.

AmigaDOS Command Reference

In PC-DOS, the asterisk character can be used to substitute for any string of characters in a filename. In AmigaDOS, the asterisk is used as an escape character that allows for the insertion of quotation marks (and other asterisks) in a filename. AmigaDOS also uses the asterisk to refer to the console device that's currently active.

PC wildcards can be used with more commands than AmigaDOS pattern matching, which is mostly confined to the COPY, DELETE, DIR, and LIST commands. AmigaDOS patterns, however, are much more flexible. They allow you to match names that start with the same group of characters, end with the same group of characters, or have the same characters in the middle (preceded by any number of characters and followed by any number of characters).

The most important pattern matching characters are the question mark (?) and the pound sign (#). The pound sign followed by a single character will match any number of repetitions of that character (including none).

For example, *#CLUTTER* matches:

CLUTTER
CCCCLUTTER
LUTTER

The question mark is used to replace any single character (but not the null string, or no character). For instance, *?LA?S* matches:

GLASS
2LABS

but not

LABS

When these two characters are paired together (#?), it creates a pattern that matches any number of any characters (or no characters at all).

For example, you could use *GLAD#?* if you wanted a pattern that matched all filenames starting with the letters *GLAD*. If you wanted to LIST all of the icon information files (whose names always end in *.info*), you could use the pattern *#?.INFO* to find them.

In addition to the pound sign and question mark, there are three other characters that have special meaning when used for pattern matching. Parentheses ( ) may be used to group a number of characters together into a single pattern element. If a pound sign is followed by a group of characters within parentheses, it will match any number of repetitions of that pattern group (including none). Thus, *#(HO)* matches these filenames:

HO
HOHO
HOHOHOHO

If you didn't use the parentheses, however, #HO would match:

HO
HHO
HHHHO

The *#H* can only substitute for repetitions of the letter *H*.

The vertical line (|) is used when you want either of two patterns to match the characters in the filename. For example, *Y|Z* matches:

Y
Z

while the pattern *WARM|COLD* matches:

WARM
COLD

and the pattern *MO(B|N)STER* matches:

MONSTER
MOBSTER

(Note how the parentheses were used to set off the *B|N* as a distinct pattern).

Use of the vertical line is particularly handy when you want to copy a whole list of files with a single command:

COPY LIST|DIR|COPY|DELETE|COPY RAM:

Under 1.2, some commands did not work properly with patterns that were more than 31 characters in length. This limit is no longer present, starting with version 1.3

The percentage sign (%) is used to represent the null string (no character). Remember, a pattern starting with the pound sign will match any number of repetitions of the following character, including none at all.

The pattern *Z#AP*, then, matches:

ZAP
ZAAAP
ZP

If you want to match only a single appearance of the character or none at all, you can use the form *(A|%)*, which stands for either *A* or the null character (no character at all). Using the same example, *Z(A|%)P* would still match:

ZAP
ZP

but would not match:

ZAAAP

which uses the *A* more than once.

AmigaDOS Command Reference

Combining the percentage sign with the question mark in the form *(?|%)* forms an expression that matches any character or no character at all. The pattern *(?|%)A?X* matches:

LAPX
APX

but not:

MAPPX

There's one final character that addresses a problem created when using these special AmigaDOS characters. Since these characters have meaning in the language of pattern matching, it makes it difficult when you want to match a filename containing one of those characters. In order to match a filename containing a question mark, for example, you must precede the question mark with an apostrophe (') to let the pattern matching mechanism know that you want to match an actual question mark, not use the question mark as a substitute for any other character.

The pattern *?OW'?* matches filenames like:

HOW?
COW?
WOW?

Since you've used the apostrophe itself as a special character, you need to use two apostrophes to represent an apostrophe that is part of the filename. You would therefore need a pattern like *?ON''T* to match filenames like:

DON'T
WON'T

Finally, if a pattern contains space characters, it must be enclosed by double quotation marks.

Pattern Matching Summary

#c	Matches any number of repetitions of the character *c* (including none)
	N#O matches N, NO, NOO, and NOOOOOOOOOOO
#(group)	Matches any number of repetitions of *group* (including none)
	#(TOM) matches TOM and TOMTOM
?	Matches any single character (but not the null character)
	K?NG matches KING and KONG (but not KNG)
#?	Matches any number of repetitions of any character (including none)
	#?.BAS matches any filename ending in .BAS
P1|P2	Matches either pattern *P1* or *P2*
	B(A|O)Y matches BAY and BOY

AmigaDOS Command Reference

%   Matches the null string (no character)
          (S|%)TOP matches STOP or TOP
(?|%)   Matches any character or no character
          (?|%)LOT matches SLOT, CLOT, and LOT
( )   Used to set off a group of characters as its own distinct pattern
          (M|P)A matches MA or PA
          M|PA matches M or PA
'   Used in front of one of the special characters to show that you want to match it, not invoke its special meaning
          ?ON"T matches WON'T and DON'T

AmigaDOS Templates

AmigaDOS contains a handy feature that can be used to jog your memory if you forget the command syntax of any AmigaDOS command (except the SAY command). By typing the command name followed by a question mark, the command's *template* is displayed onscreen. The template is a shorthand summary of the parameters and keywords associated with the command.

When a command's template is displayed, AmigaDOS treats the next line entered from the keyboard as if it were preceded by the command whose template has been called. Hitting RETURN without typing anything invokes the waiting command with no arguments.

Let's take a look at the template for the COPY command.

COPY ?

displays on the screen:

FROM/A,TO/A/K,ALL/S,QUIET/S:

AmigaDOS command arguments are separated by commas in command templates. The first part of each argument is either the argument name or the keyword associated with the argument. Keywords are followed by *qualifiers* (/A, /K, and /S), which tell you more information about the argument. When you invoke an AmigaDOS command, keywords, if used, must be typed exactly as presented; often you must type additional information following the keyword (depending on the command).

/A The argument is *required*.
/K The argument *must* contain the keyword.
/S The keyword is optional and, if specified, stands by itself.

A keyword in an argument template may have more than one qualifier associated with it (such as the TO keyword in the example above).

AmigaDOS Command Reference

Some commands allow you to use different keywords to invoke the same option. For example,

DATE ?

shows

TIME,DATE,TO=VER/K:

TIME and *DATE* are the parameter names of the first and second arguments of the DATE command. Values for these arguments are set by the user. The TO and VER keywords may be used interchangeably and require additional information to be specified after them.

If the arguments you use with an AmigaDOS command don't match the template, the message *Bad arguments* is displayed.

Redirected Output

The characters < and > may be used to redirect the output and input of AmigaDOS commands. AmigaDOS commands normally expect input to come from the system's keyboard and send output to the system's screen. Input and output redirection is temporary, lasting only until the invoked command completes. Here are some examples.

LIST the files and directories in *what a/silly/mess* directory on drive df1:. Send the output of the LIST command to the system's printer:

LIST > PRT: "df1:what a/silly/mess"

Send the output of the DATE command to a file called *tempdate* on the system's RAM disk:

DATE > RAM:tempdate

Use the Amiga's line editor (EDIT). Edit the file called *myfile* using the commands stored in the file *mycommands*. Store the edited data in *newfile:*

EDIT < mycommands FROM myfile TO newfile

The Shell program on the 1.3 Workbench disk supports not only the two existing redirection operators, but a third one as well. The characters >> can be used to append information into an existing file. For example, if you wanted to add a listing of a directory called MORESTUFF to an existing file called DIRECTORIES, you could use the command

DIR >>DIRECTORIES MORESTUFF

Note that if a file called DIRECTORIES does not exist, this command won't create one.

AmigaDOS Command Reference

Format of the AmigaDOS Command Reference

The remainder of this section is a command-by-command listing of AmigaDOS. For the most part, its format is self-explanatory. However, under the "Format" heading (perhaps the most important part of each command's listing), there are several typographical devices used to show you what is required and what is optional.

- Keywords that are required are in uppercase boldface roman type. **ASSIGN** and **COPY** are examples.
- Keywords that are optional are in uppercase boldface italics. *LIST* is an example.
- Optional entries are enclosed in brackets—[ ].
- Parameters are in lowercase italics. These denote where you'll enter something. If required, the parameter is not enclosed in brackets. If optional, it is enclosed in brackets.

Thus,

COPY [*FROM* fromname] [*TO* toname] [*ALL*] [*QUIET*]

indicates that the keyword **COPY** is required, that the keywords *FROM*, *TO*, *ALL*, and *QUIET* are all optional, and that the two parameters *fromname* and *toname* are also optional.

Of course, complete explanations of each keyword and parameter are provided under the "Explanation of Parameters and Keywords" heading.

ADDBUFFERS Command

Purpose
Sets aside a portion of the system RAM to be used exclusively as disk buffer space. This disk buffer keeps information frequently accessed from the disk in the computer's memory. Thus, the system accesses the physical disk less often, significantly speeding up disk operation. The ADDBUFFERS command allocates buffer space in 512-byte increments. Although additional buffer space increases disk performance somewhat, floppy disks reach a point of diminishing returns at the level of about 30 additional buffers (15K of buffer space). Hard drives that are formatted using the Fast File System will always benefit from the addition of more disk buffers, however.

Additional buffer space means that more of the information read from disk remains in memory where it can be accessed more quickly. Therefore, added disk buffer space only speeds up access to frequently-used files. It won't speed up operations like a file copy, where the information to be copied is only used once.

Keep in mind that any memory you allocate for buffer space will be subtracted from the free memory you have to run programs. Some programs that require the full memory of a 512K Amiga may not operate when a significant amount of memory has been allocated for disk buffer space.

Format
ADDBUFFERS *drive n*

Explanation of Parameters and Key Words

drive   This is the device name of a physical disk drive, either a floppy drive (df0:, df1:, and so on) or a hard drive (dh0: jh0:, and so on). Note that if you add buffers for an electronic RAM drive, you may actually slow down the operation of that drive since all of its information is already stored in RAM.

n   The number of 512-byte buffers to add. Floppy drive performance peaks first at about 30 buffers (15K of memory), and again at about 100 buffers (50K of memory).

ADDBUFFERS Command

Examples
1. Add 30 disk buffers for use by the internal disk drive:

ADDBUFFERS df0: 30

2. Add 100 disk buffers for use by the BridgeBoard hard drive:

ADDBUFFERS jh0: 100

ASK Command

Purpose
ASK allows input from the user to control the actions taken by an interactive sequence file. It prints a prompt string and then waits for the user to type the response Y or YES, N or NO, or RETURN (same as NO). When the user has responded, the command exits with a return code of 5 for a YES response, or 0 for a NO response. The IF WARN command can thus be used to detect the results of this operation and to direct script execution accordingly.

Format
ASK *promptstring*

Explanation of Parameters and Key Words
promptstring   The prompt message that's written to the current active output stream (usually requesting a yes or no answer). If this prompt message contains spaces, *promptstring* should be contained within quotation marks.

Example
A command file that requests the user to specify a yes or no answer, and then prints a text string that indicates what his choice was:

```
ASK "What is your choice? (Yes/No)"
IF WARN
    Echo "Your choice was YES"
ELSE
    Echo "Your choice was NO"
ENDIF
```

ASSIGN Command

Purpose
: Builds, removes, and lists associations between logical device names and filing system directories, physical devices (DF1:, PRT:, and so on), and disk volume names.

Format
: **ASSIGN** *devname dirname*
  [LIST][EXISTS][REMOVE]

Explanation of Parameters and Keywords
: *devname*   The logical device name that you wish to assign to a directory, physical device, or disk volume. After making the assignment, you can use this device name in place of specifying the entire directory, device, or volume until you change the assignments or reboot the computer.

  Certain assignments are automatically made by the operating system when DOS is initialized. These are the logical devices S:, L:, C:, FONTS:, DEVS:, LIBS:, and SYS:. These correspond to the directories of the same names, which have special significance to AmigaDOS (see Chapter 4 for more information on logical devices). If corresponding directories don't exist on the boot disk, the assignment is made to the root directory of the disk. If a specified logical device name already has a directory, physical device, or volume name associated with it, the new ASSIGNment replaces the old. If you try to assign a the same logical device names as an existing volume, however, the assignment will fail (for example, you can't assign the logical device MyDisk: when a disk whose volume name is MyDisk is already mounted). Any associations built by ASSIGN apply to all CLIs, and all are lost when the system is shut off or rebooted.

  If you want to remove an assignment without replacing it, use the command form ASSIGN *devname*.

  dirname   The directory path, physical device, or disk volume name that will be represented by references to the specified *devname*. For example, if you used the directory *df0:Daves/Wordprocessing/Documents* a lot, you might find it more convenient to be able to type *Docs:* instead of the entire phrase

ASSIGN Command

df0:Daves/Wordprocessing/ Documents. To make the assignment, type

```
ASSIGN docs: df0:Daves/Wordprocessing/
   Documents
```

Notice that the full pathname of the directory to be assigned was specified. ASSIGN searches the directory path starting with the current directory, so the path should be fully spelled out if the target directory is located anywhere but in the current directory.

If you just want to remove an assignment without replacing it, use the command form ASSIGN *devname* with no *dirname* specified.

[*LIST*]   If you type ASSIGN without specifying a logical device name, it displays the list of current assignments. If you wish to both make or remove assignments *and* show the new assignment list, use the optional LIST keyword at the end of the command line.

[*EXISTS*]   If you add the EXISTS keyword after the name of the logical device, the ASSIGN command will display assigment information for that device name only. If the device is not found, the command exits with a return code of 5 (WARN). This feature can be used in sequence files that take one action if the device name is found, and another if it is not found.

[*REMOVE*]   This optional keyword may be used to remove a physical device (such as df0: or prt:) from the list of mounted devices. It does not free up resources (such as disk buffers) used by that device, so it cannot be used to release memory, for example, that could normally be reclaimed by physically disconnecting a second disk drive. It is useful mostly for experimental purposes, like disconnecting the internal disk drive (df0:) and MOUNTing it with a different disk format (such as the Fast File System).

Examples

1. List the current logical device name/file directory associations:

ASSIGN or ASSIGN LIST

ASSIGN Command

Sample Display:

```
Volumes: RAM DISK [Mounted]
         CLI WorkDisk [Mounted]
Directories:
S         CLI WorkDisk:s
L         CLI WorkDisk:l
C         CLI WorkDisk:c
FONTS     CLI WorkDisk:fonts
DEVS      CLI WorkDisk:devs
LIBS      CLI WorkDisk:libs
SYS       CLI WorkDisk:

Devices:
DF1   DF0   PRT   PAR   SER
RAW   CON   RAM
```

2. Associate the logical device name *Rick:* with the directory *:AmigaWord/Proposals/RickWork*

ASSIGN Rick: :AmigaWord/Proposals/RickWork

After executing this ASSIGN statement, a file called *ACME* in the *AmigaWord/Proposals/RickWork* directory may be referenced by referring to the logical device name or the full directory specification for the file.

TYPE Rick:ACME

yields the same result as

TYPE :AmigaWord/Proposals/RickWork/ACME

If an ASSIGN or ASSIGN LIST was now executed, the directory association

RICK   Volume: CLI WorkDisk Dir: RickWork

would be present in the Directories section of the table.

3. Remove a logical device/directory assignment.

ASSIGN Rick:

removes the association built by the ASSIGN statement in the second example.

ASSIGN Rick: LIST

removes the association built by the ASSIGN statement in example 2 and lists the remaining logical device associations still in effect.

4. Check for the existance of a logical device name or disk volume name in a sequence file.

```
ASSIGN >nil: empty:EXISTS
IF WARN
    ECHO "The directory name doesn't exist"
ELSE
    ECHO "The directory name exists"
ENDIF
```

This script file, when executed, prints a message telling whether or not a volume named EMPTY: exists. In your own script, you might take a specified action at the points where the ECHO command appears.

AVAIL Command

Purpose Prints a report of system memory resources, broken down by memory type. For each type (CHIP, FAST, and TOTAL), AVAIL reports the amount of available (free) RAM, the amount in use, the maximum (total) amount, and the largest contiguous block that is available for allocation.

Format **AVAIL** [*FAST* or *CHIP* or *TOTAL*]

Explanation of Parameters and Keywords

[*FAST* or *CHIP* or *TOTAL*]   When one of these keywords is used with the AVAIL command, the command returns a single number that indicates the total number of available bytes of that type of memory. This value can be used by script files for comparisons, using either the EVAL or IF GT commands.

If the AVAIL command is given without any of the optional keywords, a more complete summary of available system RAM is printed. This summary includes a breakdown by RAM type and lists the total amount, amount used, amount free, and largest contiguous free block.

Examples

1. Print a complete summary of system RAM:

AVAIL

The summary is printed in the following format:

Type	Available	In-Use	Maximum	Largest
chip	909984	130168	1040152	909952
fast	3442976	751264	4194240	2097120
total	4352960	881432	5234392	2097120

In this summary, the first column shows free (available memory), the second column shows the memory in use, and the third shows the total (maximum) memory, so that the sum of the first two columns should equal the value in the third. The final column shows the largest contiguous available block of memory and is a subset of the first column, available memory.

Contiguous memory is important because if free memory is highly fragmented (broken up into small pieces scattered here and there in the memory map), it may not be possible to load and run additional programs, even if the total amount of free memory might indicate that it is possible.

2. Show only the total available chip memory:

`AVAIL chip`

In the example above, the number returned would be 909984.

BINDDRIVERS Command

Purpose
: Looks for *device drivers* (software instructions on how to interact with external hardware devices connected to the Amiga's expansion port) in the Expansion subdirectory of the startup disk (the disk to which the logical device name SYS: is assigned) and then integrates these drivers into the operating system so that it knows how to control the devices. As of this writing, devices that are added to the system in this way include the IBM-compatible Bridgeboard, and nonautoboot hard drives.

  The BINDDRIVERS command is usually issued in the *startup-sequence* script file in the *s* directory, so that external devices are added as part of the startup process. If there are no device drivers in the Expansion directory, however, the BINDDRIVERS command can be omitted from the startup-sequence file.

Format
: **BINDDRIVERS**

Explanation of Parameters and Key Words
: None

Example
: Load device drivers in the *Expansion* directory of SYS:

  BINDDRIVERS

BREAK Command

Purpose
: Sets attention flags, which interrupt a process as if the user had pressed specified CTRL-key combinations in an active window.

Format
: **BREAK** *tasknum* [C] [D] [E] [F] [ALL]

Explanation of Parameters and Keywords
: *tasknum*   The number assigned by the system to the CLI process that you wish to interrupt (for more information, see the STATUS command).

  [C] [D] [E] [F] [ALL]   The attention flag(s) associated with the interrupt type that you wish to issue. You may trigger up to four CTRL-key attention flags. If the BREAK command is issued with no flag keys specified, only the CTRL-C flag is enabled. Issuing the BREAK command simulates selecting a CLI process with the mouse and pressing the specified CTRL-key keystrokes. BREAK may be used to interrupt a background CLI task initiated by the RUN command.

Examples
: **1.** Trigger all valid attention flags (CTRL-C, CTRL-D, CTRL-E, CTRL-F) for process number 4:

  `BREAK 4 ALL`

  2. Trigger the CTRL-C and CTRL-E attention flags for process number 1:

  `BREAK 1 C E`

  3. Trigger the CTRL-C attention flag for process number 5:

  `BREAK 5`

CD Command

Purpose	Sets or changes the current directory or drive. Also used to display the current drive and directory.
Format	**CD** [*name*]
Explanation of Parameters and Keywords	[*name*] The name of the directory path or logical device name that you wish to make the current directory. A pathname may be fully specified or relative to the current default directory. Specifying a full pathname such as :*major/minor/tiny* does not make any assumptions about what the current directory is. If the current directory was set to *major/minor*, the former pathname could be switched to by a relative reference, namely CD *tiny*. You can also move the current directory back (up) one level by typing CD followed by single or multiple slashes (/). For instance, if the current directory is *major/minor/tiny*, typing CD // changes the current directory to *major*. You can specify a logical device name in lieu of a pathname. This lets you change the default disk or change directories to a directory path associated to a logical device name (see the ASSIGN command for more information). CD specified by itself with no path or device name lists the current directory setting. The complete path is specified, starting with the volume name.
Examples	**1.** Change the current directory to the root directory of the volume mounted in df1: CD df1: *Note:* AmigaDOS is somewhat different from the DOS of many other microcomputers in that the way it treats a default drive is volume- rather than device-oriented. For instance, assume you had a disk volume called *Hi There* in an external Amiga drive, and you changed the default drive to df1: by typing CD DF1:. After changing the default drive, typing DIR would give you a directory listing for *Hi There*. If *Hi There* is ejected from the drive and another volume called *Salutations* is inserted and you type DIR

again, the system will ask for the *Hi There* volume to be reinserted in the drive.

How can you avoid this? Entering another CD DF1: causes AmigaDOS to read the volume label of the disk in the external drive again and forget any volumes it previously defaulted to.

2. Change the current directory to *df0:particle/quark/charm*, and then back to *df0:particle*:

CD particle/quark/charm
CD //

3. List the current directory setting:

CD

4. Change the current directory to the the path associated with the logical device name *Rick:*

CD Rick:

5. Change directories to the root directory of the current drive:

CD :

CHANGETASKPRI Command

Purpose Changes the multitasking priority of a CLI task and of subsequent tasks started from that CLI. The Amiga multitasking operating system is set up so that each task is assigned a priority number from -128 to 127. Processor time is divided among the tasks, with each task executing in turn for a few fractions of a second. Tasks with the same priority number get an equal "time-slice," but tasks with higher priority execute more often and end up getting more of the processor's time. Normally, a CLI has a priority of zero. Raising its priority makes it (and the programs that run from it) run at a higher priority than other CLI tasks, while lowering makes it run at a lower priority and get less processor time. Under most circumstances, you shouldn't raise a task's priority higher than 5, nor lower it to less than -5. This will ensure that it doesn't preempt important system tasks like the input handler (which checks the keyboard and the mouse), nor will it have so low a priority as to get completely shut out.

Format **CHANGETASKPRI** *priority* [*tasknum*]

Explanation of Parameters and Key Words

priority The priority number for the task. This number may range from -128 to 127, but generally should be kept within the range of -5 to 5. Normally, CLI tasks run at a priority of 0.

[*tasknum*] The task number whose priority is to be changed. Normally, the CLI prompt of an interactive CLI process shows its task number. You may also check the task number of a process with the STATUS command. If no task number is used, the priority of the current CLI is changed by this command.

Examples

1. Increase the priority of the current CLI task to 5:
CHANGETASKPRI 5

2. Decrease the priority of CLI task number 5 to -1:
CHANGETASKPRI -1 5

COPY Command

Purpose
: Copies one or more files or directories to a device, and as an option, lets you give the copy a name different from the orginal. If the destination device already contains a file of the same name, the new copy replaces that file. COPY can create duplicate copies of a file on the same disk as the original if different names are used for copies in the same directory, or if the files are copied to different directories.

Format
: **COPY** [*FROM fromname*] [*TO toname*] [*ALL*] [*QUIET*] [*BUF or BUFFER =num*] [*DATE*] [*COM*] [*NOPRO*] [*CLONE*]

Explanation of Parameters and Keywords

[*FROM fromname*]   Specifies the directory or file(s) you want copied. The keyword FROM is not needed as long as the source and target files are named in the correct order *(fromfile*, then *tofile)*. If you change the order (COPY TO *tofile* FROM *fromfile*), the keyword FROM is required.

When a directory is specified as the FROM source, all files within the directory are copied. If no directory is specified but the TO keyword is used (for instance COPY TO RAM:), the current directory is assumed to be the source and all files are copied. As of version 1.3, a pair of double quotation marks (" ") can also be used to refer to the current directory.

When you're copying individual files, and not an entire directory, you may use pattern matching to copy every file in the directory that matches the pattern. However, you cannot use pattern matching with directory names. If you attempt to copy directories with patterns, nothing actually is done.

If a physical disk drive is specified, the root directory of the drive is used as the FROM source. If a logical device name is specified, the directory path associated with it is used as the FROM source (see the ASSIGN command for more details).

[*TO toname*] Secifies the TO target (where you want to put the FROM files you are copying). The key-

COPY Command

word TO is necessary only if the TO destination is listed *before* the FROM source.

When copying a single file, a device name or directory or filename can be used as the destination. A pair of double quotation marks (" ") can be used to specify the current directory as the destination. When *toname* is a directory or device name, the name of the new file will be the same as the old name. If the target file is in the same directory as *fromname*, you must specify a *toname* that's different from the original (since you can't copy a file to itself or have two files of the same name in the same directory). If the file is to be copied to a directory or a disk drive different from the one on which *fromname* resides, *toname* may be the same as or different from the original filename. If a file of the same name already exists in the target area, the existing file will actually be deleted and a new file with the same name is created and copied to. For this reason, a file that has been protected from deletion with the PROTECT command cannot be copied to.

If a directory is being copied to the same disk, a different directory path must be used for *toname*. In versions prior to 1.3, AmigaDOS assumes that the TO directory already exists, and the COPY will fail if it does not. Version 1.3 creates the new directory if it doesn't already exist and then copies the file or files.

If a logical device name is specified, the directory path associated with it is used as *toname* (see the ASSIGN command for more details).

If *toname* is a physical disk drive, the root directory of the disk in that drive is assumed to be the target directory.

toname may be other physical devices known to the system. For instance, copying files to RAM: places a copy of the files on a RAM disk (see Chapter 4 for more details on RAM:). The contents of a file may also be copied to an attached printer by specifying PRT: as the target.

[ALL]   If you use this keyword, any files, subdirectories, and the files in the subdirectories located in *fromname*'s directory will be copied to the *toname* directory. Subdirectory entries corresponding to those found in the FROM directory will automatically be

COPY Command

created in the TO directory (you might say that this command does the MAKEDIRty work for you).

[*QUIET*]   When copying multiple files (due to the use of pattern matching or the ALL keyword), the name of the files being copied and directories created are displayed unless this keyword is specified.

[*BUF or BUFFER = num*]   The BUFFERS option can be used to set the number of 512-byte buffers that are used during the copy. The default is 200 buffers or 100K bytes. You may want to use fewer buffers when copying a large file to the RAM in order to avoid running out of memory. Similarly, you may want to increase the number of buffers when copying a large file from one disk to another on a single-drive system with a lot of RAM, to reduce the number of disk swaps during the copy.

[[*DATE*]   If the optional DATE keyword is used, the creation date of the original file is copied to the new file. By default, a new creation date is set when a file is copied.

[*COM*]   If the optional COM keyword is used, the FILENOTE comments from the original file are copied to the new file. Normally, the new file is created without comments.

[*NOPRO*]   By default, a copy of a file retains the same protection bits of the original. The NOPRO keyword can be used to create a copy that has only the default protection bits (read, write, execute, and delete) set.

[*CLONE*]   The CLONE keyword can be used to make the file copy an exact duplicate of the original, with the same creation date, comments, and protection bits set. Its the same using both DATE and COM keywords.

Examples

1. Copy a file called *myfile1* to *myfile2* in the same directory:

COPY FROM myfile1 TO myfile2

or

COPY TO myfile2 FROM myfile1

or

COPY myfile1 myfile2

COPY Command

    Note that the FROM and TO keywords are optional, *unless* you reverse the order of the filenames (by putting the name of the destination file before that of the source).

2. Copy all files in the root directory of floppy disk 0 (df0:) to disk drive 1 (df1:):

COPY df0: df1:

3. Copy all files on disk drive 1 to disk drive 2, including subdirectories. Don't display the status of each copy operation:

COPY df1: df0: ALL QUIET

4. Copy a file called *burgers* in the current directory to a file of the same name in a different directory called *fast/food,* which is on the same disk:

COPY burgers fast/food

5. Copy all files in the current directory to a RAM disk, retaining the original creation date of each file:

COPY TO RAM: DATE

or

COPY " " RAM: DATE

6. Copy all files ending in *.bas* from the current directory to the directory *Basicfiles* on df1:.

COPY #?.bas TO df1:Basicfiles

    Note that if the root directory of the volume in df1: does not already contain the directory *Basicfiles,* the copy will fail. If it isn't present, you must use MAKEDIR first to create the directory.

7. Copy selected files from the C: directory to the current directory.

COPY C:DIR|DELETE|COPY|LIST|RUN ""

DATE Command

Purpose
Used to display, change, or store the current setting of the system date and time. If you haven't bought and connected a separate clock/calendar accessory, AmigaDOS checks the boot-up disk for the date of the most recently modified or created file and sets the system date a bit in advance of that.

Format
DATE [*date*] [*time*] [*TO* or *VER name*]

Explanation of Parameters and Keywords

[*date*]   The day of the month, the month, and the year to which the system date will be set. A specific desired date is typed in as *DD-MMM-YY*. *DD* is a two-digit number, with a leading zero if necessary, representing the day of the month to be set. *MMM* is the first three letters of the desired month, and *YY* is the last two digits of the year.

AmigaDOS also allows indirect references for setting the date. YESTERDAY, TODAY, and TOMORROW are valid values for *date*. YESTERDAY moves the present system date back by one day, TOMORROW moves the present value of the system date forward one day, and TODAY leaves the date unchanged.

The days of the week, SUNDAY through SATURDAY, can also be used as values for *date*. If the day specified is different from the current day of the week setting, the system date is advanced to match the specified day of the week. For instance, specifying WEDNESDAY when the current system day of the week is SUNDAY advances the system date by three days.

Specifying *date* does not alter the current system time.

[*time*]   The time of day to which the system clock is to be set. The time should be entered in the form *HH:MM:SS*, representing hours, minutes, and seconds of the desired clock setting. All three are typed as two-digit numbers, with leading zeros if necessary (as of version 1.3, the leading zero became optional, but it is still required with all earlier versions). If seconds, or minutes and seconds are omitted, they are set to zero. System time is kept in 24-hour format,

DATE Command

also referred to as *military time*. Thus, 1:00 p.m. is expressed as 13:00, and midnight as 00:00. Specifying *time* does not alter the current system date.

[*TO* or *VER* *name*]   The TO and VER options allow you to store the present system date and time to *name*, which may be a disk file or a physical device such as a printer. TO and VER are equivalent keywords and may be used interchangeably. If TO or VER is used when setting the time and/or date rather than just reading its current status, a blank file overwrites the specified file since the DATE command sends no output when used to change a setting. AmigaDOS does remember the date and time the blank file was written, however.

Examples

1. Display the current system date and time:

DATE

2. Set the system date and time to September 8, 1987, 10:05 a.m.:

DATE 08-Sep-87 10:05:00

3. Change the current system date to the next day, and change the current system time to 4:00 p.m.:

DATE TOMORROW 16:00

4. If the current system day of the week is not Wednesday, change the system date to that of the next Wednesday. Leave the time alone:

DATE WEDNESDAY

   Note: If the current system day of the week is Wednesday, the date remains unchanged.

5. Copy the current system date and time to a file named *Timestamp*:

DATE TO Timestamp

6. Change the system date and time to August 19, 2001, 2:00 a.m.:

DATE 2: 19-Aug-01

   Note: Since date and time have different formats, the order in which they are specified may be reversed. Also, AmigaDOS treats year references from 78 to 99 as 1978 to 1999, and from 00 to 77 as 2000 to 2077.

DATE Command

If you accidentally set the year to a number from 0 to 77, all files you subsequently create in that session will have a date stamp from the twenty-first century. The next time you set the clock to the correct date—say, 14-JUN-89—all files stamped 2077 will appear on the directory with the date-stamp *Future* since 2077 is in the future from the point of view of 1989. This renders the date-stamp useless since you won't even be able to tell the order in which the files were created. Version 1.3 of the Workbench introduced the SETDATE command in order to help you get rid of bogus date stamps.

DELETE Command

Purpose Removes files and directories from the designated drive. If no drive is designated, the current default drive is assumed. If no directory path is specified, the files and/or directories are deleted from the current directory. DELETE accepts patterns as well as specific filenames, and as of version 1.3, the 31-character limit for wildcards has been removed. See "Pattern Matching (Wildcards)" in Chapter 3 for more information.

Format DELETE name,,,,,,,,,[ALL] [Q or QUIET]

Explanation of Parameters and Keywords

name The name of the file(s) or directory entry(s) to be removed. Up to ten file or directory names may be entered within a single DELETE command. A pattern may be used in lieu of specific file or directory names. When an attempt to delete an item is unsuccessful, DELETE continues until it has attempted to process all specified items.

[*ALL*] When this keyword is used, DELETE erases all files and subdirectories contained within the directory as well as the directory itself. Attempts to DELETE directories that contain any files or subdirectories will fail unless those files and subdirectories are deleted first or the ALL keyword is used.

[*Q* or *QUIET*] Suppresses the status reports that are issued as each file's deletion is attempted during a DELETE that erases more than one file.

Examples

1. Erase the file *unwanted:*

DELETE unwanted

2. Erase the files *oranges, kiwi, peaches,* and *herbs:*

DELETE oranges kiwi peaches herbs

3. Erase the directory *phonebook* and all files and subdirectories within it. Don't report on the status of each deletion attempt:

DELETE phonebook ALL QUIET

DELETE Command

4. Erase the current directory and all the files and subdirectories within it:

DELETE #? ALL

5. Delete all files in the current directory that start with the letter *a*, *b*, or *c*:

DELETE (a|b|c)#?

DIR Command

DIR Command

Purpose — Lists the file and subdirectories with the present directory or another specified directory. The list is normally grouped into a list of subdirectories, followed by a sorted list of files. Options available for use with this command allow you to use a special interactive mode and/or ask for an extended listing that lists the contents of subdirectories as well. The directory listing may be aborted at any time by the CTRL-C key combination (hold down CTRL and press C).

Format — **DIR** *dirname* [*OPT A* or *OPT D* or *OPT I* or *OPT AI*] [*ALL*] [*DIRS*] [*FILES*] [*INTER*]

Explanation of Parameters and Keywords

dirname   The name of the directory or logical device whose contents you want displayed. An AmigaDOS pattern may also be used to display multiple directories. If no directory or AmigaDOS pattern is specified, the current directory is displayed.

[*OPT A* or *OPT D* or *OPT I* or *OPT AI*]   When the OPT A keyword is used, the display includes the contents of any subdirectories residing in the directory being listed. This lets you see everything in a directory with a single command. OPT D displays only the names of subdirectories within the specified directory, and not those of the files.

OPT I invokes the special interactive mode of DIR. In interactive mode, your system pauses as each subdirectory entry or file is listed, displaying a question mark to the right of the entry. When in interactive mode, you may use any of the following subcommands:

Key(s)	Function
<RETURN>	Doesn't do anything with the current item. Goes on to the next item in the DIR listing.
T <RETURN>	Types (lists) the file. To pause the display while listing, hit the space bar or any key. To resume after pausing, press the BACKSPACE key or CTRL-X. When you want to abandon the listing

DIR Command

of the file contents before the complete file has been listed, type CTRL-C. You'll be returned to the interactive mode. T is an invalid option for subdirectories.

DEL <RETURN>   Erases the file. Subdirectories may be erased only if they're empty.

E <RETURN>   Enters a subdirectory. Displays the files and subdirectories within a subdirectory. The listing remains in interactive mode. Not a vaild option for a file.

B<ENTER>   Moves back to the previous directory after you have descended into a new directory with the E command.

Q<ENTER>   Quit. Abandons the DIR listing and goes back to the CLI prompt.

As of Workbench 1.3, a new "COMMAND =" option was added to interactive mode, which allows almost any AmigaDOS command to be executed from interactive directory mode.

OPT AI combines both the A and I options, resulting in an interactive listing of all files and directories within the specified directory.

[*ALL*]   As of Workbench 1.3, this is an acceptable synonym for OPT A.

[*DIRS*]   Starting with version 1.3, this may be used instead of OPT D.

[*FILES*]   This is a new option that was added with Workbench 1.3. It allows you to display only the files within a directory and not the subdirectories.

[*INTER*]   As of Workbench 1.3, this is an acceptable synonym for OPT I.

Examples

1. List the current directory:

DIR

2. List all files and directories on disk drive df1: in interactive mode:

DIR df1: OPT AI

3. List all files and directories in directories beginning with the letter Z:

DIR Z#? OPT A

DIR Command

4. Display all directories and subdirectories that are contained within the root directory of the current disk:

DIR : ALL DIRS

DISKCHANGE Command

Purpose

Lets AmigaDOS know when you've changed the disk in a 5¼-inch disk drive. With version 1.2, AmigaDOS added support for 5¼-inch drives as DOS devices, using the MOUNT command. Unlike the normal 3½-inch drives, however, these disk drives don't have a sensing mechanism that can tell the Amiga when a disk has been removed or inserted. Therefore, when the system issues a prompt like *Please insert volume Programs in drive 1*, it has no way of telling if you've complied. You must enter the DISKCHANGE command to let AmigaDOS know you've changed the disk so that, in turn, it can check to make sure you've compiled, and then continue.

See the MOUNT command for more information about mounting 5¼-inch drives as DOS devices.

DISKCHANGE can also be used for removeable-media drives that are not yet supported by AmigaDOS, such as high-density floppies, removeable hard drives, and floppies that use the Fast File System. This is only a temporary measure, however—hopefully there will be better support for such devices in version 1.4. Another use of DISKCHANGE is to notify Workbench of a change in the volume name of a disk that was made using the CLI RELABEL command.

Format

DISKCHANGE *drive*

Explanation of Parameters and Key Words

drive   The device name of the 5¼-inch disk drive. Since the internal drive is always df0:, the 5¼-inch drive will usually be df1: (if there's no external 3½-inch drive), or df2: (if there *is* an external 3½-inch drive).

Example

Inform DOS that you've changed the disk in the sole external disk drive, which happens to be a 5¼-inch drive:

```
DISKCHANGE df1:
```

DISKCOPY Command

DISKCOPY Command
(moved to SYSTEM drawer in Workbench 1.2)

Purpose
Makes duplicates of the entire contents of 3½-inch floppy disks. DISKCOPY can be used to make copies of your work to new disks or to used disks containing files that are no longer needed. When you use DISKCOPY, any information previously stored on the destination disk is erased. While many other computer systems require that new disks be specially prepared before use, AmigaDOS DISKCOPY automatically prepares, or *formats*, disks as the information from the original disk is copied. In fact, copying an existing disk takes about the same amount of time as formatting a new one. Use DISKCOPY regularly to make backup copies of your work and non–copy-protected program disks.

Though DISKCOPY copies entire disks, it takes about the same amount of time to copy a disk full of data as to copy one which has only a few short files on it. If the amount of data you want to copy is relatively small, using the COPY command may be faster than DISKCOPY.

While DISKCOPY is usually used to copy the contents of one floppy disk to another, it can be used with other devices, as long as the source and the destination disks are of identical format and storage capacity. Thus, it's possible to use DISKCOPY to copy the contents of the RAD: RAM disk to or from a floppy, if that disk has been set to 80 tracks, 11 blocks per track (the same as a floppy).

Format
DISKCOPY [*FROM*] source drive **TO** destination drive [*NAME* volname] [*NOVERIFY*] [*MULTI*]

Explanation of Parameters and Keywords
[*FROM*] source drive   The name of the drive in which the disk you wish to copy will be mounted. If your system has only one drive, this will be df0:. If you have two drives, you may use df0: or df1:. (Technically AmigaDOS supports up to four drives—df0:, df1:, df2:, and df3:. The production version of the Amiga 500, introduced in 1987, supplies only the power required by a total of two drives. While heavi-

DISKCOPY Command

er-duty external power supplies are available for the 500 as well as drives requiring less power, most users will find two 3½-inch disk drives to be fully adequate. If *source drive* is the first argument of the DISKCOPY command, the FROM keyword is optional.

TO *destination drive*   The TO keyword *must* be used with the DISKCOPY command. This is the name of the drive in which the disk to be copied to will be mounted. If your system has only one drive, this will be df0: (the same as your FROM device). Single-drive DISKCOPY operations require that both the source and destination disks be removed and reinserted multiple times. If you have 512K, each disk must be inserted three times. On an old 256K Amiga 1000 system, DISKCOPY requires eight insertions of each disk—1000 owners are strongly advised to upgrade memory, and/or get a second disk drive. If your system has two drives, no disk swapping during the copy process is required as long as you specify different drives for the FROM and TO devices.

[**NAME** *volname*]   The volume name that will be given to the copy of the original disk. If the volume name contains spaces, it must be enclosed by quotation marks. If *volname* is not specified, the copy will have the same name as the original. AmigaDOS can still distinguish between volumes with the same name based upon information stored on the duplicate disk. The NAME keyword is required if a volume name is specified.

When DISKCOPY is invoked, you'll be prompted to insert the disks required to complete the copy operation. Status messages keep you advised as each track is copied. A standard AmigaDOS formatted 3½-inch disk requires 80 tracks of information to be read and written.

You can stop the copy process after issuing the command—when the system is waiting for the disk(s) to be inserted—by pressing CTRL-C followed by the RETURN key. You'll then be returned to the CLI prompt. If you press CTRL-C after the copy process has started, the copy is abandoned, and all information already on the destination disk is lost.

DISKCOPY Command

[*NOVERIFY*] The NOVERIFY option, added in Workbench 1.3.1, allows you to copy the disk without verifying writes. The default condition is that each track is verified as it is written.

[*MULTI*] The MULTI keyword, added in Workbench 1.3.1, allows you to make multiple copies of the disk.

Examples

1. Make a copy of a disk with a single-drive system. The copy is to have the same volume name as the original:

DISKCOPY FROM df0: TO df0:

2. Make a copy of a disk on a dual-drive system, copying the original from the external drive to the Amiga's internal drive. The copy is to have the same volume name as the original:

DISKCOPY FROM df1: TO df0:

3. Make a copy of a disk with a dual-drive system, copying the original from the internal drive to the external drive. The copy is to be named *King Keizers Lament*:

DISKCOPY df0: TO df1: NAME "King Keizers Lament"

Note: In this example the optional FROM keyword has been omitted. Quotation marks enclose the copy's volume name since it includes spaces.

DISKDOCTOR Command

Purpose

Reconstructs the directory and file structure of corrupted disks. A disk can become corrupted because of a defect in the media, exposure to magnetic fields, or operator error (such as removing the disk while the red drive light is still on). When this happens, AmigaDOS is unable to read the disk correctly and it displays a system message, such as *Volume Programs has a Read/Write error, Volume Programs is not validated, Disk is unreadable, Checksum error*, or even *Not a DOS Disk*.

Since each directory item contains duplicate information about the preceding and following entries, it's sometimes possible to reconstruct the corrupted disk information. DISKDOCTOR restores as much information as can be salvaged. Since it cannot correct media defects or magnetic damage, however, you should always use the COPY command to copy all of the files onto another disk, and you shouldn't use the damaged disk until it's been formatted again.

As of version 1.3, DISKDOCTOR can be used to salvage disks that have been formatted with the Fast File System, but only if the DOSTYPE keyword in the file DEVS:Mountlist has been set to 0x444F5301.

Format

DISKDOCTOR *drive*

Explanation of Parameters and Key Words

drive   The device name of the drive containing the damaged disk. Note that DISKDOCTOR may be used with hard drives or hard drive partitions (dh0: or dh1:), as well as with floppy disk drives (df0: or df1:), but should be used only as a last resort on hard disks.

Example

Attempt to restore the data on a damaged floppy disk in the external disk drive:

```
DISKDOCTOR df1:
```

DISKDOCTOR Command

Note: After DISKDOCTOR is finished with the disk, copy the files onto a new disk. Do *not* use DISKCOPY to transfer the files since it will copy corrupted information as well. Instead, use the FORMAT command to initialize a new disk; then use the COPY command in the form:

COPY df0: TO df1: ALL

where *df0:* contains the "doctored" disk, and *df1:* contains the newly formatted disk. If the corrupted disk was bootable, you may use the INSTALL command on the new disk to also make it bootable.

ECHO Command

Purpose ECHO is used in command files to display a message on the system screen. This is most often helpful when the RUN command is being used to carry out a background operation whose completion would otherwise not be readily apparent to the user. See Chapter 5 for more information on using ECHO.

Format **ECHO** *string* [*NOLINE*] [*FIRST num*] [*LEN num*]

Explanation of Parameters and Keywords

string The message to be written to the currently active output stream. While the current output stream will usually be the system display, it may also be a file or device. If it contains spaces, *string* should be contained within quotation marks.

There are special characters that ECHO recognizes as output controls. *N can be used to designate a new line character, while *E specifies the ESCAPE character.

[*NOLINE*] Normally, the ECHO command appends a new line character to the end of the string. The NOLINE option, introduced in Workbench 1.3, allows you to omit the new line after printing the string, so that the next word that is output to the CLI console appears on the same line as the text that was ECHOed.

[*FIRST num*] Workbench 1.3 also introduced a substring capability that allows you to print only a selected part of the text string. The FIRST keyword is used to designate the first character within the string that is to be printed. For example, if the echo string is "This is a test," FIRST 3 designates character 3, the "i" in "This," as the first letter to be printed.

[*LEN num*] Another substring option introduced in version 1.3. The LEN keyword is used to designate the length of the substring that is to be printed. In the above example, FIRST 5 LEN 4 would print the "is a" portion of the string. If no FIRST keyword is used to indicate the starting position of the substring, LEN backs up "num" number of characters from the end of the string. In the example above, if there were no FIRST, LEN 4 would print "test".

ECHO Command

Examples

1. A command file that executes a background SORT of a file called *sortsource* on the external drive to a file called *sortdest* on the same drive, and notifies you when the operation is complete:

RUN SORT FROM df1:sortsource TO df1:
   sortdest + ECHO "Sort Complete"

2. A command file that executes a background COPY of all files and subdirectories in a directory called *work/mydir* on the current default drive to a directory called *storage/archive* on the same drive:

RUN COPY FROM :work/mydir TO :storage/
   archive ALL QUIET + ECHO "That's All Folks"

3. Create a one-line file called *:Joey* that contains the text string *I have the power*:

ECHO > :Joey "I have the power"

4. Print the "middle" portion of the string "stuck in the middle with you":

ECHO "Stuck in the middle with you." FIRST 14 LEN
   6 "

ED Command

Purpose
: The ED command is used to edit the contents of a file using AmigaDOS's full-screen editor. See Chapter 6 for complete information on using the full-screen editor.

Format
: **ED** [*FROM*] name [*SIZE*] n

Explanation of Parameters and Keywords
: [*FROM*] name   The name of the AmigaDOS file which you wish to edit using the full-screen editor. If name is the first argument in an ED command statement, the FROM keyword need not be specified. If the file already exists, its contents are loaded into the editor's workspace. If the file doesn't already exist, it is dynamically created by the editor.

  [*SIZE*] n   SIZE n is used to set the size of the editor's workspace. If n is the second argument in an ED command statement, the SIZE keyword need not be given. If no value for n is specified, the editor's default workspace is 40,000 bytes. To edit files larger than that, specify SIZE n with a value for n larger than the size of the file to be edited. If the workspace size selected is not large enough, the editor will display the message SIZE of n too small.

Examples
: **1.** Invoke AmigaDOS's full-screen editor to edit a file called *WorkInProgress* in the *Current/Stuff* directory:

  `ED :Current/Stuff/WorkInProgress`

  2. Invoke AmigaDOS's full-screen editor to edit a 90,000-byte file called *Big* in the root directory of drive df1:.

  `ED df1:Big SIZE 100000`

EDIT Command

EDIT Command

Purpose

The EDIT command is used to edit the contents of a file using AmigaDOS's line editor.

Unless you're a real fan of line editors, give AmigaDOS's full-screen editor (ED) a try first. The full-screen editor is both more flexible and easier to use than EDIT. In all fairness, EDIT *does* have the ability to edit binary files and can execute a prestored list of line editor commands, which may be handy features for some users. See Chapter 7 for detailed information on EDIT.

Format

EDIT [*FROM*] fromname [*TO*] toname [*WITH*] withname [*VER*] vername [*OPT* option]

Explanation of Parameters and Keywords

[*FROM*] *fromname*   The name of the file whose contents will be edited. If *fromname* is the first argument in the EDIT command, the FROM keyword is optional. EDIT requires *fromname*, and it must already exist.

[*TO*] *toname*   The name of the file to which the edited text is saved when a Q or W subcommand is executed from within the line editor. If *toname* is the second argument in an EDIT command (following *fromname*), the TO keyword is optional.

If *toname* is different from *fromname*, the contents of the file used as input to the editor will not be replaced by a save from within the line editor. If *toname* is not specified and a save is executed from within EDIT, the contents of the original file will be moved to a temporary file called *:t/edit.backup*, and EDIT will rename its work file (where it temporarily holds edited data) to *fromname*.

[*WITH*] *withname*   This option lets you specify a file that will be used as input to the line editor's command processor. The contents of *withname* should be a series of valid line editor subcommands. If *withname* is the third argument in an EDIT command (following *fromname* and *toname*), the WITH keyword is optional. IF *withname* is not specified, the line editor expects manual input from the keyboard.

EDIT Command

[VER] *vername*   Lets you specify where you want messages and verification output produced by the line editor sent; *vername* may be a file or logical device. If *vername* is the fourth argument in an EDIT command (following *fromname*, *toname*, and *withname*), the VER keyword is optional.

[OPT P*n* or OPT W*n* or OPT P*n*W*n*]   These options let you set the maximum line length (W*n*) and number of lines (P*n*) that EDIT will keep memory resident. The default maximum line length is 120. The default number of lines is 40. Multiplying the value for P*n* by W*n* yields the amount of memory that EDIT reserves as a temporary work area. If either P*n* or W*n* is to be specified, the OPT keyword must be used.

Examples

1. Edit a file called *mysource* in the current directory, using AmigaDOS's line editor. The edited data, if saved, will be stored under the same filename. The number of lines is to be set to 40 and line width to 120 (EDIT's default values):

EDIT mysource

2. Edit a file called *bigsource* in the current directory, using AmigaDOS's line editor. The edited data, if saved, will be stored under the filename *edited bigsource*. The number of lines is to be set to 1000 and line width to 120:

EDIT FROM bigsource TO "edited bigsource"
  OPT P1000

3. Edit a file called *universe* in the current directory, using AmigaDOS's line editor. When EDIT starts up, execute the list of line editor commands contained in a file called *autocommands* in the *myprocess/nebula/* directory on drive df1:. The edited data, if saved, will be stored under the same filename. Send all messages and verification displays from the line editor to the system printer. The number of lines is to be set to 40 and line width to 250:

EDIT universe WITH df1:myprocess/nebula/
  autocommands VER PRT: OPT W250

ENDCLI Command

Purpose
: ENDCLI terminates the current Command Line Interpreter. ENDCLI should be issued only to a CLI or Shell that has been created with the NEWCLI or NEWSHELL command or to a CLI or Shell that has been opened from the Amiga Workbench environment by double-clicking a CLI or SHELL icon.

Format
: **ENDCLI**

Explanation of Parameters and Keywords
: None

Example
: Open a new CLI window and issue a directory command within the new CLI. Close the CLI window with the ENDCLI command, returning to the CLI from which the NEWCLI command was issued:

NEWCLI

Note: A new CLI window will appear on your screen. The next two commands will appear within the new window as they're typed:

DIR
ENDCLI

ENDSKIP Command

Purpose
: ENDSKIP was added to Workbench 1.3 to designate the end of a SKIP clause in a batch file. When ENDSKIP is encountered within a SKIP clause, execution continues at the line following the ENDSKIP, and the condition flag is set to WARN.

Format
: **ENDSKIP**

Explanation of Parameters and Keywords
: None

EVAL Command

EVAL Command

Purpose The EVAL command, added in Workbench 1.3, is used to evaluate simple integer expressions with one or two arguments, and to print the resulting expression in a user-specified format. It is mainly used to perform calculations in scripts, to aid in chores such as counting loops.

Format EVAL value1 [OP = operator] [VALUE2 = value] [TO filename] [LFORMAT = string]

Explanation of Parameters and Keywords

value1 The first value in the expression to be evaluated. This value may be expressed as a decimal number (the default), a hexadecimal number (indicated with a leading 0X or #X) or an octal number (indicated by a leading 0 or a leading #, followed by other digits). You may also use the ASCII value of a text character, by prefacing it with a single apostrophe (for example 'a for 97, the ASCII value of the letter "a").

[OP = operator] A symbol that indicates the mathmatical operation to be performed on the value or values. The supported operations and their symbols are:

+	Addition
−	Subtraction
*	Multiplication
/	Division
mod	Modulus
&	Bitwise AND
|	Bitwise OR
~	Bitwise NOT
<<	Bitwise shift left
>>	Bitwise shift right
−	Negation
xor	Bitwise exclusive or
eqv	Bitwise equivalence

The keywords OP = do not have to be included if the values and operator are presented in the correct order (value1 operator value2). If you change this order, the OP = and VALUE2 = keywords must be included to indicate which is the operator and which the second value.

EVAL Command

[*VALUE2 = value*]   The second value in the expression that is to be evaluated. It may be expressed in any of the forms mentioned above. The keywords VALUE2 = do not have to be included if the values and operator are in the correct order (value1 operator value2). They only need to be included if you change the order in which they're presented.

[*TO filename*]   This optional keyword is used to send the output of this command to the file whose name is indicated by filename.

[*LFORMAT = string*]   This optional keyword is used to specify the format of the text string that this command prints. By default, the program prints the answer in decimal format, but through the use of a text string, you may specify hexadecimal (%X), octal (%O), decimal (%N), or ASCII character (%C). The hexadecimal and octal format strings require a number after the letter, indicating how many digits should be printed (such as a string of "%X8" indicates that the answer should be printed as eight hex digits). You may also include any additional text you want in the format string. The command option

LFORMAT = "The answer is %N"

will cause the command to print the words "The answer is" in front of the value that it calculated. Note that by default, EVAL does not terminate its output with a new line character. If you want the cursor to skip to a new line after the output is printed, you should include the characters "*N" within the format string and put the format string in quotes. If there are any spaces within the format string, the entire string should be placed within quotes as well.

Examples

1. Calculate the value of 10,000 divided by 9, and print the answer as four hexadecimal digits followed by a new line character.

EVAL 10000 / 9 LFORMAT = "%X4*N"

EVAL Command

2. Use EVAL in a command sequence file to decrement a loop counters, causing the script to execute exactly five times:

```
setenv temp 1
lab loop
echo "Loop #" NOLINE
type env:temp
eval <env:temp >nil: to = ram:temp value2 = 1
op = + ?
copy ram:temp env:temp
if val $temp NOT GT 5
skip loop back
endif
echo "*N I'm done.Five loops is my limit.*N"
```

EXECUTE Command

Purpose

The EXECUTE command is used to invoke AmigaDOS command sequence files. Command sequence files contain a prestored series of commands that are executed sequentially once the command file has been started by EXECUTE. EXECUTE can also pass information to the command sequence file to be used as arguments for the commands contained therein.

Command files may be nested by issuing an EXECUTE as one of the commands in the command sequence file. See Chapter 5 for more information on sequence files.

Format

EXECUTE *name [arg1 arg2,,,,]*

Explanation of Keywords and Parameters

name   The name of the command sequence file to be invoked, *name* is a required parameter and may be any valid AmigaDOS filename.

EXECUTE sometimes needs to create temporary files in the course of executing a script. Under version 1.2, these files were created in the :T directory. The version on Workbench 1.3 uses the T: directory if one has been ASSIGNed, otherwise it uses :T. Also, as of version 1.3, EXECUTE will substitute the characters <$$> with the task number of the CLI from which it is run. This feature is helpful in creating unique temporary filenames.

[arg1 arg2,,,,]   Arguments to be passed to the command sequence file. Arguments may be any valid AmigaDOS string (including filenames and logical and physical devices).

Examples

1. Invoke a command sequence file called *commikazi* on drive df1:.

   EXECUTE df1:commikazi

2. Invoke a command sequence file called *games*. Pass the arguments *lacrosse, bowling, prt:* and *df1:what/the/heck* to the command sequence file:

   EXECUTE games lacrosse bowling prt: df1:
     what/the/heck

EXECUTE Command

Note: The command sequence file being called must be written so that it will receive passed arguments. Before the command file is started up, EXECUTE examines the file for special directives and characters that tell it how to insert the passed information in the command sequence file's command stream.

Command sequence lines that contain directives for EXECUTE begin with a period (.).

Directives

.K *subname1 subname2....* or **.KEY** *subname1 subname2....*   defines substitution names for passed arguments. EXECUTE scans for these names, delimited by the angle bracket (< and >) characters in subsequent lines of the command file, and substitutes passed arguments in their stead. Each substitution argument may be further qualified by /A, /K, or /S (see "AmigaDOS Templates" earlier in this reference section for information on these qualifiers).

.BRA *n*   Substitutes character *n* for the < character. This comes in handy if < is to be part of a substitution name, or if you want to use the reduction operator.

.KET *n*   Substitutes character *n* for the > character. This comes in handy if > is to be part of a substitution name, or if you want to use the reduction operator.

.DOL *n* or **.DOLLAR** *n*   Substitutes character *n* for the command file's normal default delimiter ($). Substitution arguments may assume a default if no corresponding argument is given to EXECUTE by the user. For instance, <*animal$squirrel*> substitutes the string *squirrel* for the substitution argument *animal*.

.space   Defines a comment line.

.DEF *subname string*   Assigns the value *string* to all occurrences of the substitution argument *subname*.

EXECUTE Command

Examples

1. When the following EXECUTE command is issued:

EXECUTE sortvar ingress egress

and the contents of the command sequence file *sortvar* is:

```
.KEY SFILE/A TFILE/A HEX/S
IF HEX EQ " "
SORT <SFILE$mysource> <TFILE$mysorted>
ELSE
SORT <SFILE#mysource> <TFILE#mysorted
  > OPT H
ENDIF
```

EXECUTE will substitute *ingress* everywhere it finds the substitution argument *SFILE* enclosed within < and >, and it will substitute *egress* everywhere it finds the substitution argument *TFILE* enclosed within < and >. Note that in this example, the dollar sign ($) is used to provide default filenames in case *SFILE* and *TFILE* are not specified. If the HEX keyword is passed with EXECUTE, the H option of SORT is used.

2. The following example illustrates how using various dot commands can affect the appearance of the same command file. The function of the command file remains unchanged:

```
.DOT !
!KEY SFILE/A TFILE/A HEX/S
!BRA (
!KET )
!DOL #
IF HEX EQ ""
SORT (SFILE#mysource) (TFILE#mysorted)
ELSE
SORT (SFILE#mysource) (TFILE#mysorted)
  OPT H
ENDIF
```

FAILAT Command

Purpose	The FAILAT command is used within command sequence files and RUN command statements to alter the failure level threshold of the system.
	When AmigaDOS commands encounter an error upon execution, a numeric return code is set (usually 5, 10, or 20). The higher the return code, the greater the severity of the error. If a return code that exceeds the current failure level threshold is encountered during execution of a command sequence file or multiple command task set up by a RUN, execution stops. The default failure level threshold of AmigaDOS command sequence files and RUN background tasks is 10.
	Resetting the current failure level threshold can come in handy. By setting FAILAT very high, you can test return codes with the IF command in a command sequence file and react according to the return code encountered without aborting script execution when a relatively high return code is encountered.
	Once the command sequence file or RUN sequence has ended, the current failure level threshold is reset to 10.
	See Chapter 5, "Command Sequence Files," and the RUN command for more information.
Format	**FAILAT** n
Explanation of Parameters and Keywords	n The new failure level threshold. If n is not specified, FAILAT displays the current failure level threshold.
Examples	1. Display the current failure level threshold:
	FAILAT
	2. Temporarily set the current failure level threshold to 55:
	FAILAT 55

FAULT Command

Purpose
The FAULT command provides English-language explanations for many of the error codes that AmigaDOS generates. When AmigaDOS runs into a problem, it usually displays a description of the problem or a requester box telling you what needs to be done. In some cases, nothing appears but a fault code. Further questioning of the system using the WHY command might produce a message like *Last command failed with error 220*. In these cases, the FAULT command can give you more information about the nature of the problem.

Format
FAULT $n_{,,,,,,,,,,}$

Explanation of Parameters and Keywords
$n_{,,,,,,,,,,}$ The error number (fault code) that you want explained. Up to ten error numbers may be specified within one FAULT command. If no information is available on the error, the system simply repeats the error number. For instance, entering **FAULT 999** results in the display:

Fault 999: Error 999

Examples
1. Display the error message corresponding to fault code 216:

FAULT 216

AmigaDOS responds with:

Fault 216: directory not empty.

2. Display the error messages associated with fault codes 220, 103, and 226:

FAULT 220 103 226

AmigaDOS responds with:

Fault 220: comment too big
Fault 103: insufficient free store
Fault 226: no disk in drive

FF Command

Purpose
FF (Fast Fonts) is a program that was written by Charlie Heath of Microsmiths and was originally included with his TxEd text editor. It was first included on the Workbench disk with release 1.3. This program is used to speed up the display of text to the screen when a standard 8 × 8 pixel or 10 × 9 pixel fixed-width font is used. It can also be used to replace the standard system fonts with custom fonts as long as they are of the proper size, and are fixed width (not proportional).

Format
FF [-0] [-N] [fontname]

Explanation of Parameters and Keywords

[-0]   This optional switch is used to turn the fast-text routines on. The command FF, without this optional switch, serves exactly the same purpose.

[-N]   This optional switch is used to temporarily disable the fast-text routines, which can be turned on again by running FF once more.

[fontname]   The name of the font descriptor file of the fonts to replace the TOPAZ80 and TOPAZ60 fonts. This file has a name like Siesta.font. The directory that corresponds this font descriptor file (in the example given, the fonts:Siesta directory) should contain either a file named 8, a file named 9, or both. These files should contain the font information for a fixed width 8−×−8 pixel font and a fixed width 10−×−9 pixel font respectively. If fonts of the correct type are found in this directory, they will be substituted for the default system fonts. If not, the system Topaz font will be used.

Examples

1. Turn on the fast text routines:

FF -O

2. Turn on the fast text routines using the Siesta/8 and Siesta 9 fonts:

FF Siesta.font

FILENOTE Command

Purpose

FILENOTE lets you store comments about AmigaDOS files. Any comments stored using FILENOTE remain distinct and separate from the actual contents of the file. When files are first created, there are no comments associated with them. When a file with comment attached by FILENOTE is duplicated using the COPY command, the comment is not associated with the new file. When a file is RENAMED, comments attached to the file are attached to the new filename. When the contents of a file with a comment are updated, comments remain unchanged. If a comment is already attached to a file and a FILENOTE command with a new comment is issued, the new comment replaces the old.

Comments stored using FILENOTE may be viewed by using the LIST command. Any comments about the file appear on the screen beneath the file's name and are preceded by a colon (:). If the file is accompanied by an icon (.info) file, it's possible to read and edit the comment field from the workbench by clicking on the icon and selecting the "Info" item from the Workbench menu.

Format

FILENOTE [*FILE*] *filename* [*COMMENT*] *string*

Explanation of Parameters and Keywords

[*FILE*] *filename*   The name of the file that is to have a comment attached. The FILE keyword is optional if *filename* is the first argument of a FILENOTE statement. Only one filename may be specified. FILENOTE does not support AmigaDOS patterns.

[*COMMENT*] *string*   Defines the comment assigned to the specified file. The COMMENT keyword is optional if *string* is the second argument of a FILENOTE statement (following *filename*); *string*, the comment to be attached to the file, can be up to 80 characters in length (79 characters for version 1.3 and up), and must be enclosed in quotation marks if it contains spaces.

FILENOTE Command

Examples

1. Attach the comment *Don't delete this file until September 8, 2001* to the file *fedtax86*:

`FILENOTE FILE fedtax86 COMMENT "Don't delete this file until September 8, 2001"`

2. Attach the comment *Lattice C Object Code – Almost Works* to the file named *PinBallDemo* in the directory *Lattice/Code/Work* on drive df1:.

`FILENOTE df1:Lattice/Code/Work/PinBall Demo "Lattice C Object Code – Almost Works"`

FORMAT Command
(moved to SYS:SYSTEM directory in Workbench 1.2)

Purpose

Initializes a floppy disk as a blank AmigaDOS disk. A volume name, which must be specified by the user, is assigned to the disk after the initialization process is complete. *Caution: If a used disk is formatted, all information on it will be erased.*

FORMAT prompts you to insert the disk to be formatted in the desired drive and hit the RETURN key. This is your last chance to change your mind about the FORMAT request. Hitting CTRL-C and then RETURN aborts the process at this point. Once the disk is inserted and the RETURN key is pressed, the FORMAT process *cannot* be interrupted.

A status display reports as each cylinder on the disk (0–79) is initialized. After initialization, another display appears as each cylinder is verified. After verification is complete, the volume name is assigned.

It's not necessary to FORMAT a disk before using the DISKCOPY command—DISKCOPY formats as it copies. Thus, if all you want to do is copy the contents of a disk, it's much faster to use DISKCOPY than to first format the destination disk, INSTALL the system information on the formatted disk, and use the COPY ALL command to copy all of the files one by one. In fact, it's even faster to use DISKCOPY to duplicate a blank formatted disk than it is to format a new one. One situation in which you may wish to copy a disk using the FORMAT–COPY ALL approach is where the files on the source disk have been deleted and rewritten so many times

FORMAT Command

that the contents of the disk have become scattered. When this occurs, the time required to access each file may increase noticeably. By copying each file to a newly formatted disk, the contents of the disk will be consolidated.

Format

FORMAT DRIVE *drivename* **NAME** *string* [*NOICONS*] [*QUICK*] [*FFS*]

Explanation of Parameters and Keywords

DRIVE *drivename*   The disk drive in which you will insert the disk to be formatted. The DRIVE keyword *must* be used. The valid values for *drivename* are df0:, df1:, df2:, and df3:. The values used most often will be df0: (your Amiga's internal disk drive) and df1: (the optional Amiga 1010 external disk drive).

NAME *string*   The volume name assigned to the formatted disk. The NAME keyword is mandatory. *string* is the name you want to call the disk, and it must also be specified. *string* can be up to 30 characters long and must be enclosed in quotation marks if it contains spaces.

[*NOICONS*]   The NOICONS option allows you to create a disk that is totally blank. If you don't use this option, a Trashcan drawer and icon will be placed on the newly formatted disk.

[*QUICK*]   The QUICK option (new for Workbench 1.3) can be used to quickly reformat a disk that has already been formatted once. Using this option, FORMAT only formats the tracks containing the root block, the boot block, and the bitmap blocks.

[*FFS*]   This keyword is used for MOUNTed drives, to override the DosType setting in the Mountlist. Thus, if the DosType was set for the old file system, or no DosType was specified, you could still format the drive with the Fast File System by using the FFS keyword. This option should be sparingly used, since it's much safer to set the DosType correctly in the first place.

GETENV Command

Examples
1. Format a disk in drive df0:, naming the volume *Backup9*:

FORMAT DRIVE df0: NAME Backup9

2. Format a completely blank disk in drive df1:, with the volume name *Just Another Blank Disk*:

FORMAT DRIVE df1: NAME "Just Another Blank Disk" NOICONS

GETENV Command

Purpose
GETENV prints the value of an environment variable. An environment variable is a named text string stored in an environment space that is accessible to all tasks. As of Workbench 1.3, there is no formal environment handler; rather, it is simulated through the use of an ENV: directory that is created on the RAM: disk. For now, "GETENV test" is really the same as "TYPE ENV:test". In future versions, however, the environment variables will be stored in system RAM and manipulated by their own device handler.

Format
GETENV *varname*

Explanation of Parameters and Keywords
varname   The name of the environment variable to get. Under the Workbench 1.3 system, this is the name of a text file that is stored in the ENV: directory. Using the GETENV command prints the contents of this text file.

Example
Print the contents of an environment variable named *Cubby*:

GETENV Cubby

ICONX Command

Purpose
ICONX allows you to execute a script file of CLI commands from a Workbench icon. In order to use ICONX, you must create a text file that contains the CLI commands you want executed, and create a PROJECT icon for that file whose default tool is set

ICONX Command

to the correct path for ICONX (for instance C:ICONX). The Notepad program may be used for creating both the text file and the icon, as long as you stick the default text font and style. You will have to change the default tool in the icon from Notepad to ICONX, by selecting the icon, and then using the INFO menu item from the Workbench menu.

ICONX changes the current directory to the one containing the project icon before it executes the script. It also opens a console window on the Workbench screen which can be used for receiving input or displaying output. You can specify the size of this window in the project icon's TOOL TYPES field, by entering a line in the format

"WINDOW=CON:10/10/300/100/Name"

If you don't wish the window to be visible, set the width and height to one pixel. If you don't want the script window to close immediately after the script has finished executing, perhaps so the user can read some text in the window, you may specify a delay by entering a line in the icon's TOOL TYPES field using the format "DELAY=3". The delay number indicates how many seconds the window should remain open. A delay number of 0 indicates that the window should remain open until the user enters the CTRL-C key combination.

It is possible to pass filenames as parameters to the script file by using the Workbench's extended selection facility. By holding down the Shift key, selecting the file icons, and then double-clicking the script file icon, the names of the files will be passed to the script. In order to receive these names, however, the script must use the .key keyword at the beginning of the script.

Format None (this is a CLI command designed to run from a Workbench icon).

Explanation of Parameters and Keywords None

IF-ELSE-ENDIF Commands

IF-ELSE-ENDIF Commands

Purpose
: The IF command and its associates (the ELSE and ENDIF commands) are used within AmigaDOS command sequence files to carry out groups of commands within the command sequence file *if* one or more conditions are met. If an IF statement is satisfied, the commands following the statement are executed sequentially until an ELSE or ENDIF statement is encountered. If the IF conditional is not satisfied and an ELSE statement is encountered before an ENDIF, the commands between ELSE and ENDIF are executed.

  The IF command allows multiple conditionals to be specified. If any of the conditional keywords (with the exception of NOT) is satisfied, the IF is held to be true.

  For every IF command there must be an associated ENDIF.

  The ELSE command, if used, must appear between IF and ENDIF commands.

Format
: **IF** [*NOT*] [*VAL*] [*WARN*] [*ERROR*] [*FAIL*] [*string1* **EQ** *string2*] [*string1* **GT** *string2*] [*string1* **GE** *string2*] [*EXISTS name*]

Explanation of Parameters and Keywords
: [*NOT*]   Reverses the results of the IF test. If any of the conditionals is true and NOT is also used, the IF statement will not be satisfied. If all the other specified conditionals are false and NOT is used, the IF statement will be satisfied.

  [*WARN*]   Is satisfied (true) if the return code of the previous command is greater than or equal to 5.

  [*ERROR*]   Is satisfied (true) if the return code of the previous command is greater than or equal to 10.

  [*FAIL*]   Is satisfied (true) if the return code of the previous command is greater than or equal to 20.

  [*string1* **EQ** *string2*]   Is satisfied (true) if *string1* is identical to *string2*. Case is ignored in the comparison. This test can be reversed to test inequality by use of the NOT keyword. It can be changed to a nu-

IF–ELSE–ENDIF Commands

meric comparison by placing the VAL keyword in front of the first string. *string1* and *string2* are normally text strings that are enclosed in double quotation marks if there is a space character in the string. However, under version 1.3, either or both strings may be substituted by the contents of an environment variable by using a dollar sign ($) in front of the variable name. Thus, the IF command substitutes the expression $TEST with the text string that is contained within the environment variable named TEST.

[*string1* **GT** *string2*]   This option was introduced in Workbench 1.3. The test is satisfied (true) if the characters in *string1* come after the characters in *string2* in alphabetical order. Case is ignored in the comparison. This test can be reversed to test the LESS THAN OR EQUAL condition by use of the NOT keyword. It can be changed to a numeric comparison by placing the VAL keyword in front of the first string. As with EQ, the strings may be text strings in quotes or the name of an environment variable prefaced with a dollar sign.

[*string1* **GE** *string2*]   This option was introduced in version 1.3. The test is satisfied (true) if the characters in *string1* come after the characters in *string2* in alphabetical order, or if the two strings are identical. Case is ignored in the comparision. This test can be reversed to test the LESS THAN condition by use of the NOT keyword. It can be changed to a numeric comparison by placing the VAL keyword in front of the first string. As with EQ, the strings may be text strings in quotation marks or the name of an environment variable prefaced with a dollar sign.

[**VAL**]   This option was introduced in Workbench 1.3. When this keyword is placed in front of a comparison expression (EQ, GT, GE), it is changed to a numeric rather than a string comparison. Normally, these tests compare each character of the string in alphabetical order. Thus, the string "91" is shown to be greater than the string "099", since the leading "9" of the first string comes after the leading "0" of the second string. If you compare VAL "91" and "099" however, "099" is correctly shown to be greater.

IF–ELSE–ENDIF Commands

[*EXISTS* name]   Is satisfied if *name* exists; *name* may be any AmigaDOS file, directory or logical device.

Examples

1. Using IF–ENDIF statements, build a command sequence file that deletes any file except the file *DontDoIt*:

```
.KEY nerf/a
IF <nerf> EQ DontDoIt
ECHO "I refuse to delete that File"
QUIT
ENDIF
DELETE <nerf>
```

Note: Actually this example will delete *DontDoIt* if the value *:DontDoIt* or *DF0:DontDoIt* is passed to the command file as the value of *nerf* when the command sequence file is executed. The EQ option of IF compares the text strings, not the internal block IDs of the files. Multiple EQ statements could have been added to the IF statement to check for filename variants.

IF–ELSE–ENDIF sequences may be nested within one another.

2. Using nested IF–ELSE–ENDIF statements, build a command sequence file that attempts to delete the file *broccoli*. If any errors are encountered, report on their severity.

Note: The commands of this example have been indented to highlight the IF–ENDIF command groupings.

```
FAILAT 100
IF EXISTS broccoli
  DELETE broccoli
  IF WARN
   IF NOT EXISTS broccoli
     ECHO "File deleted - error encountered"
     QUIT
   ELSE
     ECHO "Fatal error - file not deleted"
     QUIT
   ENDIF
```

IF–ELSE–ENDIF Commands

```
    ELSE
     ECHO "File deleted"
     QUIT
    ENDIF
ELSE
   ECHO "File not found"
ENDIF
```

3. Using IF–ELSE–ENDIF statements, build a command sequence file that will copy all files in the directory *mywork/text/AmigaProject* on drive df1: to the directory *mywork/text/backup* on the same disk drive. If the *AmigaProject* subdirectory does not exist, create it. Start up the program called *Textcraft* in the root directory of drive df0:.

```
FAILAT 100
ASSIGN MYDIR: TO df1:mywork/text
IF EXISTS MYDIR:AmigaProject
ECHO "Copying Documents to Backup Area"
COPY MYDIR:AmigaProject TO MYDIR:
   backup ALL
SAY backup completed boss
SKIP STARTUP
ELSE
MAKEDIR MYDIR:AmigaProject
ECHO "AmigaProject Directory Created"
ENDIF
LABEL STARTUP
RUN df0:Textcraft
```

4. For an example of the VAL and GT keywords, see example 2 under the EVAL command.

INFO Command

INFO Command

Purpose

Display information about disk volumes and the system RAM disk. A typical INFO display shows the following information about each disk volume currently mounted on a physical drive attached to the Amiga. INFO will also report on the status of RAM:, the Amiga's memory-based RAM disk, if it's being used. A typical INFO display might look like this:

```
Mounted disks:
Unit  Size  Used  Free  Full  Errs  Status       Name
DF1:  880K  1089  669   61%   0     Read Only    Graphics Demos
DF0:  880K  740   1018  42%   0     Read/Write   CLI Disk
RAM:  22K   43    0     100%  0     Read/Write

Volumes Available:
Graphics Demos [Mounted]
CLI Disk [Mounted]
```

INFO tells you what disk volumes are in use and the amount of storage currently allocated to them. Amiga 3½-inch disks have a capacity of 880K (901,120 bytes) of information. Each AmigaDOS disk contains 1758 usable sectors with each sector holding 512 bytes of information. INFO reports the number of sectors already used on each disk, the number of free sectors available for use, and the percentage of the disk used. The size of RAM: will vary depending upon how much information has been copied to it. Storage used for RAM: reduces the amount of real memory available for programs to run in. When RAM: is used, it will always show as being 100-percent full.

INFO also reports on the number of "soft" disk errors encountered in using the disk volume during the current session. Soft errors are those of a temporary nature. An example of a soft error is a temporary failure in reading some information from a disk. When the error is first encountered, many systems will try to read the information again for a predefined number of times. If one of the retries is successful, the original read error is considered a temporary, or soft, failure. If all retries fail, the error is considered a permanent, or hard, failure.

INFO Command

The status of each volume will be either *Read/Write* or *Read Only*. Read/Write indicates that the volume may be read or written to. New files may be added and existing files on the disk may be read, updated, and deleted. A volume is made Read Only when its write-protect window has been uncovered. The write-protect window is located on the front left of a 3½-inch disk and is usually uncovered by sliding a small plastic shutter toward the front edge of the disk.

Write-Protect Window

The files on Read Only volumes can be read, but not updated or deleted. New files may not be added. Any attempt to write to a Read Only disk will result in an error. While RAM: cannot be write-protected, all files residing in RAM: can be protected from deletion by using the PROTECT command.

INFO also displays the name of the disk currently residing in each physical disk drive. RAM: never has a volume name associated with it. A list of *Volumes Available* is also presented, indicating the status (mounted or unmounted) of disk known to the AmigaDOS filing system during the present session.

Format | **INFO** [*devicename*]

Explanation of Parameters and Keywords | [*devicename*]   This option was added in Workbench 1.3. It allows you to obtain information on a single device or volume by typing its name after the info command.

INFO Command

Examples
1. Display information about the disk volumes known to the filing system:

    INFO

2. Redirect the INFO display to an attached printer:

    INFO > PRT:

3. Display information about the disk in the internal disk:

    INFO DF0:

INSTALL Command

Purpose
The INSTALL command makes a formatted disk capable of a minimal startup of the AmigaDOS environment (assigning SYS: to the booted disk). The key words to keep in mind here are *minimal startup.* While a blank formatted disk that has had an INSTALL command issued to it will bring up the AmigaDOS window and command line prompt, none of the AmigaDOS commands will function unless invoked with their full pathnames.

If you wish to copy a bootable disk by formatting a new disk and copying each file from it one by one, you'll have to INSTALL the system information on the new disk in order for it to be accepted at the *Insert Workbench Disk* prompt.

With Workbench 1.3, additional functions were added to INSTALL to help the user identify and destroy "viruses", self-replicating computer programs that may be stored on the initial (boot) block of the disk without the user's knowlege.

Format
INSTALL [*DRIVE*] *drive* [*NOBOOT*] [*CHECK*]

Explanation of Parameters and Keywords

[*DRIVE*] *drive*   The disk drive in which the disk you wish to make bootable resides. The DRIVE keyword is optional. Valid values for *drive* are df0:, df1:, df2:, and df3:.

[*NOBOOT*]   This keyword, added in version 1.3, can be used to clear the boot block but not make the disk bootable. This can be used to get rid of unwanted information stored by viruses on the boot block without making the disk bootable. Note that the NOBOOT option will write out a new boot block even if the disk is not set up in the standard DOS format.

[*CHECK*]   This option, added in Workbench 1.3, is used to check if the disk is bootable, and if it contains the standard Commodore-Amiga boot code. When the CHECK keyword is used, the command prints the message "No bootblock installed" if the disk is not bootable, "Appears to be normal V1.2/V1.3 bootblock" if the disk is bootable and

INSTALL Command

contains standard boot code, or "May not be standard V1.2/1.3 bootblock" if the disk is bootable and contains nonstandard boot code. The command also sets a return code of zero if the disk is not bootable or has standard boot code, and a code of 5 (WARN) if it contains nonstandard boot code.

Examples

1. Install boot files on the disk presently inserted in disk drive df1:.

INSTALL DRIVE df1:

2. Install boot files on the disk currently residing in the internal system drive df0:.

INSTALL df0:

Note: INSTALL, as implemented in AmigaDOS, does not prompt you for the disk to be inserted. For most owners of single-drive systems, this makes a direct INSTALL to drive df0: difficult. Typically, the place where AmigaDOS commands are found by the system (the C: command directory) is assigned to df0:. If you insert the disk you wish to install to ahead of time and then type INSTALL DRIVE df0:, you'll be prompted to insert the disk with the command library on it in any disk drive. Once you do so, INSTALL puts boot files on the disk with the command library, which was *not* where you wanted the files installed and was bootable to begin with.

The following procedure will get single-drive users around this limitation. Put your Workbench or CLI disk into the drive and type:

INSTALL ?

When the command template (DRIVE/A etc.) appears, eject that disk from the internal drive and insert the disk you want to install or check. Type

DF0:

3. Check the boot code on the disk that is currently in drive df1:.

INSTALL DRIVE df1: CHECK

JOIN Command

Purpose

JOIN lets you merge the contents of up to 15 files into one file. The files are merged in the order given to JOIN.

Format

JOIN *name1 name2 ,,,,,,,,,,,,,* **AS** or **TO** *destname*

Explanation of Parameters and Keywords

name1 name2 ,,,,,,,,,,, The names of the files you want merged together. A minimum of two files must be given, with a space between each name. Up to 15 files may be merged by a single JOIN command.

AS *or* **MDBOTO** *destfile* The name of the file that the contents of all files preceding the AS or TO keyword (one of which is required) will be merged into; *destname* can be a new or old file but it cannot be any of the files that precede the AS or TO keyword. If *destname* already exists, its previous contents will be replaced. The TO keyword was added in Workbench 1.3.

Examples

1. Merge two files (*Dick* and *Jane*) in the current directory into a file (*HusbandAndWife*) in the same directory:

JOIN Dick Jane AS HusbandAndWife

2. Merge four files, from various drives, devices, and directories into one:

JOIN myparty :spritzers/white/chablis df1:soft drinks/cola/moxie RAM:mydate AS ":party/animal/March 25 1986"

LAB Command

Purpose
: LAB is used within command sequence files to define a location in the command file that may be jumped to by the SKIP command. See Chapter 5 for complete information on command sequence files.

Format
: **LAB** *string*

Explanation of Parameters and Keywords
: *string*   A "signpost" that can be used by a SKIP command to jump to the spot in the command file where a specific LAB statement is located. Once jumped to, command file execution continues with the commands following the LAB statement.

Example
: Define a location called *DontDo* that may be jumped to by a SKIP instruction:

```
IF EXISTS work.backup
SKIP DontDo
COPY work work.backup
LAB DontDo
RENAME work work.old ...
```

LIST Command

Purpose — Display the name, size, protection status, time and date of creation, and the Amiga filing system block numbers of *(a)* a directory, *(b)* a selected portion of a directory, or *(c)* a single file. LIST also displays any comments attached to a file by a FILENOTE command.

Here's an example of a typical LIST output:

```
Directory ":" on Wednesday 12-Dec-85
bagel                      20      rwed   Today       00:57:23
c                          Dir     rwed   Yesterday   23:49:01
fonts                      Dir     rwed   Yesterday   23:49:01
lox                        1921    rwe-   10-Dec-85   14:29:54
: A history of Nova Scotia's Finest
libs                       Dir     rwed   Yesterday   23:49:01
t                          Dir     rwed   Yesterday   23:49:01
2 files - 4 directories - 7 blocks used
```

The file and directory names are listed at the left. To the right of each name is additional information about the file. The first number indicates each file's size in bytes (directories are shown by the letters *Dir*).

The protection flags currently turned on for each item (see the PROTECT command for further information) are listed next, and then finally, the date and time the item was created or last updated. Any comment attached to a file or directory by the FILENOTE command appears directly beneath the file's information line in the LIST display and is preceded by a colon (:).

With 1.3, a formatting option was added that allows you to output the directory listing in a customized text display.

Format — **LIST** *listname* [*P* or *PAT pattern*] [*KEYS*]
  [*DATES*] [*NODATES*] [*TO device* or *filename*]
  [*SUB string*] [*SINCE date*] [*UPTO date*] [*QUICK*]
  [*BLOCK*] [*NOHEAD*] [*FILES*] [*DIR*]
  [*LFORMAT = string*]

LIST Command

Explanation of Parameters and Keywords

listname   This can be the device name or volume name of a disk, a directory, or the name of a specific file. With Workbench 1.3, this name may include a pattern. Thus, "LIST #?.info" gives a list of all the files ending in those five characters. This eliminates the need for the PAT option, below.

[*P* or *PAT* *pattern*]   When you use this option, the P or PAT keyword must precede the pattern. A pattern allows you to specify a number of files, each of which has some common characteristic (see Chapter 3 for more information on creating AmigaDOS patterns). Since the 1.3 version of LIST allows you to use patterns in *listname*, this option is no longer needed.

[*KEYS*]   Specifying this option includes the block number associated with each file and directory displayed. The AmigaDOS filing system automatically assigns and uses block numbers to keep track of things. Each file and directory has a single, unique block number. The block number on the display appears to the left of the file length (or *Dir*).

[*DATES*]   Includes file and directory creation date and time information in the LIST display. DATES is usually optional since LIST defaults to displaying creation dates and times unless either QUICK or NODATES is used.

[*NODATES*]   Instructs LIST to suppress the display of file and directory creation date and time information. NODATES is optional.

[*TO* *device* or *filename*]   Selects where the output of LIST is to be sent; *device* or *filename* may be any valid AmigaDOS filename or a logical device known to the system. If a file of the same name already exists, the existing file will be deleted and a new file with the same name is created. For this reason, if TO *device* or *filename* is a file that has been protected from deletion with the PROTECT command, LIST will fail. If TO *device* or *filename* is not specified, LIST's output is displayed on the system screen.

[*S* *string*]   To use this option, the SUB keyword must precede *string*, which can be any character string. LIST then displays only those filenames or directories that include *string*. If spaces are included in *string*, quotation marks must enclose it. Since the 1.3 version allows patterns in the *listname*, this option is rendered unncessary.

[*SINCE date*]   Displays information only for those files and directories created or modified on or after *date; date* may be specified in the format *DD-MMM-YY*, or as an indirect reference of YESTERDAY, TODAY, or TOMORROW. The days of the past week, SUNDAY through SATURDAY, can also be used as *date*. See the DATE command for more information.

[*UPTO date*]   Instructs LIST to display information only for those files and directories created or modified on or before *date*, which is subject to the same restrictions as the SINCE keyword.

[*QUICK*]   Instructs LIST to display only file and directory names. However, if the DATES and/or KEYS keywords are specified as well, LIST displays file and directory names along with the information associated with DATES and/or KEYS.

[*BLOCK*]   This option, added in version 1.3, specifies that the file sizes be displayed in terms of 512-byte blocks, rather than bytes.

[*NOHEAD*]   This option, new in Workbench 1.3, allows you to suppress the "Directory..." heading on the first line, and the "x files −x directories −x blocks used" footnote on the last line of the listing.

[*FILES*]   This option, added in version 1.3, allows you to list only files and not directories.

[*DIR*]   This option, also added in version 1.3, allows you to list only the directories and not the files.

[*LFORMAT = string*]   The LFORMAT option was added in Workbench 1.3 to allow you to customize the text output of the LIST command. This feature lets you use LIST to quickly generate script files. In order to send the output to a script file, however, you must use the redirection operator (>) instead of the TO option.

When you use LFORMAT, the output of the LIST command is totally controlled by the format string that appears after the keyword. This format

LIST Command

string can contain any text you want to appear in the listing.

At the place in the text string that you want the listing to appear, you use the substitution string %S. This substitution string may be used more than once in the text, allowing you to use the listing name more than once per line. If you use the string twice, the first time the pathname will be substituted for %S, and the second time the file or subdirectory name will be substituted. If you use it three times, the first occurrence will be replaced by the pathname, and the second and third by the file or subdirectory name. If you use it four times, the first and third will be replaced by the pathname, and the second and fourth by the file or subdirectory name.

Examples

1. Display standard LIST information about the contents of the current directory on the screen:

LIST

2. Output all standard LIST information and the block number of each item in the current directory to the system printer:

LIST KEYS TO PRT:

or

LIST > PRT: KEYS

3. Display standard LIST information about each file in directory *water/sports* whose name contains the character string *skin*:

LIST water/sports SUB skin

or

LIST water/sports/#?skin#?

   Note: Information for both *Snorkel & Skin Diving* and *SkinnyDipping* would be displayed by this example.

4. Output just the names and date information for items in the current directory beginning with the letters *compute* that were created or last updated on or before November 4, 1985. Send the output to a file called *MySelections*:

LIST compute#? QUICK DATES UPTO 04-
    Nov-85 TO MySelections

LIST Command

5. Create a script file that, when executed, will set the pure bit of every file in the C: directory:

LIST >RAM:TEMP C:#? LFORMAT "protect %S +p"

    This creates a script file called RAM:TEMP that contains a PROTECT command for each file in the C: directory. To set the pure bit in each file, you need only EXECUTE RAM:TEMP.

LOADWB Command

Purpose LOADWB is used to start the Workbench program. This command is usually issued automatically at boot time, as part of the s:*startup-sequence* batch file. When the Workbench is started, it notes the search paths that are currently in effect, and sets these same paths for each CLI or Shell that is started from a Workbench icon.

Format **LOADWB** [*DELAY or -DEBUG*]

Explanation of Parameters and Keywords [*DELAY or -DEBUG*]   The DELAY option was added in version 1.3 to create a three-second pause before the program returned. This pause allows the floppy disk activity that LOADWB initiates to stop before the next command in the script is executed. If there is no pause and the next command starts before LOADWB finishes using the disk, both commands have to share the floppy disk, which causes disk access to slow down and the disk heads to make a loud "thrashing" noise.

The -DEBUG option enables a new Workbench menu, which is normally not displayed. This menu contains two items of interest to programmers. The first item, Debug, executes the ROMWACK debugger, a program that communicates through a 9600-baud terminal connected to the serial port. If no such terminal is connected, you cannot make use of this command. The second item, Flushlibs, causes Workbench to expunge any libraries, devices, fonts, or other resources that are resident in memory but are not currently being used. This frees up the memory used by these resources.

Either DELAY or -DEBUG may be used, but not both at the same time.

Examples 1. Load the Workbench environment and close the CLI window:

```
LOADWB DELAY
ENDCLI >NIL:
```

2. Load the Workbench environment with the DEBUG menu activated:

```
LOADWB -DEBUG
```

LOCK Command

Purpose
: LOCK was added to Workbench 1.3 to enable or disable write protection of a hard drive parition that uses the Fast File System. Once write protection is set, it remains in force until reset with another LOCK command, or until the system is rebooted. If an optional password is used to lock the drive, the same password must be used to unlock the drive.

Format
: **LOCK** drive [**ON** or **OFF**] [password]

Explanation of Parameters and Keywords
: *drive*   The device name of a disk or disk partition that is formatted with the Fast File System. It isn't possible to LOCK a hard disk that is formatted with the old file system.

  [*ON* or *OFF*]   These optional keywords can be used to write-protect the disk (LOCK ON) or write-enable the disk (LOCK OFF). If neither is specified, the disk will be write-enabled.

  [*password*]   An optional four-character password of the user's choosing. If a password is used as part of the LOCK ON command, the same password must be used in the LOCK OFF command in order for the disk to be write-enabled.

Example
: 1. Write-protect hard drive DH0:, which uses the fast file system, with a password of *fish*.

  LOCK dh0: ON fish

  To turn off the write protection, you would use the command:

  LOCK dh0: OFF fish

  or just

  LOCK dh0: fish

MAKEDIR Command

MAKEDIR Command

Purpose

MAKEDIR creates directory entries, allowing you to divide an AmigaDOS disk into a type of multileveled filing cabinet.

Suppose you wanted to separate your written correspondence by category and recipients. Your business correspondence usually deals with accounts payable and receivable, with some occasional miscellaneous letters. Your personal correspondence is mostly letters to your family and friends, letters concerning your bills, and some other occasional things. You might decide that you want things organized like this:

Planned Directory Form

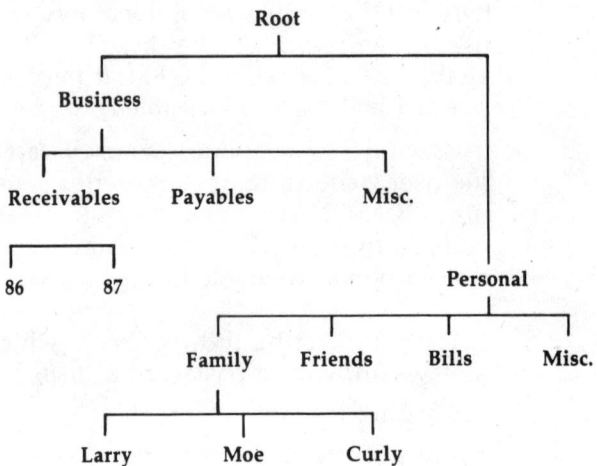

MAKEDIR Command

Assuming that you begin with the root directory of an AmigaDOS disk, this is one of the possible sequences of AmigaDOS commands that will set up such a directory structure:

```
MAKEDIR Business
MAKEDIR Business/Receivables
MAKEDIR Business/Receivables/88
MAKEDIR Business/Receivables/89
MAKEDIR Business/Payables
MAKEDIR Business/Misc
MAKEDIR Personal
CD Personal
MAKEDIR Family
MAKEDIR Friends
MAKEDIR Bills
MAKEDIR Misc
CD Family
MAKEDIR Larry
MAKEDIR Moe
MAKEDIR Curly
CD //
```

Let's examine how this was created, starting with the business correspondence. Note the top-down order in which the directories were created. MAKEDIR builds only one subdirectory at a time. When you type MAKEDIR Business/Receivables/88, the only directory entry created is 88, the rightmost portion of the specified directory path. For the command to execute successfully, both the *Business* directory and a subdirectory within it called *Receivables* must have already been created.

As the business correspondence MAKEDIR commands illustrate, you can expend a lot of keystrokes typing pathnames. Just look at all the times you had to type *Business*. You can use the CD command to cut down significantly the number of keystrokes required. Look at the sequence of commands again, paying particular attention to the last half—that used to build the personal correspondence directories. After the MAKEDIR Personal used to create the directory for personal letters, a CD Personal changed the current directory so that the pathname *Personal* could be omitted from all subsequent MAKEDIRs.

MAKEDIR Command

CD was used again to "drop down" into the *Family* subdirectory and keep unnecessary keystrokes to a minimum. Note that once again, care has been taken to ensure that the directories are built from the top down. A final CD // at the end backs you up two levels to your starting point (see the CD command for more information on its use).

For information on removing directory entries, see the DELETE command; for more information on directory structures, see Chapter 3, "The Filing System."

Format

MAKEDIR *name*

Explanation of Parameters and Keywords

name   The name of the directory to be created; *name* must be specified. MAKEDIR fails if *name* is the name of a file or subdirectory that already exists in the "parent" directory (the next highest directory in the hierarchy). MAKEDIR also fails if a nonexistent pathname is specified.

Examples

1. Create a subdirectory called *YellowPages* in the current directory:

`MAKEDIR YellowPages`

2. Create a subdirectory called *Dictionary* in the root directory of the disk inserted in drive df1:.

`MAKEDIR df1:Dictionary`

3. Create a subdirectory called *Encyclopedias* in the root directory of the current drive, create five subdirectories within *Encyclopedias*, and then change the default directory to the root of the current drive:

```
MAKEDIR :Encyclopedias
CD :Encyclopedias
MAKEDIR "World Book"
MAKEDIR Grolier
MAKEDIR Britannica
MAKEDIR "World Book"
MAKEDIR "Funk & Wagnals"
CD :
```

MAKEDIR Command

4. Create a subdirectory call *Lightning* on the Amiga's RAM disk:

`MAKEDIR RAM:Lightning`

5. ASSIGN a logical device name *QWIK:* to the directory created in example 4, and create a subdirectory called *WarpSpeed* in it:

`ASSIGN QWIK: RAM:Lightning`
`MAKEDIR QWIK:WarpSpeed`

Note: This results in creating the same subdirectory as

`MAKEDIR RAM:Lightning/WarpSpeed`

MOUNT Command

Purpose Makes AmigaDOS recognize an external hardware device (such as a 5¼-inch disk drive or a second serial port) as a DOS device. It can also be used to add a virtual device like a recoverable RAM disk, or a speech output device. This command is most often issued as part of the *startup-sequence* script file in the *s* directory of the Workbench disk, so that the device is automatically configured each time that the Amiga boots up.

MOUNT looks for a description of the device requested in the file *DEVS:Mountlist,* or an optional FROM file. The *Mountlist* file is a text file that describes various attributes of the device. This file shares some of the traits of C language source code files; if more than one description appears on a line, they must be separated by semicolons; hexadecimal numbers must start with the characters *0x*; and comments must start with the characters /* and end with */. Each entry in the *Mountlist* ends with the pound sign character (#).

The standard Workbench disk comes with a sample *Mountlist* file that can be used to mount an external 5¼-inch drive as device DF2:. This device description looks like:

```
DF2: Device = trackdisk.device
     Unit = 2
     Flags = 1
     Surface = 2
     BlocksPerTrack = 11
     Reserved = 2
     Interleave = 0
     LowCyl = 0;      HighCyl = 39
     Buffers = 20
     BufMemType = 3
#
```

The most important line is the first, which tells AmigaDOS that the device driver for this device is *trackdisk.device.* Since this device driver is an intrinsic part of the operating system, it need not be loaded in from disk. External device drivers can be loaded from disk if necessary, however. AmigaDOS will look for such drivers in the path specified, or in

MOUNT Command

the DEVS: directory if no path is included in the device driver name.

The rest of the information tells AmigaDOS what kind of disk drive this is—it's double-sided (*Surface* = 2), has 40 tracks per side (*LowCyl* = 0; *HighCyl* = 39), with 11 sectors of 512 bytes per sector (*BlocksPerTrack* = 11). This means that the total available storage on the drive is 440K (.5K × 2 × 11 × 40).

As configured, this list assumes you have an external 3½-inch drive, so it mounts the external drive as DF2:. If you don't have a 3½-inch drive as DF1:, you'll want to mount the 5¼-inch drive as DF1: (it should always be last in the chain). To do this, make two changes to the *Mountlist* file.

First, change the device name from DF2: to DF1:. Second, change the unit number from 2 to 1. Now the command MOUNT DF2: mounts the 5¼-inch drive as DF2:.

The MOUNT command can also be used to mount devices other than file storage devices. The *Mountlist* file in the DEVS: directory contains a sample mountlist for an additional serial device name AUX:

```
AUX: Handler = L:aux-handler
     Stacksize = 1000
     Priority = 5
```

Instead of describing the storage capacity of the device, this list merely shows where to find the handler (a program whose purpose is similar to that of the device driver), the size of the stack used by that program, and the priority at which it runs. Note that this *Mountlist* example by itself can't be used to mount an external serial device. For one thing, there really isn't a handler file in the L: directory called *aux-handler*. For another, you'd still need a hardware interface for the serial device.

The 1.2 and greater versions of CLI commands such as FORMAT and DISKCOPY have been altered so that they work with devices that have been mounted. Note, however, that you still can't use DISKCOPY between devices that aren't identical in storage size and layout. Thus, while you can use

MOUNT Command

DISKCOPY between two 5¼-inch drives, two hard disk partitions of equal size, or two 3½-inch drives, you can't use DISKCOPY from a 5¼-inch drive to a 3½-inch drive.

Format

MOUNT *device* [**FROM** *filename*]

Explanation of Parameters and Key Words

device This is an AmigaDOS device name, such as DF2:, DH0:, or AUX:, which refers to either a hardware device like a disk drive or serial port, or a logical device such as a RAM disk. The device name should be the same as the label given an entry in the *Mountlist* file, and the device driver or handler file indicated by that *Mountlist* should be available to the system. Some of the standard MOUNTable devices are described in Chapter 4.

There are a number of keyword options that can be used in the *MOUNTLIST* file to describe a device. Not all of them are required for all devices—in fact, most are optional. Keywords include:

Handler =	The name of the device handler file.
FileSystem =	The name of the filesystem file.
Device =	The name of the device driver file.
Priority =	The task priority of the process; 5 is customary for handlers, 10 for file systems.
Unit =	The unit number of the device.
Flags =	Flags setting for OpenDevice call (usually 0).
Surfaces =	Number of write surfaces.
BlocksPerTrack =	The number of disk blocks (sectors) per track (cylinder).
Reserved =	The number of blocks used for boot block (usually 2).
PreAlloc =	The number of blocks reserved at the end of a partition; used with a few IBM-style hard drives. Usually set to 0.
Interleave =	Interleave value (controls DOS interleave, not physical hard drive interleave).
LowCyl =	Starting cylinder to use for this device.
HighCyl =	Ending cylinder to use for this device. Total number of cylinders = HighCyl − LowCyl + 1.
Stacksize =	The amount of working memory to allocate to the process.

MOUNT Command

Buffers =	Number of cache buffers to use with the device.

BufMemType =	Type of memory to use for cache buffers.
	   0 or 1 = Any
	   2 or 3 = CHIP
	   4 or 5 = FAST

Mount =	If this value is positive, MOUNT loads the handler or driver software as soon as the device is MOUNTed, rather than the first time the device is accessed.
MaxTransfer =	The maximum number of blocks transferred at one time; used with Fast File System devices.
Mask =	Address mask that specifies the memory range that can be used for DMA transers; used with Fast File System.
GlobVec =	If the handler is written in BCPL, it needs a global vector. A value of 0 sets up a private global vector; anything else indicates that the handler is written in C or assembly language and no global vector is needed. If this keyword isn't used, the shared AmigaDOS global vector is used.
Startup =	A string passed to the handler, device, or file system on startup. This string is passed as a BPTR to a BSTR.
BootPri =	The boot priority of a bootable device, expressed as a number between −129 and 127. A value of −129 indicates that the device isn't bootable, as is appropriate for use with the recoverable RAM disk if you don't want to boot from that device on reset.
DosType =	Indicates the format of the file system used. If the Fast File System is used, this value should be set to 0x444F5301.

[**FROM** *filename*]   This option, added in version 1.3, allows you to specify a file other than DEVS:Mountlist as the place to look for the description of the device to be MOUNTed.

Example

Mount an external 5¼-inch disk drive as device DF1:
`MOUNT DF1:`

NEWCLI Command

Purpose

NEWCLI opens a new CLI window on the system display. The new window sports the same gadgets (drag gadget, back gadget, front gadget, and sizing gadget) as a CLI process that's started either by double-clicking the CLI icon from the Amiga Workbench or booting up a specially prepared CLI disk. A window created by NEWCLI becomes the current active window immediately after NEWCLI is executed. It will have the same default directory as the CLI from which NEWCLI was executed.

Every CLI window represents an independent CLI environment. You may change the active CLI window by moving the mouse pointer within any CLI window and clicking.

The default window title of CLI windows opened by NEWCLI with no title specified is *New CLI*. The new CLI's prompt line will be preceded by the message *New CLI task n*, where *n* is the task number assigned to the new CLI window.

The task number associated with the new CLI window is different from all other CLI windows currently open on the screen. For instance, if two CLI windows are created by issuing one NEWCLI command, the command-line prompt of the first CLI is 1> and the command-line prompt of the second is 2>. The CLI prompt of a window created by issuing another NEWCLI is 3>. A new CLI (task 3) can be created by issuing a NEWCLI from *either* of the two original CLI windows.

The resolution of the AmigaDOS screen display is 640 pixels (picture elements) wide and 200 pixels high. Think of an invisible 640 × 200 grid superimposed over your Amiga's display. AmigaDOS creates new CLI windows in a location that starts at the top left edge of the screen and extends 640 pixels wide × 100 pixels high. All new CLI windows are created in the same place—in the same size—unless you specify otherwise. This means that the third CLI window appears on top of the second, and you'll have to drag one out of the way if you want to use both.

NEWCLI Command

The obvious question is, aside from impressing your friends and running a computerized version of a three-ring circus, what good is NEWCLI? One obvious use is preventing a helpful display of information from scrolling off the screen. If you're attempting to clean up or reorganize a directory full of files, having to issue repetitive DIR commands to refresh your memory can be tedious, especially considering AmigaDOS's less than speedy directory searches. Opening a new window with NEWCLI and issuing a DIR command brings up a directory display that can be sent out of sight and recalled at will by using the front and back gadgets of the two active windows. Your file maintenance commands can be issued from the original CLI, whose scrolling display will not affect the directory display in the new CLI window.

You can even start a process in one CLI window and, while it's executing, make another existing CLI the active environment and start up another process in it. Multiple AmigaDOS functions can be set churning away in separate windows. While this multitasking is somewhat similar to the facilities offered by the RUN command, opened CLI windows remain available until closed by the ENDCLI command.

AmigaDOS currently supports a maximum of 20 open CLI windows.

Format

NEWCLI [*AUX:* or *CON: hpos/vpos/width/height/windowtitle*] [**FROM** *filename*]

Explanation of Parameters and Keywords

[*AUX:* or *CON: hpos/vpos/width/height/windowtitle*]   CON: lets you specify the size, position, and title of the new CLI window (if the NEWCON: device has been MOUNTed, NEWCON: can be substituted for CON:). CON: is required if *any* of the following parameters are specified.

- *hpos* is the horizontal position of the top left corner of the window (expressed as the number of pixels in from the left edge of the screen). If a value for *hpos* is omitted, it's assumed to be zero.

NEWCLI Command

- *vpos* is the vertical position of the top left corner of the window (expressed as the number of pixels down from the top edge of the screen). If a value for *vpos* is omitted, it's assumed to be zero.
- *width* and *height*, which must be specified, give the size of the window in pixels. The maximum size for a CLI window is the screen size, 640 × 200 pixels. The minimum is 90 × 25 pixels. Unless a window of exact size is required, it's usually easier to resize and drag a default size NEWCLI window (200 × 100 pixels) to a desired size and screen location rather typing the required size parameters.
- *windowtitle*, which is optional, allows you to enter the text of a title to appear in the title bar. If you want to set *windowtitle*, all preceding parameters must also be set. If you don't enter any text for *windowtitle*, the title bar is left blank. Even if you want the title bar to be blank, the last slash (/) following *height* is required. Titles with spaces can be entered, but quotation marks must enclose the entire list of NEWCLI parameters—see example 3 below. (The default title, if you do not specify *any* parameters, is *New CLI*.)

Although CON: and NEWCON: windows are the most likely targets of a NEWCLI window, you may also direct the input and output of a CLI window out the serial port by mounting the AUX: device and then issuing a "NEWCLI AUX:" command. Such a CLI will only be able to effectively run text-based programs that direct their output to the CLI window and cannot be used to cancel requesters like *Insert volume Workbench in any drive*.

[**FROM** *filename*]   This option allows you to specify a batch file that is to be executed automatically when the CLI opens, just like the *s:startup-sequence* file executes when the initial CLI window opens. As of version 1.3, if you do not specify a startup file, NEWCLI attempts to execute a default startup file, *s:CLI-Startup*, if such a file is present in the s: directory. Use of the default startup file allows you to retain settings like the CLI prompt that do not carry over from one CLI to the next.

NEWCLI Command

Examples

1. Create a new CLI window using AmigaDOS's defaults. The upper left corner of the new 200 × 100 window will be located at the top left corner of the screen. The new window will be titled *New CLI*:

`NEWCLI`

2. Create a 250 × 125 pixel CLI window in the upper left corner of the screen. The new window is to have no title:

`NEWCLI CON://250/125/`

3. Create a new CLI window 450 × 40 pixels, located 25 pixels to the right and 30 pixels below the upper left corner of the screen. The new window is to have the title *Flying High with CLI*:

`NEWCLI "CON:25/30/450/40/Flying High with CLI"`

4. Create a new CLI that uses the serial port for input and output:

`NEWCLI AUX:`

NEWSHELL Command

Purpose NEWSHELL opens an interactive Shell using a NEWCON: console window if the Shell-Seg has been made resident and the NEWCON: device MOUNTed. This Shell is an enhanced CLI that was introduced in version 1.3. It supports features such as command aliases, resident commands, and a prompt that reflects the current directory.

In order to open a Shell window, the Shell-Seg program must have been made resident with the command

RESIDENT CLI L:Shell-Seg SYSTEM pure

If Shell-Seg has not been made resident, the NEWSHELL command will open a normal CLI window instead of a Shell window, but will still try to use a NEWCON: window. If the NEWCON: device hasn't been MOUNTed, NEWSHELL will use a CON: window instead.

Format **NEWSHELL** [*AUX: or NEWCON: hpos/vpos/width/height/windowtitle*] [**FROM** *filename*]

Explanation of Parameters and Keywords [*AUX: or NEWCON: hpos/vpos/width/height/windowtitle*]   NEWCON: lets you specify the size, position, and title of the new Shell window (if the NEWCON: device has not been MOUNTed, CON: can be substituted for NEWCON:). See NEWCLI, above, for details.

As with NEWCLI, NEWSHELL can be used to open an interactive Shell through the serial port, with the command "NEWSHELL AUX:".

[**FROM** *filename*]   This option allows you to specify a batch file that is to be executed automatically when the Shell opens, just like the *s:startup-sequence* file executes when the initial CLI window opens. If you do not specify a startup file, NEWSHELL attempts to execute a default startup file, *s:Shell-Startup*, if such a file is present in the s: directory. Use of the default startup file allows you to retain settings such as command aliases that do not carry over from one Shell to the next.

NEWSHELL Command

Example

Create a new Shell window 450 × 100 pixels, located 25 pixels to the right and 30 pixels below the upper left corner of the screen. Shell-Seg has already been made RESIDENT and NEWCON: has been MOUNTed. The new window is to have the title *My Shell:*

NEWSHELL "NEWCON:25/30/450/100/My Shell"

PATH Command

PATH Command

Purpose Changes or displays the search path used by AmigaDOS to locate a command file. When you type a command at the CLI prompt, AmigaDOS first looks for the command file in the current directory—if the file is not there, DOS looks for it in whatever directory was assigned as the C: directory. (See Chapter 2 for more information on search paths.) The PATH command allows the user to specify additional directories to be searched after the current directory but before the C: directory.

It also can be used to display the current search path.

Format **PATH** [*SHOW*] [*ADD*] dir [,dir, dir...]
[*RESET* dir, dir, dir...] [*QUIET*]

Explanation of Parameters and Key Words

[**SHOW**] This optional key word displays the search path that AmigaDOS is currently using. Typing the command **PATH** accomplishes the same thing. The current search path is displayed in the following format:

Current directory
Workbench 1.3:System
C:

[**ADD**] *dir* The optional ADD key word allows you to add from one to ten additional directories to the current search path. The same effect may be achieved by typing **PATH**, followed by one or more directory names. The *dir* parameter is the name of the directory or directories to add. This directory may be specified relative to the current directory, or the entire pathname may be used to specify it. If more than one directory is added, each directory name is separated by a space. Each new directory that's added gets searched after the other user-specified directories, but before the C: directory.

[*RESET dir*] The optional RESET key word is used to delete the current search path and optionally to replace it with one or more directories. The optional *dir* parameter is the name of the directory to be added to the search path. This directory may be

PATH Command

specified relative to the current directory, or the entire pathname may be used to specify it. If more than one directory is added, each directory name is separated by a space. If no directory names are specified, the default search path is reset to the current directory and the C: directory.

[*QUIET*]   This optional keyword was added in version 1.3. It can be used in combination with the SHOW option to supress the "Please insert volume *xxx*" requester for disks that aren't currently mounted. When the QUIET option is used, only the volume name will be diplayed for paths in unmounted volumes.

Examples

1. Add the *System* and *Utilities* directories on the root directory to the current search path:

PATH ADD :System :Utilities

or

PATH :System :Utilities

2. Display the current search path, suppressing the "Please insert volume" requester for unmounted disks:

PATH SHOW QUIET

or

PATH QUIET

3. Reset the search path to the current directory and the C: directory:

PATH RESET

4. Replace the current search path with the *Demos* and *Utilities* directories in the root directory of the disk in the external 3½-inch disk drive:

PATH RESET df1:Demos df1:Utilities

PROMPT Command

PROMPT Command

Purpose
: The PROMPT command changes the prompt for the currently active CLI or Shell. The default prompt for any given CLI is *n>*, where *n* is the task number associated with that CLI. For instance, if only one CLI has been started, its prompt is 1>. If two more CLI windows are then started with the NEWCLI command, their prompts will be 2> and 3>. When used with a Shell window, PROMPT can automatically display the current directory as part of the command prompt.

Format
: **PROMPT** *prompt*

Explanation of Parameters and Keywords
: *prompt*   The string you want to substitute for the active CLI's prompt. If no value for *prompt* is specified, the CLI prompt will be changed to >. *prompt* may be a maximum of 59 characters. If it contains spaces, the entire prompt must be enclosed by double quotation marks. Note the ANSI escape sequences shown in the table in Chapter 2 can be used in the prompt string to change the prompt to a different color, or italics.

    There's a special substitution string allowed with the value specified for *prompt*. If *prompt* contains the two-character combination %N, the task number associated with the current CLI is substituted for those two characters. The Workbench 1.3 Shell adds another substitution string. When the characters %S are used in a Shell prompt, they are replaced with the current directory path.

Examples
: **1.** Change the current CLI prompt to *Ready]*:

    PROMPT Ready]

    2. Change the current CLI prompt to *Really Ready* (with a trailing space):

    PROMPT "Really Ready "

PROMPT Command

3. Change the current CLI prompt to *CLI n Ready* (with a trailing space, and where *n* is the current CLI's task number):

PROMPT "CLI %N Ready "

4. Change the current Shell prompt to show the Shell task number and current directory, separated by angle brackets (>):

PROMPT "%N>>%S>> "

5. Change the current CLI prompt to >:

PROMPT

PROTECT Command

Purpose — PROTECT allows you to alter the attributes of AmigaDOS files and directory entries. Originally, there were protection flags associated with each of four attributes. These flags are *r, w, e,* and *d*; they tell the system if the file or directory entry may be read (r), written over (w), executed (e), or deleted (d). In Workbench 1.3, three more flags were added. These flages are *s, p,* and *a*. They indicate whether the file is a script that may be directly executed from a Shell (s), a pure command file that may be made resident (p), or if the file has remained unchanged since the last archival backup (a).

The LIST command is used to examine the status of a file or directory entry. In the display provided by the LIST command, there's room for eight characters to the left of the date information. Seven of these characters, *sparwed*, correspond to the seven protection status flags. When a file or directory entry is first created, the last four flags are turned on and they can be modified thereafter using PROTECT. The three new bits must be set either by the user or by a backup program.

If a flag character is present in the LIST display, it is said to be *on*, and the operation may be carried out. The Read flag lets you read from a file or directory entry, the Write flag lets you update the file or directory with new information, the Delete flag allows the file or directory entry to be removed altogether, and the Execute flag is meaningful only for files that are actual programs for the Amiga. The Execute flag allows DOS to execute (run) the program. If you set the Execute flag on a nonprogram file (like a text file, for instance), you cannot expect DOS to load and run the file. The Script bit will allow you to execute a script file just by typing the name of the file at the Shell prompt. Remember, this only works with a Shell window, not a CLI, and the file name must be of a valid script file. The Pure bit is used in connection with the Resident Shell command, and indicates that a command is suitable for being made resident. The Archive bit is used mostly by back-up

PROTECT Command

programs, to indicate which files have not changed since the last back up.

If a flag is off, the LIST display shows a dash (–) in place of the flag character.

It is important to note that of the initial four bits (rwed), only the Delete and Execute flags work. You can set the others, but DOS does not act on those settings.

Format

PROTECT [*FILE*] *name* [*FLAGS*] [*S*][*P*][*A*][*R*][*W*] [*E*][*D*][*ADD or* +] [*SUB or* –]

Explanation of Parameters and Keywords

[*FILE*] *name*   The name of the file whose protection flags are to be modified; *name*, which is mandatory, may be any valid AmigaDOS filename or directory name. The FILE keyword is optional.

[*FLAGS*] [*S*][*P*][*A*][*R*][*W*][*E*][*D*]   The protection flags that will be turned on by PROTECT. The FLAGS keyword does not have to be entered—it's optional. The protection flags to be turned on must be specified as a single string in any desired order. Remember that if a flag is set to *on*, the operation associated with the flag can be carried out. If no flags are specified, all flags are turned off. These are the operations associated with each flag:

S—Script
P—Pure
A—Archive
R—Read
W—Write
E—Execute
D—Delete

Note: Some AmigaDOS commands (notably COPY) will actually delete an existing file and create a new one with the same name rather than overwriting a file. For this reason, COPY and other commands that behave in this manner will fail for files that are protected from deletion.

[*ADD or* +]
[*SUB or* –] Version 1.3 of the Protect command now allows you to add or subtract individual bits rather than requiring you to set all of a file's flags at once. To set specific flags, you can name the flags and follow them with the keyword ADD, or just put a plus

PROTECT Command

sign (+) in front of the initials. To turn off specific flags, follow the list with the keyword SUB, or precede it with a minus sign (−).

Examples

1. Make the file *S:Script* executable directly from a Shell window:

PROTECT FILE Script S ADD

or

PROTECT Script +S

2. Protect the file *Public Knowledge* in subdirectory *:info/expose* from being deleted. If it's a program, let it be executed. The file may be read but not written to:

PROTECT ":info/expose/Public Knowledge" RE

3. Protect a file called *transitory* on the system's RAM disk from being read, written to, deleted, or executed:

PROTECT RAM:transitory

4. Reset a file called *Enough Already* on drive df1: to the protection attributes it had upon creation:

PROTECT "df1:Enough Already" DWER

5. Protect a directory entry called *shuttle/columbia* from being deleted:

PROTECT shuttle/columbia WER

QUIT Command

Purpose
: The QUIT command is used within command sequence files (see Chapter 5 for complete information on command files). The QUIT command allows you to exit a command sequence file and, optionally, to set the return code.

Format
: **QUIT** [*returncode*]

Explanation of Parameters and Keywords
: *returncode* The return code that is reported when the command sequence file is terminated by a QUIT. If *returncode* is nonzero, the message

    quit failed returncode *returncode*

    is displayed on the screen, with the number specified substituted for *returncode*. If *returncode* is set to zero or is not specified, no message is displayed on termination of the command sequence file by QUIT.

Examples
: **1.** Exit a command sequence file using the QUIT command. The QUIT in the following example is executed only if the file *wolfbane* is found on drive df1:. No return code is to be set:

```
IF df1:wolfbane EXISTS
ECHO "Get the silver bullets"
QUIT
ENDIF
TYPE :Transylvania/here/I/come
```

2. Exit a command sequence file using the QUIT command. A return code of 88 is to be set:

```
ECHO "This is just a silly example"
QUIT 88
LIST
```

    The LIST command in the above example will never be executed. The message *quit failed returncode 88* will be sent to the system display when the QUIT 88 is executed.

RELABEL Command

RELABEL Command

Purpose
RELABEL lets you change the volume name associated with a floppy disk. Volume names are initially assigned when a disk is formatted by the FORMAT command or created by a DISKCOPY operation.

Note: RELABEL does *not* prompt you for the disk to be inserted. If you have a single-drive system and insert the disk you want to relabel ahead of time and then issue the RELABEL command, you'll be prompted to insert the disk with the command library on it in any disk drive. Once you do so, RELABEL promptly renames the volume with the command library on it. The following procedure will work for single-drive system owners.

COPY :C/RELABEL TO RAM:

Change disk now.

RAM:RELABEL df0: *NewName*

Format
RELABEL [DRIVE] drive **[NAME]** name

Explanation of Parameters and Keywords

[DRIVE] *drive*   The disk drive in which the disk to be relabled is mounted. The DRIVE keyword is optional if *drive* precedes the volume name in the RELABEL statement.

[NAME] *name*   The volume name which will replace whatever name is currently associated with the target disk; *name* may be up to 30 characters long. If the volume name contains spaces, quotation marks must enclose it. The NAME keyword is optional if *name* follows *drive*.

Note: Under AmigaDOS Versions 1.0 and 1.1, RELABEL fails if no drive is specified or if *name* is omitted. However, RELABEL does succeed (in a strange kind of way) if the NAME keyword and *name* are specified, and if anything else is entered on the line. For instance,

RELABEL gorko NAME "This is Weird"

and

RELABEL NAME "This is Weird" *garbage*

RELABEL Command

both relabel the volume located in the present default drive with the specified name *This is Weird*. Life—and AMigaDOS—can be strange. (It's the opinion of the authors that this is either a bug or a feature of AmigaDOS with deep transcendental meaning.)

Examples

1. Relabel the disk in drive df1: as *Various Programs:*

RELABEL DF1: "Various Programs"

2. Relabel the disk in drive df0: as *Home on the Range:*

RELABEL NAME "Home on the Range"
  DRIVE DF0:

Notice that in this example, both NAME and DRIVE were specified since their order was switched in the RELABEL statement.

REMRAD Command

Purpose
: Allows you to remove the recoverable RAM disk device, RAD:, from the system without turning off the power. Although this device's ability to survive a warm boot can be very handy, it also presents a problem when you decide to deallocate the memory set aside for the RAM disk. REMRAD commands the device to delete all of its files and release most of its memory. The next time the system reboots, the recoverable RAM disk is removed entirely.

Format
: **REMRAD**

Explanation of Parameters and Keywords
: None

RENAME Command

Purpose
: RENAME allows you to change the name of AmigaDOS files and directories. AmigaDOS's RENAME function also lets you move files from one directory to another on the same disk and reorganize directory structures at will.

Format
: **RENAME** [*FROM*] *fromname* [*TO* or *AS*] *toname*

Explanation of Parameters and Keywords
: [*FROM*] *fromname*   The file or directory that's to be renamed. The FROM keyword is not required if *fromname* is the first argument of a RENAME statement.

  [*TO* or *AS*] *toname*   The new name to be given to the file or directory specified by *fromname*. The TO and AS keywords may be used interchangeably and are optional if *toname* is the second argument of a RENAME statement. If *fromname* already exists, RENAME will fail.

  Note: fromname and *toname* must reside on the same disk volume.

  RENAME's ability to manipulate AmigaDOS directory structures makes this one of the most powerful AmigaDOS commands and, consequently, a command that should be used with great care. An entire directory, including all files, subdirectories, and files within its subdirectories may be moved to another location in the volume's directory tree structure with a single RENAME.

  For instance, suppose the directory structure of a disk volume looks like this:

RENAME Command

Animals, Part One

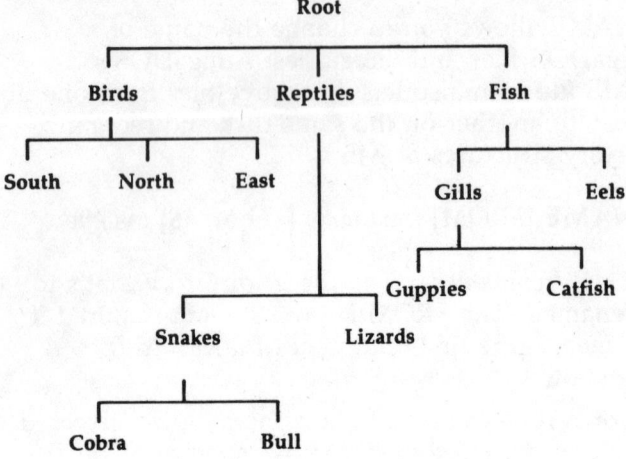

Issuing the following RENAME command:
```
RENAME :FISH/GILLS :REPTILES/SNAKES/BULL
  /PETS
```
results in a new directory structure.

Animals, Part Two

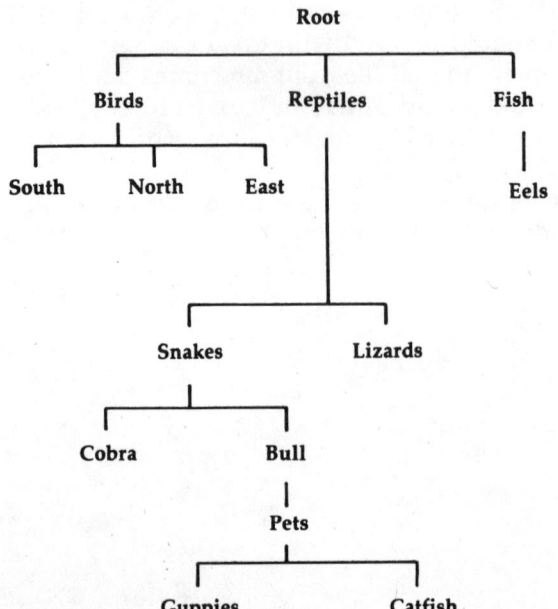

RENAME Command

Examples

1. Rename a file called *birddog* to *hounddog*:

RENAME birddog hounddog

2. Move a file called *Lights Out* to a directory called *HeavyMetal/JGeils*. The filename is to remain the same:

RENAME "Lights Out" ":HeavyMetal/JGeils/Lights Out"

3. Move a directory called *LaserDiscs* and all the files and subdirectories within it to a directory called *Phils/Video*. The directory name is to remain the same:

RENAME LaserDiscs Phils/Video/LaserDiscs

4. Move a file called *Apple* in the *fresh/fruits* directory to a directory called *Desserts/Light*. The filename is to be changed to *Rome*:

RENAME fresh/fruits/Apple Desserts/Light/Rome

5. Move a directory called *Ancient Computers* and all the files and subdirectories within it to a directory called *8-Bit Processors*. The directory name is to be changed to *Ancient History*:

RENAME "Ancient Computers" "8-Bit Processors/Ancient History"

RESIDENT Command

RESIDENT Command

Purpose The RESIDENT command is used to load programs into memory and to keep them resident there where they may be executed without having to load them from disk each time. This not only saves the time required for loading the command, but also can save memory in a multitasking environment, since several Shell windows can execute the same program code simultaneously without having to load a separate copy of the program for each Shell. Note, however, that commands may be made resident only from a Shell window and not from a regular CLI.

Format **RESIDENT** *name filename* [*REMOVE*] [*ADD*] [*REPLACE*] [*PURE*] [*SYSTEM*]

Explanation of Parameters and Keywords

name   An optional resident name for the program. For example, you may choose to call your resident version of the DIR program by the letter D. If no resident name is specified, the filename is used as the resident name.

filename   The name of the file to be made resident. The full pathname should be used.

Not all commands may be made resident. Resident commands must be reexecutable, which means that they must be able to be run a number of times in a row without being reloaded or reinitialized. They must also be *reentrant*, which means that the same copy of the program must be able to be executed from different Shells simultaneously. Many of the programs in the C directory of Workbench 1.3 can be made resident, and their files have the pure protection bit set to indicate this fact.

[*REMOVE*]   This keyword is used to remove the indicated resident name from the resident list. This operation will succeed only if the resident command is not currently in use.

[*ADD*]
[*REPLACE*]   Either of these keywords acts like the default RESIDENT command with no options specified. That is, if these keywords are used without a

RESIDENT Command

filename (RESIDENT ADD or RESIDENT REPLACE), the command lists the programs on the resident list. If either is used with a filename, the RESIDENT command tries to place that file on the resident list. If there is another file with the same filename or resident name already on the list, the new command will replace the old one, unless the old one is already in use and cannot be deleted.

[*PURE*]   Normally, a command cannot be made resident unless its file has the pure bit set (see PROTECT). When the PURE keyword is used however, RESIDENT is forced to load the program whether or not the pure bit is set, and to print the warning message "Pure bit not set". Of course, the file still must be an executable program—RESIDENT can't make a data file resident.

Using the PURE option to make a possibly unsuitable command resident is a hazardous proposition that can lead to a system crash. Therefore, if you wish to experiment with making commands resident, try to do so under conditions that won't lead to catastrophic data loss. Don't experiment with RESIDENT and then go to work on your most important project.

[*SYSTEM*]   This option is used to add a command to the system porition of the resident list. Once added, this command cannot be deleted by the user. The most common use of this keyword is to add the Shell-Seg program that enables Shell windows in place of ordinary CLI windows. The command you use to make the Shell-Seg resident is:

RESIDENT CLI L:Shell-Seg SYSTEM

If used without a filename, the SYSTEM keyword can be used to list the resident system commands along with the resident user commands.

RESIDENT Command

Examples

1. Make the DIR command resident, using the resident name D:

RESIDENT D C:DIR

2. Remove the EXECUTE command from the resident list:

RESIDENT execute REMOVE

3. List all of the commands (including the system commands) on the resident list:

RESIDENT SYSTEM

RUN Command

Purpose
The RUN command may be used to create a system CLI task that executes in the Amiga's background (in other words, the task doesn't present you with an interactive CLI window). RUN allows multiple AmigaDOS commands to be executed in sequence. Once all commands given to a RUN statement are executed, the background task disappears.

When RUN is initiated the system prints the message

[CLI n]

where *n* is the task number assigned to the background task. Immediately after the message is issued, control is returned to the CLI from which RUN was issued. The background task keeps running until all commands are completed or until the task is interrupted by the BREAK command. The commands are executed sequentially. If any command fails with an error code, the background task terminates and removes itself.

As of Workbench 1.3, RUN checks the resident list before looking in the current directory for a command so that it uses the resident copy if available. Also, if the output of the RUN command is redirected to the NIL: device, the existence of a background task will no longer prevent the closing of the CLI window from which that task was launched.

Format
RUN *command+command,,,,,,,*

Explanation of Parameters and Keywords
command+command,,,,,,, This is the AmigaDOS command you want executed in the background. More than one command may be strung together in a RUN sequence. To build a RUN with multiple commands, end each command line with a plus sign (+) and press RETURN. RUN treats the plus sign as a command delimiter. The cursor will jump to the beginning of the next line, at which point you may enter another command. Keep ending each command line with a + until you've entered the last one for this RUN sequence. End the last command line with a RETURN (without a + preceding it). RUN

RUN Command

then begins processing the commands—one by one—in the background. You may receive messages and requester boxes from background tasks.

Examples

1. Print a complete directory and file listing of the current drive to the printer. The print operation is to be executed in the background:

RUN DIR > PRT: OPT A

2. Format a blank disk in drive df1: and then install boot files on the newly formatted volume. Print a message on the screen when the format and install are done. The operations are to be executed in the background by a single task:

RUN FORMAT DRIVE DF1:NAME EMPTY +
INSTALL DF1: +
ECHO "Format and Install Finished"

3. Execute the command sequence file *My Command File* located on the system RAM disk. The command file is to be executed in the background by a single task:

RUN EXECUTE "RAM:My Command File"

4. Start the *Clock* program as a background task and redirect the output of the RUN command to NIL: so that you can close the CLI while *Clock* is still running:

RUN >NIL: Clock

SAY Command
(Moved to SYS:SYSTEM drawer in Workbench 1.2, and to SYS:UTILITIES in Workbench 1.3)

Purpose

The SAY command is used to invoke the Amiga's built-in speech synthesis capabilities. The quality and speed of speech may be controlled by the user. SAY has two modes—*interactive* and *direct*.

In direct mode, the text to be spoken or an AmigaDOS file containing the text to be spoken is specified on the command line with the keyword SAY.

Interactive mode is entered by typing **SAY** by itself. Two windows will appear on the system screen.

The *Phoneme window* initially displays the option codes that may be used to control the quality and speed of the synthesized voice. As text is spoken, the phoneme codes that SAY uses are displayed.

The *Input window* is where text you wish spoken is displayed as it's typed in. The text is passed to SAY when the RETURN key is pressed. The interactive mode is exited by typing a line consisting only of a RETURN keystroke.

The SAY command was added to AmigaDOS in Release 1.1.

Format

SAY [*options*] [*text*],,,,,,,,,,,

Explanation of Keywords and Parameters

[*options*]   Control the quality, pitch, speed, and source of the text to be spoken. SAY identifies *option* by a leading dash (–). These are valid options for SAY:

Option	Function
–m	Use male voice.
–f	Use female voice.
–r	Use robot voice (monotone).
–n	Use natural voice.
–s###	Set speech rate to ### (valid values are 40–400).
–p###	Set pitch of voice to ### (valid values are 65–320).
–x *file*	Say contents of *file*. The –x option may not be invoked in the interactive mode of SAY; *file* must be an AmigaDOS file in the current directory and may not contain *any* spaces or be enclosed in parentheses.

SAY Command

Multiple options, separated by spaces, may be specified at one time.
[*text*]   The text to be spoken.

Examples

Try all these examples in interactive mode.

1. SAY a phrase using a high female voice at a relatively slow rate:

SAY −f −p250 −s130 Why don't you come up and see me sometime

2. SAY the contents of the file *gettysburg*:

SAY −x gettysburg

3. Have your Amiga carry on a conversation with itself:

SAY −f −p250 −s130 Hi blitter −n −p140 −s175 Hi workbench −f −p250 −s130 What's up −n −p140 −s175 Oh just talking to myself −f −p250 −s130 Not a bad idea blitter be seeing you around

Note: You'll soon discover that the options, when used in both direct and interactive modes, produce significantly different sounds.

SEARCH Command

Purpose

SEARCH lets you scan AmigaDOS files for a specified string of characters. You may SEARCH a single file, all files matching an AmigaDOS pattern, all files within a directory, and optionally, all files within a directory's subdirectories.

SEARCH displays the name of the AmigaDOS file currently being searched and, if the search text is found, all lines containing the search text. Each displayed line is preceded by a line number. As of Workbench 1.3, the command returns a code of zero if the object is found, and 5 (WARN) if it isn't, which makes the command more useful in scripts. The CTRL-C key combination may be used to stop the search.

AmigaDOS treats the carriage return character as an end-of-line character. SEARCH examines only the first 205 characters of each line. If SEARCH comes across a line longer than 205 characters, the message *LINE n truncated* displays, and SEARCH continues.

Format

SEARCH [*FROM*] name [*SEARCH*] string [*ALL*] [*NONUM*] [*QUIET*][*QUICK*] [*FILE*]

Explanation of Parameters and Keywords

[*FROM*] *name*   The file or directory that you want searched; *name* may also be an AmigaDOS pattern. (See Chapter 3, "The Filing System," for detailed information on patterns and their uses). If *name* is the first argument in the SEARCH command, the FROM keyword is optional.

[*SEARCH*] *string*   The text string that will be searched for. If *string* is the second argument in the SEARCH command, this second SEARCH keyword is optional. If *string* contains any spaces, it must be enclosed in quotation marks. Case (uppercase, lowercase) within *string* is ignored by SEARCH. A search string of *RUBBER DUCKY*, for instance, will match the text found in a file that contains the phrase *Ernie bought his rubber ducky an Amiga.*

SEARCH Command

[*ALL*]   If the ALL keyword is specified and *name* is an AmigaDOS directory, all files within the directory and its subdirectories are searched.

[*NONUM*]   This option, added in version 1.3, supresses the output of line numbers along with the strings.

[*QUIET*]   This option, added in version 1.3, supresses all output to facilitate the use of the command in scripts.

[*QUICK*]   The QUICK option, introduced in version 1.3, uses a more compact format for the output.

[*FILE*]   The FILE option, new for version 1.3, searches for a file whose name is exactly the same as *string*, rather than searching for the string within the contents of the file. If the file is found, its name is printed but, unfortunately, not its full pathname. Thus, SEARCH will let you know if the file exists.

Examples

1. Search all files within the directory called *Mayan/Civilization* and all files within its subdirectories for the phrase *ancient astronauts*:

SEARCH Mayan/Civilization "ancient astronauts" ALL

2. Search a file called *MyLetters* for the word *gorilla*:

SEARCH MyLetters gorilla

3. Search all files that end with *.bills* in the current directory for the phrase *blank disks*. Redirect the QUICK output to the system printer:

SEARCH > PRT: #?.bills "blank disks" QUICK

; (Semicolon) Command

Purpose
: The semicolon (;) command allows the insertion of informational comments in command sequence files. The comments may be on the same line as other AmigaDOS commands or they may stand by themselves on separate lines. Anything to the right of a semicolon in an AmigaDOS command line is considered a *comment*.

Format
: ; [*comment*]

Explanation of Parameters and Keywords
: [*comment*]   May be any text string, up to 254 characters in length (if the ; is the first character of a line).

Example
: Here is a simple example of a command sequence file with comments, using the ; command. Remember, everything to the right of a semicolon is considered a comment.

```
; Niagra Falls Routine
IF Curly EXISTS ; Test for a stooge
SAY Slowly I turned ; Set em up for the gag
WAIT 5 SECS ; Dramatic pause
SAY Inch by Inch
ELSE
;Sign off without gag
SAY th th th thats all folks
ENDIF
```

SETCLOCK Command

SETCLOCK Command

Purpose — SETCLOCK is used to copy the time and date from the hardware clock on the 2000 (optional on the 500) to the AmigaDOS software clock, or vice versa. It only works with Commodore's own clock/calendar.

Format — **SETCLOCK** *LOAD or SAVE or RESET*

Explanation of Parameters and Key Words — *LOAD or SAVE or RESET* One of these three keywords must be used with SETCLOCK. If the SAVE option is used, the current AmigaDOS system time and date (the one set with the DATE command) is copied to the hardware clock. If the LOAD option is used, the stored time and date is copied from the hardware clock to the system clock (this is usually performed in the startup sequence). The RESET option is used to start the clock up again if it has been turned off by some runaway program that accidently wrote to its hardware registers.

Example — Set the system time and date from the hardware clock:

```
SETCLOCK LOAD
```

SETDATE Command

Purpose

Changes the date or time associated with a file or directory. The time and date of the file creation can be displayed with the LIST command.

SETDATE is useful when the date and time associated with a directory or file doesn't reflect its true creation date, either because the date and time wasn't set correctly when the file was created or because the file was copied from another disk, in which case the date-stamp reflects the date of the *copy*, not the date of creation. It can also be use to manipulate a "make" type program, which directs a C compiler to compile files based on the date-stamp.

Format

SETDATE *name* [*date*] [*time*]

Explanation of Parameters and Key Words

name   The name of the directory or file whose date stamp you want to change. As of version 1.3, if no date or time is included with the filename, the file is set to the current system time and date.

[*date*]   The day of the month, month, and the year associated with the file. The date is usually specified as *DD-MMM-YY*, where DD is a two-digit number representing the day, MMM is a three-letter abbreviation of the month (such as FEB or JUN), and YY is the last two digits of the year. The SETDATE command, like the DATE command, also allows indirect references for setting the date, such as YESTERDAY or WEDNESDAY. For more complete details, see the DATE command.

[*time*]   The optional time-stamp for the file, expressed in the format *HH:MM:SS*, where each is a two-digit number representing the hours, minutes, and seconds. Hours are set in 24-hour format, where 1:00 p.m. is referred to as 1300 hours. If minutes or seconds are omitted, they're set to zero. If this optional parameter is omitted, the time-stamp on the file is set to 00:00:00.

SETDATE Command

Examples

1. Change the date-stamp of the *Printers* subdirectory of the *Devs* directory on the Workbench disk to show a creation date of January 5, 1987 at 1:56 p.m.:

SETDATE Workbench:Devs/Printers 05-jan-87 13:56

2. Change the date-stamp of the file *Mydata* in the current directory to midnight yesterday:

SETDATE Mydata Yesterday

3. Change the date-stamp of the file *"Au Courrant"* in the current directory to the current time and date:

SETDATE Au Courant

SETENV Command

Purpose
SETENV is used to assign a text string to an environment variable, or to delete a text string already assigned to such a variable. An *environment variable* is a named text string that is stored in an environment space that is accessible to all tasks. As of Workbench 1.3, there is no formal environment handler; rather, it is simulated through the use of an ENV: directory that is created on the RAM: disk. For now, "SETENV test TestString" is really the same as "ECHO >ENV:test TestString". In future versions, the environment variables may be stored in system RAM, and manipulated by their own device handler.

Format
SETENV *varname* [*string*]

Explanation of Parameters and Keywords

varname   The name of the environment variable to set. Under the Workbench 1.3 system, this is the name of a text file that is stored in the ENV: directory. Using the SETENV command copies the text string to this file.

[*string*]   The text string to assign to the environment variable. Like all such strings, if there are spaces in the text, the entire string must be enclosed in quotes. If no string is specified, an empty string will be copied to the variable, effectively removing the text string currently associated with it.

Example

1. Copy the name *Darlene* to an environment variable named *Cubby*:

SETENV Cubby Darlene

2. Remove the text string associated with the environment variable named *Annette*:

SETENV Annette

SETMAP Command
(located in SYS:SYSTEM drawer)

Purpose   Changes the default key map of the keyboard, allowing the use of different keyboard layouts for foreign countries.

The key map is a data table to which the Amiga refers when a key is pressed. By changing this key map, you can change which character is printed when you press a particular key. For example, the French keyboard has the letter *Q* reversed with the letter *A*, so when you use the SETMAP command to install the French key map, every time you press *A*, a *q* appears, and vice versa. Key maps can also be used to assign strings to the function keys.

The SETMAP command looks for its key map data files in the *Keymaps* subdirectory of the directory designated as the logical device DEVS: (usually the *Devs* directory of the startup disk). The standard key map files on the 1.2 Workbench disk include:

cdn	French Canadian
d	German
dk	Danish
e	Spanish
f	French
gb	Great Britain
i	Italian
is	Icelandic
n	Norwegian
s	Swedish
usa0	Emulates the standard key mapping of the 1.1 Workbench.
usa1	Includes maps for additional numeric pad keys on 500/2000
usa2	Dvorak

Note that the *usa0* key map is provided for purposes of compatibility with the 1.1 version of the AmigaDOS. Since some changes were made to the default key map in 1.2, some programs (such as the commerical telecommunications program *Online!*) require that you install the *usa0* key map before running them.

SETMAP Command

Some of the new key maps implement a new feature known as *dead keys*. A dead key is one that prints out a character only when struck preceding another character. It's often used for accented vowels. In order to produce an *a* with an accent mark over it, for example, you might hit the accent key first (the dead key). Nothing prints on the screen when you hit the accent key, but if the next key you press is an *a*, an accented *a* appears.

Complete information about the layout of the various foreign keyboards is included in *Introduction to the Amiga*. The *Keytoy* program included on the *Extras* disk in the *Tools* directory displays a graphics representation of the current key map as well.

Format

SETMAP *mapfile*

Explanation of Parameters and Key Words

mapfile   A key map data file describing the keyboard layout to be used. This file should be located in the *Keymaps* subdirectory of the directory designated as *DEVS:*. In order to restore the default key map, use the name *usa* for the mapfile. This key map is part of the operating system, and need not be read from a disk file.

Examples

1. Install the French language key map:

SETMAP f

2. Restore the default system key map:

SETMAP usa

SETPATCH Command

Purpose	SETPATCH is used to fix a few of the known bugs in the Kickstart 1.2 and Kickstart 1.3 ROMs. It should be run as the first command in the *startup-sequence* file. The command prints a list of the patches made.
Format	**SETPATCH [*r*]**
Explanation of Parameters and Key Words	[*r*] This optional switch is used to allow the recoverable RAM disk (RAD:) to recover sucessfully on machines with one megabyte of CHIP RAM. It need only be used with systems that include the 1 Mb Agnus chip (on which AVAIL shows over 512K of CHIP RAM). Note that the letter *r* should be in lowercase, as this command is case sensitive.
Example	Patch the 1.3 Kickstart routines without printing a list of the patches: `SETPATCH >nil:`

SKIP Command

Purpose
: The SKIP command is used within command sequence files to jump to a specified label. If a SKIP is executed, command execution continues immediately after the label which was skipped to.

If SKIP is executed with no label specified, command execution continues with the commands following the next LAB command in the command file.

If a SKIP is executed and the label specified is not found, or if a SKIP with no label searches to the end of the command file without encountering a LAB command, command file execution is terminated and the message *label* label *not found by SKIP* is displayed.

As of Workbench 1.3, an option was added that allows skipping backward in the file.

Format
: **SKIP** [*string*] [*BACK*]

Explanation of Parameters and Keywords
: [*string*]   The string attached to a LAB command, which SKIP searches for in the currently executing command file. The search starts at the command following SKIP and continues downward toward the end of the command file. If the matching LAB *string* command precedes the SKIP command, SKIP will not find it, and the command file terminates with an error.

If *string* is not specified, the first LAB command following SKIP will be skipped to.

[*BACK*]   This option, added in Workbench 1.3, starts the search for the specified label at the beginning of the file, not at the line following the SKIP command. You still may not SKIP backward past an EXECUTE statement, however.

Examples
: 1. Transfer control to the commands immediately following the next *LAB filecontrol* command in the current command sequence file:

```
SKIP filecontrol
```

SKIP Command

2. Transfer control to the commands immediately following the next LAB command in the current command sequence file:

SKIP

3. Transfer control to the commands immediately following the preceding *LAB Jumpback* command in the current command sequence file:

SKIP Jumpback BACK

SORT Command

Purpose

SORT performs an alphabetic sort on contents of an AmigaDOS text file. SORT is line-oriented.

Within a file, AmigaDOS treats any string of characters that ends with a linefeed character as a single line. SORT compares lines beginning with the first character, unless a different sort start position is specified via the COLSTART keyword. Lines that begin with numbers will precede those that begin with alphabetic characters in the sorted version of the original file. Lines with numbers will be in ascending order. Case is ignored by SORT. For instance, a SORT of a file containing these lines:

1,234,576
a sunny spring day
AOK
rags to riches
.Hiya.
1
R2D2 and C3PO
3.14159
.0000000001

results in this output:

.0000000001
.Hiya.
1
1,234,576
3.14159
a sunny spring day
AOK
R2D2 and C3PO
rags to riches

SORT is not particularly fast, especially when the size of the file to be sorted is longer than 50 lines. When operating on files close to 200 lines long (approximately the largest file that can be sorted using the CLI's default 4000-byte stack), SORT tends to be downright slothlike. See the STACK command description for details on how to change CLI's stack size to accommodate sorts of larger files. SORT fails if the file to be sorted is larger than the system's available free memory.

SORT Command

Format

SORT [*FROM*] *fromname* [*TO*] *toname*
[*COLSTART* n]

Explanation of Parameters and Keywords

[*FROM*] *fromname*   The name of the AmigaDOS file whose contents are to be sorted. If *fromname* is the first argument of a SORT command, the FROM keyword is optional.

[*TO*] *toname*   The name of the AmigaDOS file or logical device that the sorted lines from *fromname* will be sent to. If *toname* is the second argument of a SORT command, the TO keyword is optional; *toname* must be different from *fromname* or the SORT will fail.

[*COLSTART* n]   Lets you specify that SORT will compare lines beginning with the *nth* character in each line. If *n* is given, the COLSTART keyword *must* be used. If COLSTART n has been specified and lines are found to be equal, SORT attempts a secondary sort of the equal lines, starting with the first character of each line.

Examples

1. Sort the contents of a file called *Mixed Up* to a file called *InOrder*:

SORT "Mixed Up" InOrder

2. Sort the contents of a file called *Inventory* in the *majorappliance/washers* directory. Print the sorted output on the system printer:

SORT :majorappliance/washers/Inventory PRT:

3. Sort the contents of a file called *widgets* located on the system RAM disk, comparing lines beginning with the fifth character of each. Display the sorted output on the system screen:

SORT RAM:widgets * COLSTART 5

STACK Command

Purpose

The STACK command may be used to display or set aside the amount of stack space for the currently active CLI. The stack space is used by AmigaDOS commands and all other programs as a sort of intermediate work area. The default stack size for a CLI environment is 4000 bytes, which is large enough to execute the vast majority of AmigaDOS commands successfully.

Two AmigaDOS commands may require a stack size greater than 4000 bytes. If a SORT command is executed on a file with more than 200 lines, or if a DIR is issued against a file structure with more than six levels of directories, the stack size should be increased. The exact size is open to question. According to the developers of AmigaDOS, optimum stack sizes for a specific heavy SORT or DIR are a matter of trial and error.

You can also check the stack size of all active system tasks with the STATUS command.

Format

STACK [n]

Explanation of Parameters and Keywords

[n]   The amount of space, in bytes of memory, that you wish to assign as stack space for the currently active CLI. If n is omitted, the current stack size is displayed.

Examples

1. Display the stack size of the currently active CLI:

STACK

2. Change the stack size of the currently active CLI to 12,000 bytes:

STACK 12000

Footnote: Fun with STACK
Interestingly enough, STACK will let you specify an amount (n) greater than the total amount of memory in your system and will not crash the computer. You might as well have crashed, though, since doing so leaves no room in memory for any further AmigaDOS commands to be loaded for execution.

STACK Command

If you're really feeling adventurous and want to see what a stack failure and subsequent system crash looks like, make a copy of a CLI disk and boot it up. Type

STACK 400
DIR

You'll be presented with a rather scary looking requester box that tells you your disk has been corrupted. Click the cancel button and you can watch your Amiga give up the ghost. Don't worry, it's only temporary. Reboot with CTRL-Amiga–Amiga and you're back in business.

STATUS Command

Purpose

The STATUS command displays system information about active tasks. STATUS displays the stack size, global vector size, priority, and segment list section names associated with active tasks. A discussion of these system variables is beyond the scope of this book. For a complete explanation, see the *AmigaDOS Technical Reference Manual*.

While STATUS information will normally be of interest only to advanced programmers, there are some uses of STATUS that may come in handy to users of the RUN command. The CLI STATUS keyword can be used to check what command is currently active in both foreground and background CLI environments—something you may forget once you execute a RUN. It can also be used to find the task number of the task you wish to send a BREAK.

Format

STATUS [*tasknum*] [*FULL*] [*TCB*] [*SEGS*] [*CLI* or *ALL*] [*COMMAND* = *filename*]

Explanation of Parameters and Keywords

[*tasknum*]   The number of the task that STATUS is to report on. If *tasknum* is not specified, all active tasks are reported.

[*FULL*]   FULL displays all the information normally reported by STATUS if the TCB, SEGS, and ALL keywords were all specified. The FULL keyword is optional.

[*TCB*]   Causes STATUS to display information dealing with the stack size, global vector size, and priority of each active task known to the system. The TCB keyword is optional.

[*SEGS*]   Causes STATUS to display each active task's segment list section names. The SEGS keyword is optional.

[*CLI* or *ALL*]   Specifying either CLI or ALL causes STATUS to report on all currently active CLI tasks and display the section names of all commands currently loaded within the CLIs. The CLI and ALL keywords are interchangeable and optional.

STATUS Command

[*COMMAND* = *filename*]   This new option, added in Workbench 1.3, prints the task number of the CLI from which the program named in *filename* was run. This allows you to send that program a BREAK—for example, using a script file.

Examples

1. Display an abbreviated status report on all active tasks:

STATUS

2. Display the segment list section names of task 3:

STATUS 3 SEGS

3. Print the stack size, global vector size, priority, and segment list section names of each active task known to the system on the system printer:

STATUS > PRT: FULL

4. Send a BREAK to the task running the WAIT command:

STATUS >ram:temp COMMAND=Wait
BREAK <ram:temp >NIL: ?

TYPE Command

Purpose
The TYPE command lets you output the contents of any AmigaDOS file to the screen, a disk file, or any AmigaDOS physical device.

TYPE is most often used to examine the contents of a file, although it may actually be used to copy a file. TYPE also has the capability of reformatting its output to a special hexadecimal dump format or of including line numbers at the beginning of each output line.

TYPE's output may be paused by hitting the space bar (or any other key) and resumed by hitting the RETURN key, BACKSPACE key, or holding down the CTRL-X key combination. Its output may be canceled by breaking the command with CTRL-C.

Format
TYPE [*FROM*] *fromname* [[*TO*] *toname*] [*OPT N* or *NUMBER* or *OPT H* or *HEX*]

Explanation of Parameters and Keywords

[*FROM*] *fromname*   The name of the file you want TYPEd; *fromname* is required and may be any valid AmigaDOS filename. The FROM keyword is optional and need not be specified if *fromname* immediately follows TYPE.

[[*TO*] *toname*]   The name of the file or device you want the output of the TYPE operation sent to. The TO keyword is optional if the first argument of TYPE is *fromname* and the second argument is *toname*. If no destination for TYPE's output is specified, the output is displayed on the screen. *toname* may be an AmigaDOS file or an AmigaDOS device, such as the printer (PRT:). If *toname* is an existing file, its contents are overwritten; if *toname* is a file that does not exist, it will be created by the TYPE operation. If *toname* is a directory with files in it, TYPE fails; if *toname* is an empty directory, the directory will be deleted and a file called *toname* created.

[*OPT N* or *NUMBER* or
   OPT H or *HEX*]   Adding *OPT N* or *NUMBER* to a TYPE command instructs the system to precede

TYPE Command

each line output by TYPE with a line number. AmigaDOS treats any number of characters within a file ending with a linefeed as one line.

Specifying *OPT H* or *HEX* instructs TYPE to produce a formatted hexadecimal dump of the *fromname* file's contents. The *N* and *H* options are mutually exclusive—only one can be specified. If either option is specified using the initial instead of the full word, the OPT keyword *must* be used.

Examples

1. Output the contents of a file in the current directory called *textwiz* on the screen:

TYPE textwiz

2. Copy a file called *copyclone* in a directory called *qwikbuck* to a file of the same name in the directory called *copies* on df1:.

TYPE :qwikbuck/copyclone df1:/copies/
    copyclone

3. Produce a formatted hexadecimal dump of a file called *objectcode* on the printer:

TYPE objectcode PRT: OPT H

or

TYPE > PRT: objectcode HEX

4. List the contents of the file *namelist* with line numbers before each line to a file on the system RAM disk called *tempname*:

TYPE namelist RAM:tempname OPT N

VERSION Command

Purpose Displays the internal version number of the *Kickstart* and *Workbench* disks used to start the computer. This provides a CLI equivalent of the Version selection on the Workbench's Special menu. The internal version numbers give much more precise information about which release is in use than the mere *1.2* identifier. Programs that open one or more operating system libraries may specify the release required so that the program doesn't try to use certain features not available with earlier versions of the system. With the official 1.3 release, the VERSION command returns the following information:

```
Kickstart version 34.5 Workbench
  version 34.20
```

As of Workbench 1.3, VERSION can also be used to find the version and revision number of any library or device, and to test for a particular version in a script file.

Format **VERSION** *libraryname* or *devicename* [*versionnum*] [*revisionnum*] [*unitnum*]

Explanation of Parameters and Key Words

libraryname or *devicename*
[*unitnum*] This optional parameter can be used to specify the library or device whose version you wish to check. A library name ends in the letters ".library" (for example "graphics.library"), while a device name ends in the letters ".device" (for example "trackdisk.device"). In the case of a device, an optional unitnumber may be specified if the device has more than one unit.

[*versionnum*]
[*revisionnum*] These optional parameters may be used to verify that the version number (or revision number) is greater than the number specified. If the version number (and possibly revision number) is greater than or equal to the one specified, the command returns a code of zero. Otherwise, it returns a code of 5 (WARN).

VERSION Command

Examples

1. Display information about the Kickstart and Workbench disks used to start the computer:

VERSION

2. In a script, check to see if the version of the graphics library is greater than or equal to 34. Print a warning message if it isn't.

VERSION graphics.library version=34
IF WARN
ECHO "Wrong version of graphics"
ENDIF

WAIT Command

Purpose WAIT can be used to put a task in a state of suspended animation for a user-definable period of time or until a specified time of day. WAIT can be used in command sequence files or in conjunction with a RUN command.

When WAIT is encountered by the system, the task sits in a seemingly idle state for the specified period of time and then continues with the next command. Sending a BREAK to a WAITing task causes the WAIT to conclude.

Format **WAIT** [*n*] [*SEC* or *SECS*] [*MIN* or *MINS*] [*UNTIL* *time*]

Explanation of Parameters and Keywords

[*n*] [*SEC* or *SECS*] [*MIN* or *MINS*]   The amount of time, in minutes or seconds, that the system will wait. If *n* is omitted and the SEC or MIN keyword is specified, *n* defaults to one (1). Using the SEC or SECS keyword tells AmigaDOS to wait *n* seconds, while using MIN or MINS causes the CLI task to wait *n* minutes before continuing. SEC/SECS and MIN/MINS keywords are optional. If they're omitted, the default unit of time is seconds.

[*UNTIL* *time*]   The time of day you want the current process to wait until before continuing. If *time* is specified, the UNTIL keyword is required; *time* must be stated in the format *HH:MM*, where *HH* and *MM* are the hour and minute of the day in military (24-hour) time. If UNTIL *time* is used, the system will "wake up" sometime between *HH:MM*:00 and *HH:MM*:59.

Examples

1. Wait for one second:

WAIT

2. Wait for one minute:

WAIT MIN

3. Wait for three minutes:

WAIT 3 MIN

or

WAIT 180

WAIT Command

4. Wait until 10:15 a.m.:

WAIT UNTIL 10:15

5. Set up a background process using the RUN command that will wait until 11:00 p.m.; then copy all the files in a directory called *documents* to a directory on df1: called *backupdir*:

RUN WAIT UNTIL 23:00 + COPY :documents/
   #? to df1:backupdir

WHICH Command

Purpose
: The WHICH command, new for Workbench 1.3, can be used to display the path for a particular command. The command in question must be on the resident list, or in the current directory or search path. If there is more than one version of the command available to AmigaDOS, this command will tell you WHICH version will be found first.

Format
: **WHICH** *filename* [*NORES or RES*]

Explanation of Parameters and Keywords
: *filename*   The name of the file or directory or logical device to find. WHICH searches in the resident list, the current directory, and the search path. If a directory or logical device is specified, the ASSIGN list is also checked.

  [*NORES or RES*]   If the NORES option is selected, the resident list is not checked for the command. If the RES option is selected, only the resident list is checked.

Example
: 1. Display the directory in which the Setmap program is stored. Don't check the resident list:

  WHICH SETMAP NORES

  2. Display the directory to which the logical device WP: is ASSIGNed:

  WHICH WP:

WHY Command

Purpose
: WHY can be used to obtain additional information about failing commands. AmigaDOS is relatively friendly compared with most other computers' disk operating systems. Most DOS systems will give no error messages or, at best, minimal messages when a command fails. Even when an error message is displayed, it's often a cryptic numeric that sends you scurrying for the appendix of a DOS manual. When AmigaDOS runs into a problem, it will usually display a message telling you that the command failed, an English language description of the problem or a requester box telling you what needs to be done. Issuing a WHY immediately after a command failure can provide more detailed information on the reason for the failure.

    In some instances, WHY will indicate a numeric return code as the reason for the failure. When this happens, the FAULT command can be used to investigate the error code.

    WHY can provide meaningful information only if the previous command fails with a nonzero return code. A WHY issued after a successful command, or after a failed command which has already given you all information available, results in the message *The last command did not set a return code.*

Format
: **WHY**

Explanation of Parameters and Keywords
: None

Example
: A WHY command is issued after an EXECUTE command fails to get more information about the failure:

```
1>EXECUTE nowherefile
EXECUTE: Can't open nowherefile
1>WHY
Last command failed because object file not found
```

Appendix

AmigaDOS Error Messages

Appendix
AmigaDOS Error Messages

Eventually, you'll see an AmigaDOS error message. The code numbers and short messages listed below will appear when you use the FAULT or WHY command. A short, albeit more detailed, explanation of each is included here for your information.

103: insufficient free store
There's not enough contiguous free memory available to run the invoked task. Additional memory may be freed by closing down any unnecessary active tasks. Reboot the system and try again. If this message still appears, consider installing additional memory in your system.

104: task table full
You've attempted to run more than 20 concurrent tasks. Close down any unnecessary active tasks and try again.

120: argument line invalid or too long
The arguments you've specified with an AmigaDOS command are incorrect or do not apply. For a quick check of the argument template for any AmigaDOS command (with the exception of the SAY command), type a space and question mark (?) immediately following the command and hit RETURN. See the "AmigaDOS Command Reference" for complete specifications.

121: file is not an object module
The file you've attempted to run is not a binary program (remember, all AmigaDOS commands are actually programs extrinsic to the CLI interpreter). AmigaDOS command sequence files are *not* binary programs. Use the EXECUTE command to start up a command sequence file.

202: object in use
The directory or file specified as an argument in the invoked AmigaDOS command is being used by another active task. Wait until the task using the file or directory has freed the object, then try again.

203: object already exists
You've attempted to create a directory or file that already exists. Rename or delete the existing object if you wish to use the specified name for a new file or directory.

Appendix

204: directory not found
You've referred to a directory which does not exist. Check the complete pathname and spelling of the specified directory. LIST and DIR may be used to get a complete listing of all the directories on a disk. See the "AmigaDOS Command Reference" sections on the LIST and DIR commands for complete information.

205: object not found
You've referred to a file or device which does not exist. Check the spelling of the specified *object.directory*. LIST and DIR may be used to get a complete listing of all the files on a disk. The ASSIGN command can be used to check on the name of all logical and physical devices known to the system. See the "AmigaDOS Command Reference" sections on the LIST, DIR, and ASSIGN commands for complete information.

206: invalid window
You've attempted to open a new window on the screen with invalid width, height, or position, or you've specified a physical device which does not support display windows (for instance, SER: or PAR:).

210: invalid stream name
The filename you've specified contains one or more invalid characters (control characters) or is longer than 30 characters.

212: object not of required type
The type of the object you've specified is incompatible with the invoked AmigaDOS command or options, for example, attempting an operation on an AmigaDOS file that's normally associated with a directory. See the "AmigaDOS Command Reference" for complete information on the command and its options.

213: disk not validated
An error has occurred during the validation of a disk. The disk may be bad or the validation process was interrupted before it was completed. If the disk was in use, try copying all of the existing information on it to another disk. You cannot write to an unvalidated disk.

214: disk write-protected
You've attempted to write to a disk whose write-protection tab is in the write-protected position. If you're sure you want to write to the disk, slide the write-protect tab so the small, square cut-out is completely covered.

AmigaDOS Error Messages

215: rename across devices attempted
You've specified different devices in the FROM and TO (or AS) arguments of the RENAME command. Both arguments must reside on the same device. See the "AmigaDOS Command Reference" section on the RENAME command for further information.

216: directory not empty
You've attempted to DELETE a directory that's not empty. See the "AmigaDOS Command Reference" section on the DELETE command for further information.

218: device not mounted
You've referenced a disk volume not currently in a disk drive. Check the name specified, or locate the desired volume and insert it in one of the system's drives, then try again.

220: comment too big
You've specified a comment which exceeds 80 characters in conjunction with the FILENOTE command. Try again with a shortened version of the comment.

221: disk full
The disk that you've attempted to write to does not have enough free space to complete the specified command. Free up enough space by deleting any unneeded files and/or directories, or use another disk.

222: file is protected from deletion
You've attempted to delete a file which has been protected from being deleted by the PROTECT command. The status of a file's protection flags may be examined using the LIST command. See the "AmigaDOS Command Reference" sections on the PROTECT and LIST commands for complete information.

223: file is protected from writing
You've attempted to write to a file which has been protected from being written to by the PROTECT command. The status of a file's protection flags may be examined using the LIST command. See the "AmigaDOS Command Reference" sections on the PROTECT and LIST commands for complete information.

224: file is protected from reading
You've attempted to read a file which has been protected from being read by the PROTECT command. The status of a file's protection flags may be examined using the LIST command. See the "AmigaDOS Command Reference" sections on the PROTECT and LIST commands for complete information.

Appendix

225: not a DOS disk
You've inserted a disk that is not an AmigaDOS format disk into one of the system's drives.

226: no disk in drive
You've referenced a disk drive which does not contain a disk. Insert an AmigaDOS format disk in the specified drive and proceed.

Index

ABasiC program 16
ADDBUFFERS command 139–40
additional CLI processes, starting 17–20
ALIAS command 24
alternate character set, CLI and 14
ASK command 141
ASSIGN command 51, 57–58, 59, 62, 142–45
assignments, removing 62
autobooting 48
AUX: logical device 67
AVAIL command 146–47
background tasks 20–21, 76, 241–42
batch files. *See* command sequence files
BINDDRIVERS command 46, 48, 75, 148
block transfer commands, ED 96–97
.BRA directive 82
branching, command sequence files and 88–89
BREAK command 149
break function 15
bridge board 48–49
buffers, disk 75, 139–40
C: directory 59–60
CD command 38–40, 150–51
CHANGETASKPRI command 152
character deletion/insertion, ED and 92–93, 95
character operations, EDIT and 110
CLI 3, 7–9, 53
   alternate character set and 14
   command sequence files and 72–89
   console 11
   disk, creating 7–9
   editing commands 11–14
   environment 10–25
   environment, accessing 5–6
   escape codes 14
   icon, activating 5–6
   linefeed and 13
   pausing and restarting and 14–15
   prompt, modifying 18, 226–27
   starting additional processes 17–20
   tasks, background 20–21, 76, 241–42
   tasks, keeping track of 20
   window on Workbench 5, 76
   window, importance of keeping at least one open 20
   window, opening 17–20, 67, 76, 218–21
clock, system 33, 76, 248, 249–50
   third-party 78–79
command alias 23–25
command files, EDIT 123–24

command groups, EDIT 123
command history buffer, NEWCON: and 22
command line 11
command-line editing 68–69
commands, making resident 60
command sequence files 3, 58, 72–89
   branching, and 88–89, 255–56
   condition testing and 83–87
   error threshold 87
   interactive 141
command shell, Workbench 1.3 and 23–25
command summary, ED 101–3
command summary, EDIT 126–28
communication speed 51
communications ports 51
CON: command 19, 131–32
condition testing, command sequence files and 83–87, 192–95
console 53–56
   CLI 11
console device 42
   as input 54–55
   output window 19–20, 53–54
COPY command 40, 59, 153–56
current line, EDIT 105, 108, 111–12
cursor movement, ED 91–92, 94–95
DATE command 33–34, 78–79, 157–59
.DEF directive 80–82
DELETE command 41, 160–61
device
   description 47–48
   handlers 58
devices 46–71
   hardware 46, 63–69
   sending files to 51
   standard input and output 69
DEVS: logical device 60–61
DIR command 37, 70
directories 5, 35–40, 162–64, 150–51
   as logical devices 58–62
   creating 36–37, 59, 77, 210–13
directory path 37–40
directory
   structure 36–37
   disk listing 29
disk 26–45
   block 31–32, 203–7
   buffers 75
   changing 165
   CLI, creating 7–9
   copying 27, 64, 166–68
   corrupted 169–70
   directory, listing 29, 162–64

277

drives 46–47
formatting 26–28, 189–90
identification number 27
Kickstart 6, 48, 64
making bootable 28
volume information 26, 196–98
volume name, changing 232–33
DISKCHANGE command 165
DISKCOPY command 27, 64, 166–68
DISKDOCTOR command 169–70
DJmount 48
.DOLLAR directive 82–83
DOS directories 5
DOS, command-driven 3
drawer icons 5
ECHO command 70, 73, 171–72
ED system screen editor 72, 90–103, 173
   character deletion/insertion 92–93, 95
   command summary 101–3
   cursor movement and 91–92, 94–95
   extended mode 90, 93–100
   file management 97–98
   immediate mode 90, 91–93
EDIT system line editor 72, 90, 104–28, 174–75
   character operations and 110
   command files and 123–24
   command groups and 123
   command summary 126–28
   current line and 105, 108, 111–12
   file merging and 124–25
   from file 105
   HALT command 125
   leaving 107–8
   lines, renumbering 116
   lines, splitting and joining 121–22
   operational windows 109–10
   parameters and keywords 106
   REWIND command 125
   starting 106–7
   to file 105
   verification and 108–9
editing commands, CLI 11–14
ELSE statement 84
ENDCLI command 19–20, 56, 76, 176
ENDIF statement 84
ENDSKIP command 177
environment variable 86, 191, 251
ERROR
   keyword 86
   messages 185, 273–76
   threshold, command sequence files 87
escape codes, CLI and 14
EVAL command 178–80
EXECUTE command 25, 32, 58, 72–89, 181–83
   avoiding using 74–75
   from a command sequence file 89
extended mode, ED 90, 93–100

FAILAT command 76, 87, 184
FAIL keyword 86
FastMemFirst command 75
FAULT command 16, 185
FF command 76, 186
FFS (Fast File System) 49–50, 64–65
file
   dating 33–35
   handler 51
   management, ED and 97–98
   manipulation commands 40–41
   merging, EDIT and 124–25
   merging, JOIN command and 201, 124–25
   name, changing 40–41, 235–37
   protection level, file 32–33, 228–30
   size 31–32
   specifications 30
filenames, characteristics of 29–31, 132
FILENOTE command 31, 187–88
files 28–45
   copying 40, 59, 153–56
   deleting 41, 160–61
   in subdirectories, accessing 37–40
   RAM: disk and 50
   saving additional notes about 31
   sending to devices 51
   sorting 17, 257–58
   text 72–73
filing system 26–45
FONTS: logical device 60
FORMAT command 26–28, 189–90
formatting disk 26–28
GETENV command 86, 190
global operations, EDIT 122–23
HALT command, EDIT 125
hard disks 48–50
   interfaces 48–49
hard drive, partitioning 49
hardware devices 46
   adding to system 63–69
IBM compatibility option see bridge board
icons 3
ICONX Command 191
identification number disk 27
IF command, command sequences and 83–87, 192–95
IF EXISTS command 83–84
immediate mode, ED 90, 91–93
INFO command 27, 32, 196–98
input
   redirection of 69–71
   unfiltered 55–56
INSTALL command 28, 199–200
integer expressions, evaluating 178–80
introduction 3–9
JOIN command 41, 201
kernel rom bugs 75
.KET directive 82
.KEY directive 79–82

keyboard layout, changing 252–53
Kickstart disk 6, 48, 64
Kickstart rom 64
L: directory 58
LAB command 202
leaving EDIT 107–8
LIBS: logical device 61
limbo 56
line-editing, CLI and 11–15
line editors, history of 104–5
linefeed 52
    CLI and 13
lines
    renumbering, EDIT and 116
    splitting and joining, EDIT and 121–22
LIST command 21, 29, 31, 32, 203–7
LOADWB command 76, 208
LOCK command 209
logical devices 46, 56–62
    as directory aliases 56–57
    assignment summary 61–62
MAKEDIR command 36–37, 59, 77, 210–13
memory, available 146–47
memory-resident programs 17, 23, 32, 60, 78, 238–40
Midi musical device 51
modem 51
MOUNTable device drivers and handlers 63–69
MOUNT command 21, 46, 48, 53, 58, 63–69, 214–17
mountlist 63, 64
MS/PC DOS 3, 4, 16, 17
    Commodore disk drive for 46
multiple commands, CLI and 13
multitasking 10, 152
NEWCLI command 17–20, 67, 76, 218–21
NEWCON: console device 11, 21–23, 53, 58, 68–69
NEWSHELL command 23, 76, 222–23
NIL: logical device 56, 79
noninteractive running of programs, CLI and 20–21
operational windows, EDIT and 109–10
output redirection, 56, 65–66, 69–71
parallel port 51
parameters
    and keywords, EDIT 106
    CLI command and 79–83
PAR: logical device 51, 52
partitioning hard drive 49
PATH command 76, 224–25
path, directory 37–40
pattern matching 41–45, 132–36
    differences from MS/PC DOS 41–42
    summary 44–45
pausing and restarting, CLI and 14–15
PIPE: logical device 65–66
    downloading and 66

PopCLI program 20
power supply 46
Preferences program 6, 51, 52
printer, testing 52
program
    files, assigning device name to 62
    location, specifying 16
    running from CLI 15–17
PROMPT command 18, 226–27
PROTECT command 33, 74, 228–30
protection level, file 32–33
PRT: logical device 52
QUIT command 87, 231
RAD: logical device 63–65
ram disk 4
    directory, making default 77
RAM: disk 50–51, 58
    creating 50
RAW: logical device 55–56
redirection
    of input 69–71
    of output 56, 65–66, 69–71, 137
    operators 69–71
RELABEL command 26, 232–33
remote machine 67
REMRAD command 234
RENAME command 40–41, 235–37
RESIDENT command 17, 23, 32, 60, 78, 238–40
REWIND command, EDIT 125
root 36–37
RUN command 20–21, 76, 241–42
S: directory 58
SAY command 67, 73, 243–44
script files see command sequence files
SEARCH command 245–46
search and replace commands, ED 95–96
; (semicolon) command 247
SER: logical device 51, 52
serial port 51
    unbuffered communication through 66
SETCLOCK command 76, 248
SETDATE command 249–50
SETENV command 86, 251
SETMAP command 76, 252–53
SETPATCH command 254
shell aliases 62
SKIP command 88–89, 255–56
software devices 46
SORT command 17, 257–58
SPEAK: logical device 58, 67–68
speech synthesis 67–68, 73, 243–44
STACK command 17, 259–60
stack space, specifying more 16–17, 259–60
starting EDIT 106–7
startup-sequence file 75–79
    modifying 76–79
STATUS command 20, 261–62
subdirectories 35–40

SupraMount 48
SYS: logical device 61
system clock 76
   third-party 78-79
system library files 61
tabs and margins, ED and 98-99
task 10, 20, 261-62
task number 18
template, AmigaDOS 136-37
text files 72-73
   converting to speech 67-68
   deleting, EDIT and 119-21
   displaying, EDIT and 112-13
   inserting, EDIT and 113-14
   printing to screen with AmigaDOS 29
   replacing, EDIT and 115, 118-19
text, searching for, EDIT and 116-18
tool 5
tree 36-37
TYPE command 29, 51, 263-64
typeface, screen, CLI and 14
UNIX 4
utilities, not accessible from Workbench 3
verification, EDIT and 108-9

VERSION command 265-66
virtual disk
   fixed-size 63-65
   recoverable 64
volume name, disk 26
WAIT command 76, 267-68
warm start 50
WARN keyword 86
WHICH command 269
WHY command 16, 270
wildcards. *See* pattern matching
WordPerfect 72
Workbench 3-9, 49
   bypassing at boot-up time 7-9
   CLI window on 4-5, 76
   command shell 23-25
   concepts, DOS and 4-5
   disk 6, 48
   environment, starting 76
   starting 76, 208
   utilities, not accessible from 3
   version 1.3, console enhancements under 21-25